The Faerie Queene: a reader's guide

The Faerie Queene is the first great epic poem in the English language. It is a long and complex allegory which presents the first-time reader with many difficulties of allusion and interpretation.

This book is the only convenient and up-to-date guide to Spenser's poem, and is designed as a handbook to be consulted by students while reading the poem. Each chapter is devoted to a separate book of the poem, and sub-sections treat particular episodes or sequences of episodes in detail.

Dr Heale considers fully the religious and political context, and pays due attention to the variety of Spenser's literary techniques. She encourages close reading of the poem and a lively awareness of both its rich detail and the intricate interrelation of its episodes.

The Faerie Queene

a reader's guide

ELIZABETH HEALE

Department of English,
University of Reading

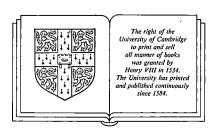

The right of the
University of Cambridge
to print and sell
all manner of books
was granted by
Henry VIII in 1534.
The University has printed
and published continuously
since 1584.

CAMBRIDGE UNIVERSITY PRESS

CAMBRIDGE

LONDON   NEW YORK   NEW ROCHELLE
MELBOURNE   SYDNEY

Published by the Press Syndicate of the University of Cambridge
The Pitt Building, Trumpington Street, Cambridge CB2 1RP
32 East 57th Street, New York, NY 10022, USA
10 Stamford Road, Oakleigh, Melbourne 3166, Australia

First published 1987

Printed in Great Britain at
the University Press, Cambridge

British Library cataloguing in publication data
Heale, Elizabeth
The Faerie Queene : a reader's guide.
1. Spenser, Edmund. Faerie Queene
I. Title
821'.3   PR2358

Library of Congress cataloguing in publication data
Heale, Elizabeth, 1946–
The faerie queene.
Bibliography: p.
Includes index.
1. Spenser, Edmund, 1552?–1599. Faerie queene.
I. Title.
PR2358.H35   1987   821'.3   86–31723

ISBN 0 521 30386 9 hard covers
ISBN 0 521 31679 0 paperback

To
Graeme and Beatrice

CONTENTS

Contents

PREFACE

This book has been designed for those reading *The Faerie Queene* for the first time. In my experience the poem presents such readers with a number of initial difficulties, owing partly to the remoteness of the sixteenth century and its ideas from our own and partly to the allegorical mode of the poem and its multiple plots. On first reading we enter a quite unfamiliar world in which the significance of characters and episodes and the logic of their sequence is far from obvious. But the poem demands and copiously rewards re-reading and close attention to its details. With more knowledge and greater familiarity much that at first seems inexplicable or insignificant finds its place and takes on meaning.

This guide in no way wishes to pre-empt the reader's own exploration and gradual discovery of the poem. Its aim is twofold: first, to provide in a convenient form information which is otherwise difficult of access, hidden in scholarly articles or sixteenth-century texts, and which I consider basic to the understanding of the poem; and secondly, to suggest the bare bones of a reading of the poem which concentrates on its coherence – the connections between episodes, their sequence, the significance of repeated patterns and details. I have attempted neither to write all that might be written about any episode, if such a thing were possible, nor to give a neutral account of various critical views. It seemed to me more important to try to provide what I hope may be a stimulating and suggestive reading and to refer the reader to more detailed and scholarly studies in the notes and bibliography.

My own biases will be clearer to those with some knowledge of Spenserian criticism than to first readers and I shall therefore try briefly to state those that I recognize. In my view, Spenser is a poet deeply concerned with the world in which he lives. In general terms this means that I stress the way his fictions are concerned with the difficulties of interpretation and action in a fallen world, and more specifically the way his analysis of the virtues reflects a sixteenth-century Protestant point of view in all its partisanship. On the question of Spenser's esotericism, I take a middle position. Spenser described his poem as a 'darke conceit', and while I do not accept that its interpretation depends on sources so recondite as to be obscure even to his contemporaries, it does seem to me that on occasion he deliberately cultivates complexity and mystery to convey a sense that he is dealing with supernatural and therefore hidden secrets. In trying to explain the allegories as clearly as possible, I run the risk of over-simplifying and falsifying the poem's carefully achieved obliquity.

My understanding of *The Faerie Queene* has been shaped by the criticism I have read, and it is now difficult to disentangle what is my own and what I owe to others. I wished to avoid overwhelming a book such as this with scholarly references, but where I am conscious of a specific debt I have tried to acknowledge it. I apologize sincerely if I have drawn on a previous writer significantly without giving due credit. I have incurred some debts that cannot be adequately repaid in endnotes. The first is to Martin Wright, who first introduced me to Spenser and tried to teach me how the poem worked as poetry; the second is to Frank Kermode, whose writing and teaching opened many new doors for me, and through whom I first discovered the magnificent resources of the Warburg Institute; the third is to my colleague Anthea Hume, whose conversations have profoundly influenced my reading of the poem. My greatest debt is without any doubt to my husband, Graeme Watson, whose support, intellectual, moral and domestic, has made this book possible.

NOTE ON TEXTS

Quotations from *The Faerie Queene* are from A. C. Hamilton's Longman Annotated English Poets edition of 1977. The notes to this edition are invaluable, and I have on occasion referred to them in parentheses in my text. Quotations from *A View of the Present State of Ireland* are from the edition by W. L. Renwick (Oxford, 1970), cited in my text as *View*. All other quotations from Spenser's poetry and from the letters between Spenser and Harvey are from the *Poetical Works*, edited by J. C. Smith and E. De Selincourt (Oxford, 1912), cited in my text as *Works*.

Unless otherwise indicated, quotations from the Bible are from the Geneva version, standard in Spenser's time. I quote from the London edition of 1607. Other frequently cited works are: Aristotle, *Ethics*, trans. John Warrington, Everyman's Library (London, 1963); John Calvin, *Institutes of the Christian Religion*, trans. H. Beveridge, 2 vols. (Grand Rapids, Mich., 1975); Sir Thomas Elyot, *The Book named the Governor*, introd. and ed. S. E. Lehmberg, Everyman's Library (London, 1962); Sir Philip Sidney, *An Apology for Poetry*, ed. Geoffrey Shepherd (Manchester, 1973), and William Perkins, *The Workes*, 3 vols. (London, 1612). Page references to these editions are given in parentheses following quotations.

Where I cite from works whose details are contained in full in my Select Bibliography, I have given only the name and page number in parentheses in my text.

To make quotations from early works easier to read without losing the flavour of their original spelling, I have silently altered *i* to *j* and *u* to *v* to accord with modern usage.

INTRODUCTION

BACKGROUNDS

1. The life

Facts about Spenser's life, especially the early years, are sparse.[1] He was probably born in 1552, and he tells us in *Prothalamion* (1596) ll. 127–9 that his place of birth was London. His parents seem to have been in relatively humble circumstances, although he claimed descent from 'An house of auncient fame' (*Prothalamion* l. 130), the Spencers of Althorp. He dedicated a number of poems to daughters of that family and seems to have received patronage from them (see, e.g., the dedication to *Muiopotmos* (1590), and *Colin Clouts Come Home Againe* (1595) ll. 536–71).

Spenser was fortunate to attend Merchant Taylors' School, which had been recently opened and was run by one of the great English educationalists of the sixteenth century, Richard Mulcaster. As was normal, Mulcaster would have grounded his boys in classical languages and texts, but unusually for his time Mulcaster put emphasis on vernacular English as a language fit for the composition of verse and fine prose. As part of his mastery of language and versification, Spenser would undoubtedly have had to compose poems at school in both Greek and Latin, and from both languages into English. He would have gained familiarity with the main classical genres and have learned to imitate them. Copiousness, the ability to enrich a topic with variety of vocabulary, was seen as a virtue, and Spenser may well have learned from Mulcaster his interest in adding to the abundance of the English language with the introduction of old and regional words.[2] Spenser would thus, at school, have had considerable practice in techniques of imitation and composition, which became fundamental to his own art. From account books, we know that Spenser attended Merchant Taylors' as a 'poor scholar' and that he received charity payments when he went up to Pembroke Hall, Cambridge, in 1569. In the same year his first verses were published: a number of translations in Jan van der Noot's *A Theatre wherein be represented as wel the miseries and calamities that follow the voluptuous Worldlings, As also the greate joyes and plesures which the faithfull do enjoy*. This

1

was an ardently Protestant work by a refugee from Spanish Catholic persecution in the Netherlands. Spenser later revised and republished some of these translations as 'The Visions of Bellay' and 'The Visions of Petrarch' in his volume *Complaints* (1591).

Spenser graduated BA in 1573 and MA in 1576, though he seems to have left Cambridge a little before the latter date. He next appears in 1578 as secretary to Dr John Young, formerly Master of Pembroke Hall and now appointed Bishop of Rochester. In 1579, letters between Spenser and Gabriel Harvey, a Fellow at Pembroke Hall, make it clear that Spenser was now in London in the service of the Earl of Leicester and apparently enjoying some literary conversations with Leicester's nephew, Sir Philip Sidney, and another aristocratic poet, Sir Edward Dyer (*Works* pp. 612, 623, 636, 638). Late in 1579, Spenser's first major published work, *The Shepheardes Calender*, appeared under the pseudonym 'Immerito'. Its printer, Hugh Singleton, was a Puritan who had recently, and probably through Leicester's protection, narrowly escaped losing his right hand for printing a work criticizing Elizabeth's possible marriage with the French Catholic Duke of Alençon. To add to the other changes and achievements of this momentous year, we can deduce from references in one of Harvey's letters to Spenser that he married (*Works* p. 632). He seems to have had two children by this marriage, Sylvanus (1582?) and Katherine.

In 1580, even more momentously, Spenser went to Ireland as secretary to the new Lord Deputy, Arthur, Lord Grey de Wilton – a post possibly obtained for him through the patronage of the Sidney family. He accompanied Lord Grey on his many expeditions: to quell a rebellion in the Wicklow Mountains where the English army was bloodily ambushed; to Drogheda; to Wexford; possibly to Ulster, and more than once to Munster, where the Desmond Rebellion kept most of the south-west of Ireland ungovernable by the English. In 1580 Spenser accompanied Grey to the siege of Smerwick on the extreme south-west tip of the Kerry peninsula, where six hundred Spanish and Papal troops had landed intending to aid the Desmond rebels. On their unconditional surrender, Grey had all the common soldiers massacred – a brutal act, but one which should perhaps be seen in the context of Smerwick's remoteness, the continual dearth of provisions for Grey's own troops, and the problem of how to march an enemy army, almost as large as Grey's own, across rebel country to the security of Dublin.

The severity of Grey's regime in Ireland made him an object of criticism at the English Court and lost him Elizabeth's support. In 1582 his repeated requests to resign were accepted and he returned to England. Spenser, like many of his fellow officials in Ireland, strongly approved of Grey and his policies (see *View* pp. 106–7). Ludovick Bryskett, a friend and colleague of Spenser's, wrote of Grey that his 'justice is a terror to the wicked, and a comforte unto the good, whose sinceritie very envie it self cannott touche, and whose wisdome might, in the oppinion of the wysest that consider his proceedinges, governe a whole Empyre' (quoted in Renwick's commentary on the *View* p. 213).[3] Spenser stayed on in Ireland after Grey's departure, having leased New Abbey in Kildare, a forfeited rebel property. Probably in 1584, Spenser became Bryskett's deputy as Clerk of the Munster Council, in which capacity he helped to divide up the confiscated Desmond lands for purchase by English 'undertakers' or settlers. In 1589 he acquired one of these portions of land himself – the 4,000-acre estate of Kilcolman, neglected and hampered by lawsuits, on which he built a 'fair stone house' (Judson p. 130), and where, probably in 1594, he married his second wife, Elizabeth Boyle, for whom he wrote the *Amoretti and Epithalamion* (published 1595).

We know from the letters between Spenser and Harvey (*Works* pp. 612 and 628) that *The Faerie Queene* had already been begun in 1580. In 1588 Abraham Fraunce printed a stanza from Book 2 in his *Arcadian Rhetorike*, so we may assume that the manuscript of some or all of Books 1–3 was circulating in London by that date. By this time *The Shepheardes Calender* had been through three editions, and Fraunce refers to it as being by Spenser, so that it seems clear that Spenser's reputation was growing in England at least among those interested in new writing. In 1590 a fellow 'undertaker' in Munster, Sir Walter Raleigh, visited Spenser at Kilcolman and then journeyed with him to London. Spenser must have hoped that Raleigh's influence with Elizabeth might bring him her patronage and possibly advancement in England. While in London, he saw Books 1–3 of *The Faerie Queene* through the press. In February 1591 he gained a pension of £50 a year from Queen Elizabeth. Spenser describes the Queen's munificence in rapturous terms in *Colin Clouts Come Home Againe* (1595), which gives fictional form to his journey from Ireland to London. In it Cynthia's shepherd, Raleigh, accuses Colin Clout, Spenser's persona, of banishing himself in Ireland 'that waste, where I was quite forgot'. However, once in London, in spite of his praise of the Queen, the life of the Court disgusts him. It is a place of 'dissembling curtesie' (l. 700) where 'each one seeks with malice and with strife,/To thrust downe other' (ll. 690–1). Colin decides to return to Ireland, whose 'utmost hardnesse I before had tryde' (l. 673). Such a rejection of the vices of the Court is conventional in pastoral poetry (see. p. 150 below), but there may be some reflection of Spenser's own experience.

While in London in 1590–1 Spenser collected together some recent and earlier work for publication in *Complaints*. In late 1595 or 1596 Spenser again journeyed to London, partly to see *The Faerie Queene* 4–6, and the reprinting of Books 1–3, through the press. In Ireland, there was growing anxiety about renewed rebellion, this time from the north, led by the Earl of Tyrone, and this was matched by the fear that Spanish and/or Papal forces might try again to land on Ireland's southern coast. In London, Spenser wrote *A View of the Present State of Ireland*, a powerful statement of the opinion he shared with many other officials and settlers in Ireland: that the imposition of law and order must be carried through with resolution and must be the first step in civilizing what seemed to them a land wasted by barbarism and strife. In this view, Elizabeth's vacillating and placatory policies did nothing but harm by prolonging Ireland's agony.[4] In 1598 Tyrone openly took up arms against Elizabeth, and rebellion spread to the whole of Ireland, including Munster which had been in recent years relatively peaceful. Spenser, like many other settlers, had to leave his house and his possessions and take refuge first in Cork and then in London. There, weeks after arriving, he died. Ben Jonson's famous words to Drummond of Hawthornden that Spenser 'died for lack of bread in King Street' may be regarded as colourful exaggeration, though no doubt he had left virtually everything behind.

Such, in brief, is the life. Two aspects in particular need a little more development before we turn to *The Faerie Queene*.

2. Spenser and Protestant politics

England under Elizabeth was a Protestant nation which felt itself threatened and isolated by the great Catholic continental powers, particularly Spain. Many Englishmen wished to see England assume the role of champion of true religion against what they saw as a grand Catholic design to destroy Protestantism. They saw evidence for this in France, where the leading Huguenots and thousands of others were massacred on St Bartholomew's Day 1572; in the Netherlands, where the largely Protestant Northern States were in revolt against Spanish domination; and above all in England, which through much of Elizabeth's reign felt threatened by Spanish invasion. Such fears came to a head in 1588 with the Armada, but they by no means passed after that date. Essex's expedition to Cadiz in 1596 (celebrated in *Prothalamion* ll. 147–9) was to destroy a new armada.

Fears of Catholic invasion were matched by anxieties about Catholic activity in England. In 1568 Mary Queen of Scots had fled to England, where she was to remain a prisoner for nineteen years until her execution. As the strongest claimant to Elizabeth's throne and a Roman Catholic, she inevitably became the focus for the hopes and plots of those of her co-religionists inside and outside England who wished to see Elizabeth removed and a Catholic, pro-Spanish monarch established in her place. There was a series of plots against Elizabeth involving Mary. In 1586, following the latest of these, the Babington Plot, Mary was tried, first by a special commission and then by Parliament – reflecting Elizabeth's uneasiness about the legitimacy of such a trial of a foreign monarch. Mary was executed the following February after considerable procrastination by Elizabeth. In addition to the anxieties centred on Mary's presence, there was the continual irritant of Jesuit missionary activity within England, which became increasingly vigorous and effective in the 1580s and 1590s.

During the reign of the Roman Catholic Mary Tudor, many Protestants had fled to the continent, where they had been influenced by the radically reformist ideas they met there and by a sense of the sufferings of their co-religionists, especially in the Netherlands. When Elizabeth succeeded to the throne in 1558 many exiles returned, hoping to influence the re-establishment of Protestantism and to put England and Elizabeth at the head of an anti-Catholic alliance that would wage an aggressive war against Spain, Catholicism's champion. In fact Elizabeth resisted such plans: the Church Settlement was more cautious than the reformers would have liked and her foreign policy was, on the whole, defensive, intervening abroad on as small a scale as possible and only when it seemed necessary to keep Spain's power at bay.[5]

Leicester, in whose household Spenser briefly held a post in 1579–80, was the most powerful patron of writers and preachers with such Puritan views and strongly advocated in Council more interventionist policies abroad, particularly in the Netherlands.[6] He came to be identified with the cause of the Netherlands and was the obvious choice as leader of the army which Elizabeth finally agreed to send over in 1586 (see pp. 141–2 below). Sir Philip Sidney, Leicester's nephew, whose friendship, on however humble a level, Spenser claimed in 1579 and to whom he dedicated *The Shepheardes Calender*, was an ardent advocate of such a militantly Protestant view of England's role in continental affairs.

Spenser's first published work, as we have seen, was a series of translations for a strongly anti-Catholic work by a Protestant exile from the Netherlands. His own *Shepheardes Calender* shows in the ecclesiastical eclogues, 'Maye', 'Julye' and 'September', that Spenser's sympathies coincided with those of the 'moderate Puritan party' (Hume p. 40). We find him, for a while at least, under Leicester's patronage. From Leicester he moved, possibly through the influence of the Sidneys, to the service of Lord Grey, similarly Puritan and anti-Catholic in his views.

At the end of his career, in 1596, Spenser wrote *Prothalamion*, a celebration of a marriage taking place at Essex, formerly Leicester House, 'Where oft I gayned giftes and goodly grace/Of that great Lord, which therein wont to dwell' (ll. 138–9). Essex, Leicester's stepson, had taken over Leicester's role as champion of a militant Protestantism, as well as his palace. Spenser celebrates his recent expedition to burn Philip's ships in Cadiz harbour: his

> dreadfull name, late through all *Spaine* did thunder,
> And *Hercules* two pillors standing neere,
> Did make to quake and feare. (ll. 147–9)

The poem places Spenser's loyalties and his hopes for advancement towards the end of his life in the same religious and political context as we saw them at the beginning – ardently Protestant and retaining a vision of England as the Protestant champion whose duty was to wage an active and aggressive war against Catholic Spain. This was a vision all but lost by the 1590s after the death of Leicester and the loss of the Puritan party's influence as Elizabeth became, in both her domestic and her foreign policy, even less sympathetic to their views. Spenser's Protestantism and the vision it entails of a special, providential role for England are profoundly important for Spenser's whole conception of his epic poem, but particularly for the allegories of Holiness and Justice in Books 1 and 5.

3. Spenser and Ireland

No aspect of Spenser's biography has caused critics such distaste as his involvement in Ireland. C. S. Lewis' famous remark that 'Spenser was the instrument of a detestable policy in Ireland, and in his fifth book the wickedness he had shared begins to corrupt his imagination' (Lewis (1936) p. 349) typifies many twentieth-century responses. Such a view is, in my opinion, naive: it depends on a wish to see Spenser as an idealizing, dreamer poet whose gaze is fixed above the murky realities of his own times, as well as on a failure to grasp the context and the complexity of his views on Ireland. Spenser, throughout his poem, is deeply concerned with practical action in a fallen world in all its difficulty. Book 5 shares such a concern but examines that practical virtue, justice, in terms of the world he knew and experienced. To dismiss Book 5 or Spenser's views on Ireland because in the twentieth century we no longer find them palatable is to cut ourselves off from some of Spenser's hardest thinking and most vigorous writing.

To the Elizabethans, Ireland was the place where all their fears and anxieties about the vulnerability of their long peace under Elizabeth took nightmare form. It was an overwhelmingly Roman Catholic nation in a state of constant turbulence, where repeated rebellions against English authority might at any time combine with a Spanish invasion force, to which it offered easy access, to bring Antichrist to the very threshold of England. In *Colin Clouts Come Home Againe*, England, in spite of its alarums, seems all that is ordered and civilized in contrast to Spenser's adopted country:

> Both heaven and heavenly graces do much more
> (Quoth he) abound in that same land, then this.
> For there all happie peace and plenteous store
> Conspire in one to make contented blisse:
> No wayling there nor wretchednesse is heard,
> No bloodie issues nor no leprosies,
> No griesly famine, nor no raging sweard,
> No nightly bodrags, nor no hue and cries;
> The shepheards there abroad may safely lie,
> On hills and downes, withouten dread or daunger:
> No ravenous wolves the good mans hope destroy,
> Nor outlawes fell affray the forest raunger.   (ll. 308–19)

To Bryskett it seemed, after the recall of Lord Grey, 'that the secrett Judgement of God hangeth over this soyle' (quoted in *View* p. 213). Spenser's grim picture reflects the ravages Ireland had undergone, particularly in the previous thirty years, as Elizabethan Deputies struggled to reduce it to, in English terms, 'civility' (a useful term, in frequent use in the sixteenth century, denoting a civilized state of society). What was from the Irish point of view a coherent, if not particularly peaceful, culture, with loyalty centred on large family groups (or septs), and with its own legal system and an economy based on cattle rearing, seemed to the English savage and unjust. Typical of the views of such recent settlers as Spenser is that of Edmund Tremayne, like Spenser a servant of the Crown, who described the behaviour of a Gaelic lord in the following terms:

When this great lord is thus in possession of his Country, he is followed of all the warlike people of the same, viz., horsemen, galloglasses, and kern, and with these multitudes he useth the inferior people at his will and pleasure. He eateth and spendeth upon them with man, horse, and dog. He useth man, wife or children according to his own list, without any means to be withstanded or again-said, not only as an absolute king but as a tyrant or a lord over bondsmen. For deciding of causes in controversies he hath a judge of his own constitution and useth the law called the Brehon Law, nothing agreeing with the law of England. If any of his people commit an offence, he is punished or pardoned as pleaseth the lord. If any of his people receive wrong or any offence be done against his Country, this great lord useth the revenge according to his own will, without making any stay for commission for the Queen or her governor. So as, in short terms, a man may say the Irish rule is such a government as the mightiest do what they list against the inferiors.[7]

In response to such apparent injustice, and disorder, Spenser, echoing the views of many other observers in Ireland, advocated a period of severe, martial suppression of the rebels, to be followed by policies designed to transfer patterns of allegiance from the sept to the Crown, partly by forcible resettlement and partly by the example of English settlers who would come to live amongst the Irish and teach them the habits of civility (see, e.g., *View* pp. 95–6, 123–5). Those who thought like Spenser regarded Elizabeth's vacillating policies, following periods of severity with general pardons, with despair. Her lack of support for Lord Grey was seen by Spenser as a particularly regrettable example of her failure of nerve (*View* pp. 105–6; and see p. 144 below).

Elizabethan attempts to bring 'the Irish from desire of wars and tumults to the love of peace and civility' (*View* p. 158) notoriously failed. In 1598, rebellion spread in support of Tyrone, and Spenser with many of his kind had to flee. For Spenser, Ireland's savagery was a tragic theme: 'I do much pity that sweet land to be subject to so many evils, as every day I see more and more thrown upon her, and do half begin to think that it is . . . her fatal misfortune above all countries that I know, to be thus miserably tossed and turmoiled with these variable storms of afflictions' (*View* p. 19). The same note sounds at the end of Book 5 of *The Faerie Queene*, when Artegall is recalled before the 'ragged common-weale' (xii.26) can be reformed, and in canto vi of the *Mutabilitie Cantos*, where the curse on Arlo Hill reflects what seemed to be a curse on the whole of Ireland and Elizabethan efforts in it (see p. 175 below). Arlo's restoration must wait for Nature, the agent of Divine Providence. Without such 'heavenly graces', it seems, all would continue to go awry in that land.

1. Design

With the first three Books of *The Faerie Queene*, Spenser published 'A letter of the Authors expounding his whole intention in the course of this worke' addressed to Sir Walter Raleigh (referred to as the 'Letter to Raleigh'), in which he states that his intention is 'to fashion a gentleman or noble person in vertuous and gentle discipline'. Because he knows 'doctrine' is more palatable 'by ensample, then by rule', he has shadowed his moral under the history of Arthur. In so doing, he claims to follow a long tradition:

I have followed all the antique Poets historicall, first Homere, who in the Persons of Agamemnon and Ulysses hath ensampled a good governour and a vertuous man, the one in his Ilias, the other in his Odysseis: then Virgil, whose like intention was to doe in the person of Aeneas: after him Ariosto comprised them both in his Orlando: and lately Tasso . . . By ensample of which excellente Poets, I labour to pourtraict in Arthure, before he was king, the image of a brave knight, perfected in the twelve private morall vertues, as Aristotle hath devised, the which is the purpose of these first twelve bookes.

Notoriously, the 'Letter' is misleading in citing Aristotle as the source for Spenser's virtues (see Tuve chap. 2), and it later goes on to give descriptions of Books 1–3 which conflict with the poem as we have it on a number of points, suggesting that the poem, or at least Spenser's overall design for it, was still in a process of evolution when he wrote the 'Letter'. Nevertheless the passage I have quoted is important because it claims grand paradigms for the poem. The authors Spenser cites – Homer, Virgil, Ariosto, Tasso – wrote heroic or epic poetry, the supreme form of poetry, written in the highest style. It was a form a poet undertook only after his skill and knowledge had properly matured. *The Faerie Queene* was intended to furnish the English language with this most prestigious form of poetry, of which Sidney wrote in his *Apologie for Poetrie* (c. 1582) that it

is not only a kind, but the best and most accomplished kind of Poetry. For as the image of each action stirreth and instructeth the mind, so the lofty image of such worthies most inflameth the mind with desire to be worthy, and informs with counsel how to be worthy. (p. 119)

Spenser's epic will celebrate not only virtue, but England itself, both in the person of Arthur, the embodiment of a past national greatness, and in the person of Elizabeth: 'In that Faery Queene I

9

meane glory in my generall intention, but in my particular I conceive
the most excellent and glorious person of our soveraine the Queene,
and her kingdome in Faery land.' Such national celebration is part
of the epic tradition. Book 6 of Virgil's *Aeneid* recounts the origins of
Rome and hails Augustus' reign as the fulfilment of Rome's imperial
destiny (787–805), and Ariosto, in *Orlando Furioso*, glorifies an
ancestor of the Este family, his patrons. It would be a mistake to see
Spenser's praise of Elizabeth as mere personal flattery, though no
doubt he had hopes of advancement by pleasing the Queen. In the
writings of innumerable poets, Elizabeth had already been
transformed into an image of perfection. For Spenser she is, as
Gloriana, the embodiment of idealized sovereignty, virtuous herself
and the inspiration for virtue in others.

The distinction maintained throughout the poem between Briton
and Faery may be seen as part of Spenser's concern to celebrate his
nation as well as particular virtues. Hume has shown that the British
characters are those with a historical role, having, however tenuous-
ly, some function as part of the royal house of England (Hume chap.
7). With a frequency and detail that may puzzle modern readers,
Spenser returns to the British/Tudor genealogy (2.x; 3.iii and x;
5.vii). Each genealogy serves a specific purpose in its immediate context, but they also establish England through its royal house as a
nation with a great destiny. As Rome in Virgil's *Aeneid* was a second
Troy, so is England (Gloriana's capital is Troynovaunt); but it is one
which far outstrips its pagan paradigms. The genealogies place the
Tudor dynasty, and thus England, at the culmination of a providential plan unfolding in history, with Gloriana's Court as its ideal
pattern.

As Gloriana signifies both 'glory' and Elizabeth, so Arthur has
both a national and a moral significance: 'in the person of Prince
Arthure I sette forth magnificence in particular, which vertue for that
(according to Aristotle and the rest) it is the perfection of all the rest,
and conteineth in it them all'. Aristotle's discussion of magnificence
is, in fact, entirely concerned with the use of wealth and throws little
light on Spenser's Arthur. Rosemond Tuve has shown how the traditions of the virtues which Spenser inherited had converted
magnificence into a form of Fortitude, the fourth of the gifts of the
Holy Spirit. According to one treatise on the virtues well known in
the sixteenth century, magnificence 'is an hye werke and happy
achyevyng. Our Lord Jhesu Cryst . . . *calleth this vertu perseveraunce* by
whyche the good knyght of God endureth the evulles *unto the ende in
that hye waye of perfectyon* whyche he hath emprysed' (quoted Tuve

p. 58). Such a synthesis of Christian values with chivalric ones is very close to Spenser's conception of Arthur. He is the perfect knight, a loyal and passionate lover (1.ix.13–15), temperate (2.viii.40–52), friendly in the fullest sense (4.viii.20ff.), just (5.viii) and courteous (6, esp. viii). But he is also, most fundamentally, a Christian knight whose memento from Redcrosse is 'his Saveours testament' (1.ix.19) and whose interventions at moments of crisis, aided by his dazzling shield, make of him an instrument of Divine Grace (e.g., 1.viii.21; 5.viii.37–8).

Arthur breaks briefly into the narrative of each book, often in the seventh or eighth canto, and then disappears until the following book. He is not the focus of the narrative in the way that, for example, Aeneas is in the *Aeneid*. Instead Spenser's poem brings together, with an eclecticism that is wholly characteristic of his methods, the aims of the epic with the techniques of chivalric romance learned from medieval and popular romances such as *Guy of Warwick* and *Sir Bevis of Hampton* (Middle English poems which were frequently reprinted in the sixteenth century), as well as from the more fashionable Italian romance of Ariosto's *Orlando Furioso* (1532). Each book follows its knight on what is both a chivalric quest through a perilous landscape and a moral journey in pursuit of a complete understanding of that book's virtue in all its facets. Thus Spenser achieves both the moral seriousness of epic and the variety and narrative complexity of romance.

From chivalric romance Spenser has adopted a structure of multiple interlaced plots. This is particularly apparent in Books 3 and 4 (see pp. 75–7 below), but it is present to a greater or lesser extent in all the books. The technique yields him a great many advantages, allowing for suggestive juxtaposition of plots and characters, a series of brief episodes in which he can present many aspects of his virtues in succession and, above all, a variety of events and actors that may sometimes seem confusing. It is at first difficult for the reader to retain a name from one canto to another, or from one book to another, or to distinguish clearly the many adventures each knight experiences. It must be emphasized that *The Faerie Queene* is not a poem which yields its full richness on first reading. Perhaps more than any other poem in the language, it demands and repays close and attentive re-reading. But to some extent the reader's initial experience of confusion is a deliberate effect of the poem. Very often Spenser confronts the reader as well as his knight with ambiguous characters and episodes whose true significance is only learned gradually. Our first meeting with the magician Archimago is an example (1.i.29–37). At first sight he seems innocuous enough, 'An aged Sire, in long blacke weedes yclad' (29). Not until half a dozen stanzas later does Spenser give the reader any sign of the hermit's true nature: 'For that old man of pleasing wordes had store,/And well could file his tongue as smooth as glas' (35). Two stanzas later Spenser makes his real nature clear to us, though not to Redcrosse and Una: 'A bold bad man'. He is not named until fourteen stanzas after his first appearance: Archimago, the arch-magician, a figure of infernal power and intentions.

Archimago's nature is made clear in the course of the narrative, but Spenser does not always make the full significance of his characters or episodes plain; nor is the difficulty simply a case of recovering a context more familiar in the sixteenth century than in the twentieth, though that may help. On occasion Spenser confronts us with allegories which depend for some of their effect on an air of mystery. We are given the sense of being in the presence of secrets half understood. Such, in my view, are the Garden of Proserpina in the Cave of Mammon (2.vii.51–64), the House of Busirane (3.xi and xii) and the Temples of Venus (4.x) and of Isis (5.vii). These episodes are complex because of the many levels of allusion, which require close and attentive reading, but they also announce themselves as places where the human understanding is at its limit – an effect produced partly through the wondering incomprehension of those who take part in the cantos and partly through their strange and specific imagery, whose meaning is unexplained and not easily explicable.

Not all Spenser's allegory is so mysterious. In most of the books, core cantos 'of instruction and vision' (Roche p. 128) create a respite from the narrative and illuminate the virtue with which they are concerned by representing it in an ideal form. Such are the Houses of Holiness (1.x) and Alma (2.x), the Court of Mercilla (5.ix) and the Vision of the Graces (6.x). Books 3 and 4 are somewhat anomalous, the equivalent cantos being, perhaps, the Garden of Adonis (3.vi) and the ambiguous Temple of Venus (4.x). With the exception of the last, these episodes, for all their allusiveness and subtlety of thought and image, are reasonably clear and ordered, offering respite and illumination to the reader as well as to the knights.

Nevertheless, complexity and, on occasion, mystery are deliberately sought effects in *The Faerie Queene*. The poem presents the reader with an experience in some respects analogous to that of the knights, who must achieve their ends in a confusing world of sudden appearances and disappearances in which the correct interpretation of events is often unsure. Cymoent's lament over her misinterpretation of Proteus' prophecy is one which many other characters and we, the readers, may wish to echo:

Introduction

> So tickle be the termes of mortall state,
> And full of subtile sophismes, which do play
> With double senses, and with false debate,
> T'approve the unknowen purpose of eternall fate.   (3.iv.28)

Eternal fate is, however, manifest in the characters' narratives, testing and teaching the best of them by means of 'many a bitter stowre' (3.iii.3) and finally bringing them to fulfil their destinies.

Spenser imitates in his poem something of the complexity and confusion of human experience, but his, too, is a complexity with a plan. We, like the heroes, are tested and taught. The interlacing plot and episodic structure confront us with example after example of the virtues we are exploring or the vices which oppose them. The virtue of each book is unfolded with an appearance of fullness and completeness into its many different facets. In Book 2, for example, anger is seen in its different forms and with different significance in Sansloy and Hudibras (ii.19), in Furor, Pyrochles and Phedon (iv; v.1–24) and finally in Guyon himself (xii.83). By observing its motives and effects in each instance, we can deduce by the end of the book its use and misuse.

Reading *The Faerie Queene* is a dynamic process. We must continually juxtapose episodes and characters, noting repeated patterns and significant changes. The unbound and oppressive Proteus of Book 3 (viii.38–41) becomes, when acting legitimately in his own hall, the patron of concord and fertility in Book 4 (xi); some of the motifs of the House of Busirane (3.xi and xii) are echoed and find their source in the Temple of Venus (4.x); the early episodes of Book 6 closely parallel the early episodes of Book 5. In my discussion of each book, I have been able to do no more than indicate a few of the links and repetitions that bind the multiple episodes and characters of the poem together.

In the 'Letter to Raleigh', Spenser describes a design for his poem of which there is little trace in the published books: 'I devise that the Faery Queene kept her Annuall feaste xii. dayes, uppon which xii. severall dayes, the occasions of the xii. severall adventures hapned, which being undertaken by xii. severall knights, are in these xii. books severally handled and discoursed.' In the poem as we have it, not all the knights undertake their adventures in the Faery Court and there is no mention of an annual feast. Whatever the origins of their quests, a rather different pattern emerges, each knight in some sense beginning where his predecessor ended, perfection not quite achieved. At the end of Book 1, Redcrosse must leave Una: 'Of ease or rest I may not yet devize' (xii.18), nor can he yet enter the New

13

Jerusalem of which he has had a glimpse (x.56–63). Instead he must return again to serve the Faery Queen for six more years. At the beginning of Book 2, Guyon and the Palmer meet and receive Redcrosse's blessing for their quest:

> But wretched we, where ye have left your marke,
> Must now anew begin, like race to runne;
> God guide thee, *Guyon*, well to end thy warke,
> And to the wished haven bring thy weary barke.   (2.i.32)[8]

Similarly, Artegall, his quest imperfectly fulfilled, hands over to Calidore at the beginning of Book 6: 'But where ye ended have, now I begin/To tread an endlesse trace, withouten guyde' (i.6). Each book in a different way enacts a similar pattern of resolution almost but not finally achieved, with the next book taking over where its predecessor left off. Interlaced through each book runs the quest of Arthur for the Faery Queen:

> From that day forth I cast in carefull mind,
> To seeke her out with labour, and long tyne,
> And never vow to rest, till her I find,
> Nine monethes I seeke in vaine yet ni'll that vow unbind.
>
> (1.ix.15)

Arthur's, too, is a quest never finally completed in the poem as we have it.

Patricia A. Parker has written of 'Spenser's vision' as sharing 'in the Virgilian melancholy, the sense of an end as elusive and distant as the ever-retreating Ausonian shores' (Parker p. 88). In the 'cantos of instruction and vision' we catch glimpses of a perfection that can never fully be achieved in the world of time in which the knights must operate. The *Mutabilitie Cantos* provide the unfinished poem with an ending which acts as an emblem of its state. Mutability endlessly dilates through time and matter; only in God's eternity can rest and perfection be achieved.

2. Voice and stanza

Whatever the larger unities and design of *The Faerie Queene*, our sense of its coherence from stanza to stanza is to a great extent an effect of style and narration. That is not to say that Spenser uses a consistent narrator such as we might expect in a novel by Henry James. On the contrary, the point of view of the narrating voice varies considerably. He clearly has access to privileged information otherwise hidden from the reader, as when he tells us that Redcrosse,

14

in spite of appearances, is inexperienced in battle: 'Yet armes till that time did he never wield' (1.i.1). Often, however, he responds to his own narration with a naive wonder and suspense:

> But ah for pittie that I have thus long
>   Left a fayre Ladie languishing in payne:
>   Now well away, that I have doen such wrong,
>   To let faire *Florimell* in bands remayne,
>   In bands of love, and in sad thraldomes chayne;
>   From which unlesse some heavenly powre her free
>   By miracle, not yet appearing playne,
>   She lenger yet is like captiv'd to bee:
> That even to thinke thereof, it inly pitties mee.   (4.xi.1)

In the proems, and sometimes in the first stanzas of a canto, the narrator makes explicit moral comments which usually offer a straightforward and reliable guide to the reader; but occasionally his comments seem to miss subtleties or striking ironies, as when, in 5.viii, he congratulates Artegall on his moral sternness in parting from Britomart in 'suite of his avowed quest' (3) comparing him favourably to Hercules who 'For his loves sake his Lions skin undight' (2). But this follows an episode in which Artegall did strip himself of his armour to serve the wrong woman (see 5.v.20–3). Spenser is using the narrating voice subtly and flexibly to prompt our own responses to the narrative, whether to alert us to the need for delicacy and complexity of judgement in contrast to the narrator's simplicity, or to guide us morally or emotionally by anticipating our pity or fear or wonder. At other times it provides us with information necessary for a correct understanding of the allegory.

In spite of the variation in use and point of view it is possible to recognize in the teller a distinctive voice:

As the anonymous storyteller of medieval romance, it is only necessary for him to suit his tone to the time and place of his story. That these are in the past age of chivalry, a more heroic time than the present, requires a respect or veneration for the values that are represented; that the events are marvellous requires also the innocence of childhood. Both constitute that ethos or character which, as Aristotle said, is almost 'the most potent of all means to persuasion'.[9]

The poet the teller represents is honestly but wearily fulfilling his task of reporting the wonders and truths revealed to him (see, e.g., 2.Proem; 6.Proem 1 and ix.1). Like Colin Clout (6.x), he is both spectator and teller, revealer of divine mysteries and 'nigh ravisht with rare thoughts delight' (6.Proem 1). Through this honest, human voice, open to all the discouragements and emotions of the mortal

15

condition, Spenser encourages us to perceive as he would like us to: as one in the midst of experience, occasionally tiring but open to the beauty and wonder of what we see, trusting no doubt to our own virtue and skill but ultimately reliant on God's illumination and guidance.

Such may be the role into which we are subtly cast by the narrating voice of the poem, but as a writer Spenser is much less innocent and much less the simple reporter of sights seen than he would have us believe. I should like to conclude this introduction by looking at a few typical stanzas of narrative in order to focus exclusively, for a moment, on the poem's art rather than its themes. The stanzas come at the conclusion of Triamond and Cambel's battle in Book 4 and describe the entrance of Triamond's sister Cambina:

> Thereat the Champions both stood still a space,
>> To weeten what that sudden clamour ment;
>> Lo where they spyde with speedie whirling pace,
>> One in a charet of straunge furniment,
>> Towards them driving like a storme out sent.
>> The charet decked was in wondrous wize,
>> With gold and many a gorgeous ornament,
>> After the Persian Monarks antique guize,
> Such as the maker selfe could best by art devize.

> And drawne it was (that wonder is to tell)
>> Of two grim lyons, taken from the wood,
>> In which their powre all others did excell;
>> Now made forget their former cruell mood,
>> T'obey their riders hest, as seemed good.
>> And therein sate a Ladie passing faire
>> And bright, that seemed borne of Angels brood,
>> And with her beautie bountie did compare,
> Whether of them in her should have the greater share.   (iii.38–9)

> And as she passed through th'unruly preace
>> Of people, thronging thicke her to behold,
>> Her angrie teame breaking their bonds of peace,
>> Great heapes of them, like sheepe in narrow fold,
>> For hast did over-runne, in dust enrould,
>> That thorough rude confusion of the rout,
>> Some fearing shriekt, some being harmed hould.
>> Some laught for sport, some did for wonder shout,
> And some that would seeme wise, their wonder turnd to dout.

> In her right hand a rod of peace shee bore,
>> About the which two Serpents weren wound,
>> Entrayled mutually in lovely lore,
>> And by the tailes together firmely bound,

Introduction

> And both were with one olive garland crownd,
>   Like to the rod which *Maias* sonne doth wield,
>   Wherewith the hellish fiends he doth confound.
>   And in her other hand a cup she hild,
> The which was with Nepenthe to the brim upfild.
>
> Nepenthe is a drinck of soverayne grace,
>   Devized by the Gods, for to asswage
>   Harts grief, and bitter gall away to chace,
>   Which stirs up anguish and contentious rage:
>   In stead thereof sweet peace and quiet age
>   It doth establish in the troubled mynd.
>   Few men, but such as sober are and sage,
>   Are by the Gods to drinck thereof assynd;
> But such as drinck, eternall happinesse do fynd.   (iii.41–3)

The apparent movement of the stanzas is from confusion and wonder to clarity. In stanza 38 we share the champions' astonished fascination at the bizarre and violent appearance of the chariot 'like a storme out sent'. In the next stanza some of the details are filled in. The chariot is drawn by grim lions, but their savagery is now curbed. The lady within the chariot 'seemed borne of Angels brood' and her 'bountie' is as great as her beauty. The two lines illustrate Spenser's flexible use of the narrating voice. In the first the perspective is still that of a spectator merely deducing from appearances, in the second we are given privileged information not available to a spectator. By stanzas 42 and 43, the narrator is able to explain all, even divine secrets.

The Stanzas may move from confusion and mere outer appearance to an explanation of hidden significance, but the reader may feel that much is still puzzling. The episode is bizarre, not only because of the exotic chariot and the rod and cup the lady bears, but because we receive apparently contradictory signals about her nature. Her chariot approaches violently, gorgeously bedecked 'After the Persian Monarks antique guize'. False Duessa's headdress was 'like a *Persian* mitre' (1.ii.13), and she took Redcrosse to the Court of Pride, whose richness exceeded even that of '*Persia* selfe, the nourse of pompous pride' (1.iv.7). The chariot is drawn by lions whose ferocity must be curbed by a strong hand; indeed, coming to 'th'unruly preace/Of people' (41), they break 'their bonds of peace'. Yet the figure within the chariot sits mildly, so still that the brimming cup in her hand does not spill. Neither hand is free to touch the reins.

The scene is not, of course, realistic; Cambina and her chariot are moving emblems. Cambina is the daughter of Agape (the charitable

17

or brotherly love of the New Testament) and comes, we are told in
stanza 40, to 'pacifie the strife' between the two knights. The rod and
cup she holds are both signs of peace and concord. The chariot,
however, is less straightforward. Why should an emissary of peace
arrive in such a violent manner in a chariot of such pagan splendour?
This the narrating voice does not explain, and it is part of the enigma
of the stanzas. We, the readers, must ponder the contradictions
and tentatively feel our way towards an explanation based on the
reiterated themes of the book. In this case, the violence may be explained by the recurring theme of *discordia concors*, the notion that concord binds together discordant elements in a tense unity maintained
only by the active power of love (Roche pp. 23–6). Where that power
fails, the bound elements will again fly apart and resume their
violence. Cambina's power of love curbs powerful forces, she can
tame savage lions and fierce warriors; but among 'th'unruly preace'
it seems she has no power, and the violence of her lions reflects the
wild, discordant confusion of the throng. The pagan splendour of the
chariot remains puzzling, perhaps suggesting the pride that accompanies violence but which Cambina's demeanour annuls.

Emblematic as Cambina and her chariot may be, they are described in terms that give them a drama and presence. The narrating
voice communicates, '(that wonder is to tell)', the astonishment of
the spectator. The narrative catches up the emblem, transforming
it into a bizarre adventure. But these stanzas also slow the action
down. We move from narrative, the fight and its interruption, to
emblematic tableaux: Cambina's appearance, followed, in stanza 49,
by the transformation of the fighters to friends, as symbolized by
their handshake, an image of concord (Roche p. 28).

The continual pull of Spenser's poem between the forward-moving
story-line and the static density of its images is built into the stanza
form itself, which contains both 'the sense of "staying" or dilation
. . . and the straightforward, linear, syntactic movement towards the
final period' (Parker p. 64). The rhyme scheme tends to focus the
stanza on the rhyming couplets in the middle and at the end, creating
an effect of fulness and closure which is emphasized by the final alex-
andrine (twelve-syllable line) and the end-stopping of each stanza. In
the passage we are examining, we can see how the stanzas function
almost like building blocks or like a suite of gorgeously hung rooms
through which we must pass to our destination. Each has its own
character: stanza 38 concentrates on the chariot and 39 on the contrast between the lions and the still lady who controls them, 42 is
devoted almost entirely to the 'rod of peace' and 43 to Nepenthe.

Introduction

Stanza 41 needs to be looked at in more detail. It breaks into the wonder and mystery of the surrounding stanzas with a note of satiric comedy. Our attention is diverted from the pain of those whom Cambina's lions 'over-runne' to the indecorum and absurd confusion of the crowd's behaviour;

> Some fearing shriekt, some being harmed hould,
> Some laught for sport, some did for wonder shout,
> And some that would seeme wise, their wonder turnd to dout.

The stanza demonstrates the ineffectiveness of Cambina's power among the rude throng and suggests the reason for it – these tow-headed plebeians are too gross and senseless. But the stanza also helps to change the mood of the reader, lightening the tension that remains from the violent and tragic fight between Cambel and the three brothers, and preparing for the release and festivity of its happy resolution.

In these few comments I have tried to suggest some of the ways in which Spenser directs and controls our responses to Cambina's dramatic entry into the narrative. The passage contains, in little, examples of Spenser's methods throughout the poem: his mixture of narrative and emblem, his cultivation of enigmas not wholly explained by the narrating voice, and his flexibility of style and point of view, allowing us to share the spectators' wonder and puzzlement in one stanza, breaking the decorum with satiric comedy in the next, and revealing divine mysteries to us in a third.

Chapter 1

BOOK 1

INTRODUCTION

1. Holiness

Cast off . . . the old man which is corrupt through ye deceivable lusts, And bee renewed in the spirit of your minde, And put on the new man, which after God is created in righteousnesse, and true holinesse.

(Ephesians 4.22–4)

Book 1 reverberates with the spiritual drama St Paul describes. Holiness is not a virtue as normally understood, a quality of the good man achieved by obeying a set of moral laws. All human activity has to be placed in the context of the Fall, the consequent corruption of man's nature and the expulsion from Eden. In the Protestant view this corruption is indelible and all-pervasive; man by his own efforts cannot save himself, cannot achieve that state of being given over to God which is the essence of holiness. The New Testament displays a paradoxical attitude to holiness. On the one hand it is something which through Christ the Christian has already been given, on the other it is a goal still to be reached. The paradox is perhaps best summed up by St Paul when he writes, to quote the New English Bible for its clarity: 'I have not yet reached perfection, but I press on, hoping to take hold of that for which Christ once took hold of me' (Philippians 3.12).

In sixteenth-century Protestantism the dramatic process by which the individual pressed on to take hold of that which he had already been given was a subject of thorough analysis. The key terms in this analysis are Election, Calling, Repentance, Justification and Sanctification.[1] The Election of a few to salvation and many to damnation was by God from all eternity, and for much of his life the individual Christian might have no knowledge of whether he was one of the elect. Not until the dramatic moment of the special, or 'effectual', Calling, in which the Holy Spirit breaks into the Christian's life, does the work of regeneration begin. Calvin vividly describes the lost and helpless condition of even the elect before Calling:

'All we like sheep have gone astray, we have turned every one to his own way' (Isa. liii.6); that is, to perdition. In this gulf of perdition God leaves those whom he has determined one day to deliver until his own time arrive; he only preserves them from plunging into irremediable blasphemy.

(Institutes II, 250)

Calling typically takes the form of illumination. The Christian is made vividly aware of his own desperate sinfulness and repents, but he is also comforted by the gift of a renewed faith in the promise of salvation. With Calling and Repentance comes assurance of the gift of Justification, in which the Christian's sins are forgiven him through Christ's atonement. That this forgiveness comes not from the sinner's own merit but as a free gift of God is central to Protestant thought:

When God justifies us through the intercession of Christ, he does not acquit us on a proof of our own innocence, but by an imputation of righteousness, so that though not righteous in ourselves, we are deemed righteous in Christ.

(Institutes II, 39)

Although justified in God's sight, the Christian is still corrupt and sinful in his own nature. But by God's Grace, the Christian is now able to begin the process of Mortification (or true repentance) and Sanctification (the renewal of God's image in him), which, according to Ephesians 4.24, 'is created in righteousnesse, and true holinesse'. Calvin tells us:

we must be holy, because 'God is holy' (Lev. xix.l; 1 Pet. i.16). For when we were scattered abroad like lost sheep, wandering through the labyrinth of this world, he brought us back again to his own fold. When mention is made of our union with God, let us remember that holiness must be the bond; not that by the merit of holiness we come into communion with him (we ought rather first to cleave to him, in order that, pervaded with his holiness, we may follow whither he calls) . . . this is the end of our calling, the end to which we ought ever to have respect, if we would answer the call of God.   *(Institutes* II, 3)

Such in outline is the Protestant 'paradigm of salvation', a story certainly on an epic scale and fraught with great spiritual drama. Spenser's Redcrosse is a type of the elect Christian. Through his initial errings and wanderings; in Orgoglio's dungeon, his 'gulf of perdition', where Grace intervenes; through his Repentance and Justification and his instruction in the course of Sanctification in the House of Holiness; and in his final defeat of Satan, he exemplifies the drama of salvation the reader might have already experienced, or might hope to face. We shall follow Redcrosse's spiritual drama in greater detail when we examine the episodes in which he is involved.

2. Secondary narrative models for Book 1

The drama of salvation as described by St Paul and interpreted by sixteenth-century Protestants provides a major source of imagery and the structural model for Book 1 of *The Faerie Queene*. Characteristically, however, Spenser weaves together paradigms and images from a variety of sources to produce his own richly allusive synthesis. We shall look briefly at three of these sources.

a. The Revelation of John the Divine

Redcrosse's spiritual drama is rendered yet more vivid by Spenser's use of the striking allegorical imagery of St John's visions. A woman 'clothed with the sunne' (12.1) is chased into the wilderness by a great red dragon with seven heads and ten horns (12.3, 13.14). In league with the dragon is the great Whore of Babylon, mounted on a scarlet beast also with seven heads and ten horns. She is 'arayed in purple and scarlet, and gilded with gold, and precious stones, and pearles, and ha[s] a cup of gold in her hand, full of abominations, and filthinesse of her fornication' (17.4). The Whore triumphs now amongst the ungodly, but, it is promised, she will be stripped naked (17.16) and destroyed, while her adversary, the woman that fled to the wilderness will be clothed in 'pure fine linen, and shining' (19.8) and married to the Lamb (Christ). John is told of the defeat of the dragon, though initially it is chained for a thousand years, to be freed again briefly before its final destruction. Finally he sees a vision of the New Jerusalem 'pure golde like unto cleare glasse' (21.18), from which flows the 'river of water of life' and beside it the 'tree of life' (22.1–2).

We shall look at Spenser's use of this imagery as we look at episodes in Book 1 in detail, but something may by said at this stage about sixteenth-century Protestants' understanding of the allegory. Most clearly, Revelation describes the temptations and ravages of Satan suffered by Christians and promises his final overthrow and the triumph of the elect. But Revelation was also understood to describe the sufferings of the Church throughout history, including those of the English Church. The woman clothed with the sun who is chased into the wilderness and finally wedded to Christ was interpreted as the Church, and by sixteenth-century Protestants as the True (Reformed) Church. Opposed to her are the Whore of Babylon and the seven-headed beast, who were universally interpreted by Protestants as the Roman Catholic Church.

Revelation thus provided Spenser with vivid images to describe the conflict of good and evil. But the images bring with them a tradition of historical allegory, so that at times episodes in Book 1 refer not only to the individual's fight with the forces of Satan, but also to the fight of God's elect through history and to the sufferings of the True Church. At times, Spenser's imagery is so specific as to suggest that he is dealing particularly with the history of the English Church and its fight with the forces of Satan in recent times. It is easy to be heavy-handed and over-insistent when following the historical allegory in Book 1. It is perhaps best to think of it as a potential dimension which the poetry sometimes opens up to us but which it often does not.

b. The Legend of St George

St John's Satanic dragon is also, in Spenser's poem, the dragon killed by St George. In characteristic fashion, Spenser multiplies the significance of his images by grafting a number of models on to one another. In the case of St George some of this work had already been done for him. A version of the St George legend possibly available to Spenser was the manuscript of Lydgate's *The Legend of St George*, in which St George is described as vanquishing 'the fiend', that is, 'the worlde, the fleshe'.[2] A ballad of 1606 similarly calls the dragon 'the Fiend' and compares St George's victory over it to that of Christ over the Devil (Variorum edition p. 390). Both Lydgate, and Caxton in his translation of the story, interpret an element of George's name to mean holiness, and Caxton further writes: 'George is sayd of Geos/Whiche is as muche to saye as erthe and orge/that is tilyenge/so george is to saye as tilyenge the erthe/that is his flesshe'.[3] George's connection with the earth is a significant detail for Spenser, who works it into his account of Redcrosse's origins. At the House of Holiness Redcrosse is told that a fairy stole him when he was still a baby:

> Thence she thee brought into this Faerie lond,
> And in an heaped furrow did thee hyde,
> Where thee a Ploughman all unweeting fond,
> As he his toylsome teme that way did guyde,
> And brought thee up in ploughmans state to byde,
> Whereof *Georgos* he thee gave to name.   (1.x.66)

I shall explore Spenser's association of Redcrosse with the earth and the flesh more fully in my discussion of the Orgoglio episode (see pp. 37–40 below).

The revelation of Redcrosse's identity is carefully handled by Spenser. The early tableau of Redcrosse killing the monster Error while Una stands to one side with her lamb clearly identifies St George to the reader, even though he is not named to us until the following canto (l.ii.12). Redcrosse does not discover his own identity until the House of Holiness when his particular connection with England is made clear:

> For thou emongst those Saints, whom thou doest see,
> Shalt be a Saint, and thine owne nations frend
> And Patrone: thou Saint *George* shalt called bee,
> Saint *George* of mery England, the signe of victoree.   (l.x.61)

St George's connection with England is familiar. Not only was he the patron saint, but he was also closely connected with the monarchy as patron of the prestigious Order of the Garter. This particularly English, and particularly royal, dimension to Redcrosse, added just before his final battle with the dragon, suggests that at this point the reader is fully justified in finding historical allegory in the events described.

c. The 'Aeneid'

Spenser signals to the reader the importance of the *Aeneid* as a model in the first stanza of *The Faerie Queene*. In Renaissance editions, Virgil's epic began with the lines

> Ille ego, qui quondam gracili modulatus avena
> carmen . . .
> . . . at nunc horrentia Martis
> arma virumque cano.

[I am he who once tuned my song on a slender oaten reed . . . but now I sing of the terrible arms of Mars and the hero] [4]

Spenser's opening lines clearly echo both these words and the pattern established by Virgil of a movement from pastoral to epic poetry:

> Lo I the man, whose Muse whilome did maske,
> As time her taught, in lowly Shepheards weeds,
> Am now enforst a far unfitter taske,
> For trumpets sterne to chaunge mine Oaten reeds,
> And sing of Knights and Ladies gentle deeds.

Spenser's debt to the *Aeneid* in Book 1 is not only a matter of specific borrowings or the imitation of actual episodes, although the underworld to which Duessa descends in canto v owes some of its details to the underworld to which Aeneas descends in *Aeneid* 6. Rather, Spenser invokes, by his initial echo of Virgil, and his own self-

conscious assumption of the role of the epic poet, the exemplary
heroic pattern embodied in Aeneas. Spenser acknowledges this in the
'Letter to Raleigh':

I chose the historye of king Arthure, as most fitte for the excellency of his per-
son . . . In which I have followed all the antique Poets historicall, first
Homere, who in the Persons of Agamemnon and Ulysses hath ensampled a
good governour and a vertuous man, the one in his Ilias, the other in his
Odysseis: then Virgil, whose like intention was to doe in the person of
Aeneas.

The significance Aeneas held for the Renaissance as the exemplary
epic hero was summed up by Ben Jonson when he wrote: 'Virgil
makes throughout the most exquisite pattern of piety, justice,
prudence and all other princely virtues' (quoted by Nohrnberg p.
30). As the model of excellence and piety Spenser, the fledgling epic
poet, might have been expected to shape not only Arthur, but Redcrosse too, in Aeneas' image, and indeed there are parallels. Redcrosse, like Aeneas, is chosen (destined in Aeneas' case, elected in
Redcrosse's) for remarkable achievements. Both spend much time in
wandering and both are caught in the sexual snares of a woman. Both
eventually achieve their quests and are rewarded with marriage.

But as a Protestant poet Spenser subtly transforms his model.
Where Aeneas was interpreted as the perfect man, able by his virtue
and piety to conquer his passion for Dido in obedience to the gods
and to endure and overcome the difficulties he faced, Redcrosse is a
type of the fallen man, unable by his own efforts to free himself from
Duessa or escape Orgoglio's dungeon, and only finally enabled to
achieve holiness and accomplish his quest through the powerful intervention of Grace. Beyond Virgil's *Aeneid* lies the idealized City of
Rome, but beyond Spenser's book lies the heavenly Jerusalem.

Virgil's epic set before his imitators a pattern of the perfect hero,
but it also provided a model for a national epic. The *Aeneid*, written
for the Emperor Augustus, tells of the remote origins from which will
grow the imperial glory of Rome prophesied at the end of *Aeneid* 6.
Spenser signals that his poem will have a similar historical and
nationalist dimension in the fourth stanza of the Proem to Book 1.
As the events of the *Aeneid* foreshadowed the glories of Rome, so the
figure of Gloriana in *The Faerie Queene* foreshadows the reign of
Elizabeth:

> O Goddesse heavenly bright,
> Mirrour of grace, and Majestie divine,
> Great Lady of the greatest Isle, whose light
> Like *Phoebus* lampe throughout the world doth shine,

> Shed thy faire beames into my feeble eyne,
> And raise my thoughts too humble and too vile,
> To thinke of that true glorious type of thine,
> The arguement of mine afflicted stile.

The historical significance of Gloriana reverberates throughout *The Faerie Queene*, but these stanzas also preface Book 1 — in which, as we have seen, Redcrosse carries a similar though intermittent historical resonance.

Una and Duessa

In the book of Revelation Spenser found an account of the struggle of good and evil which relied on dramatically opposed images: monstrous beasts from the sea and the earth versus the rider on a white horse in the heavens; Babylon versus Jerusalem; the scarlet whore versus the woman clothed with the sun. There is a similar sense of the drama of opposites in Book 1. The darkness in which evil habitually lurks (e.g., Error i.14, the darkness of Archimago's magic i.37–9, or Duessa's affinity to Night v.20–7) is opposed by the light that emanates from good, however it may be temporarily obscured (e.g., Una's brightness beneath her veil iii.4, or Arthur's uncovered shield viii.19); the showy but rotten edifice of the House of Pride is set against the strait, plain but ancient House of Holiness; Redcrosse's descent to Orgoglio's Hell-like dungeon, where he is imprisoned by blind Ignaro (viii.30–1, 37–9) is followed by his ascent of the steep hill of Heavenly Contemplation under the care of its blind but visionary guardian (x.46–7). The most strikingly opposed figures in Book 1 are Una and Duessa. The contrast is developed both in terms of their significance and in the details of their narratives.

1. Una

Una first appears before the reader elaborately described in language rich with emblematic significance:

> A lovely Ladie rode him faire beside,
> Upon a lowly Asse more white then snow.
> Yet she much whiter; but the same did hide
> Under a vele, that wimpled was full low;
> And over all a blacke stole she did throw,
> As one that inly mournd: so was she sad,
> And heavie sat upon her palfrey slow;
> Seemed in heart some hidden care she had,
> And by her in a line, a milke white lambe she lad.

> So pure and innocent, as that same lambe,
> She was in life and every vertuous lore,

26

And by descent from Royall lynage came
Of ancient Kings and Queenes, that had of yore
Their scepters stretcht from East to Westerne shore,
And all the world in their subjection held;
Till that infernall feend with foule uprore
Forwasted all their land, and them expeld:
Whom to avenge, she had this Knight from far compeld.   (i.4–5)

The details point to Una's humility (the ass) and her innocence (her whiteness). The milk-white lamb is more complex: it suggests her innocence and vulnerability, and it also suggests her identity as the lady rescued by St George, who was traditionally shown leading a lamb (Variorum edition pp. 389–90). This identification is confirmed shortly afterwards by the tableau of Redcrosse killing the monster Error as Una stands to one side (i.18–19). The lamb also links Una with Christ, the sacrificial lamb (John 1.29). The connotations of Una's association with an image of the crucified Christ are developed in the account of Una's ancestry. She inherits the lost innocence and rights of Adam and Eve before the Fall in the Garden of Eden. Her inheritance is also that of the primitive Christian Church, which in the Protestant view had ruled over East and West before the usurpation of the Roman Catholic Church. Una's association with the lamb thus suggests both her identity as Christ's True Church, to be restored by the defeat of Roman Catholicism, and the promise by which our sinful inheritance from Adam and Eve will be purged and we shall be restored to our first communion with God. Characteristically, Spenser does not name Redcrosse's lady until some of the richness of her allusiveness has been revealed to us, so that we have a sense of the wide inclusiveness of her significance before she is fixed by a name, Una (i.45), meaning One, the indivisibility of Truth. She is called Truth in the Arguments to the following two cantos.

Una's whiteness is covered by a 'blacke stole' and she is veiled (i.4), a sign of her outcast state in this world. Truth may be one and indivisible, but she is by no means unmistakable to the dimmed vision of fallen man. Redcrosse's failure, when deceived by the 'divelish arts' (ii.9) of Archimago, to tell the false from the true Una (i.50 and ii.5–6) and his abandonment of her (ii.6) condemn Una to a period of wandering. The marvellous adventures which assail Una in the 'woods and forrests' (ii.9) develop her spiritual and historical significance. Like her prototype, the woman in the wilderness (Revelation 12.13–14), she is under divine protection, though the lion who protects her has a possible historical dimension. He is described heraldically as 'ramping' (iii.41), he is a 'kingly beast' (iii.8) and 'full of kingly awe' (iii.41). He protects Una by destroying Kirkrapine (iii.19–20) and is only finally defeated by the 'lawlesse' Sansloy (iii.42–3). The language suggests that the lion may be an embodiment of kingly power, more specifically the power of the kings of England, who sported a rampant lion as their emblem.

Una may be protected for a while by kingly power, but she is threatened by the Mohammedan Sansloy, by the subtle 'trains' of Archimago as a false Redcrosse (iii.24–38), and by the nefarious trio of Corceca, Abessa and Kirkrapine (iii.13–21). The Argument to canto iii identifies Corceca as 'Blind Devotion', while her superstitious behaviour ('thrise nine hundred *Aves* she was wont to say' iii.13) and her daughter's name suggest the abuses of monasticism. But Abessa's deaf-mute condition and her name (*ab essa*) may also suggest the abuse of absenteeism, an abuse particularly current in the Elizabethan Church following the wholesale transfer of monastic lands into secular hands.

While Redcrosse succumbs to the blandishments of Duessa and contributes to the diversions of the House of Pride (i.5), Una remains helplessly in the hands of 'lawless lust' (Argument to canto vi), the pagan Sansloy. But

> Eternall providence exceeding thought,
> Where none appeares can make her selfe a way:
> A wondrous way it for this Lady wrought.   (vi.7)

Wondrous indeed! The fauns and satyrs who now come to Una's aid respond instinctively to Una's unveiled beauty, although they are unable to rise above a superstitious idolatry, despite Una's efforts to instruct them:

> her gentle wit she plyes,
> To teach them truth, which worship her in vaine,
> And made her th'Image of Idolatryes.   (vi.19)

When she forbids them to worship herself, they turn with comic ignorance to worshipping her ass instead. Anthea Hume describes the merely natural religious instinct represented by these half-human woodland creatures and cites (p. 88) an analogous passage in Calvin:

There is no nation so barbarous, no kind of people so savage, in whom resteth not this persuasion that there is a God. And even they that in other parts of their lyfe, seme very litle to differ from brute beastes, yet do continually kepe a certain sede of religion . . . Yea and ydolatrie it selfe is a substanciall profe of the persuasion.

While the satyrs are unable to progress beyond idolatry, Satyrane, whose mother is human, is able to respond to Una's instruction (vi.31) and to release her from their adoring, but too limiting, protection.

Canto vii marks the crisis in Una's fortunes, as in those of Redcrosse: tricked and pursued by Archimago, threatened by Sansloy, she mourns over the armour of the apparently dead Redcrosse (vii.22–3). With the appearance of Arthur a few stanzas later her restoration and the eventual triumph of the forces of good begin. With great delicacy Una is used by Spenser to mark the transition. At this point Una's allegorical significance is at its most muted and she seems most like us, expressing a very human sense of loss and the hopelessness of our unregenerate condition:

> For earthly sight can nought but sorrow breed,
> And late repentance, which shall long abyde.
> Mine eyes no more on vanitie shall feed,
> But seeled up with death, shall have their deadly meed.   (vii.23)

With Arthur's appearance (vii.29) there is a sense of new beginning, and the allegory reasserts itself with clarity. In her explanation to Arthur, Una recapitulates the facts of Redcrosse's quest and her own identity as the only daughter of the King and Queen of Eden (vii.43–4). In her role as the True Church, Una both represents a human institution and offers to fallen man his only hope of salvation. In words which illumine Una's significance, Calvin comments:

To prevent the truth from perishing in the world, the Church is its faithful guardian, because God has been pleased to preserve the pure preaching of his word by her instrumentality, and to exhibit himself to us as a parent while he feeds us with spiritual nourishment, and provides whatever is conducive to our salvation.   (*Institutes* II, 290)

Through Una, Redcrosse is led to his salvation, and, in turn, through Redcrosse's defeat of 'that old dragon', Satan, in which he shares by Grace in the victory of Christ, Una's parents are released from captivity, the bondage of man to sin and death.

The restoration of Una's parents to their kingdom is a spiritual event enacted in each Justified Christian, but the events of canto xii also clearly carry contemporary historical significance. Una is identified with the True Church. She is 'all lilly white, withoutten spot' (xii.22) and of a 'blazing brightnesse' (23), recalling St Paul's description of the Church as 'not having spotte or wrinkle' (Ephesians 5.27) and the allegorical description of the bride of Christ, the Church, in Revelation, as 'arayed with pure fine linen and shining' (Revelation 18.16). Her restoration through the victory of a Redcrosse knight who has now been identified as 'Saint *George* of mery England' (x.61) in part celebrates the particular achievement of Elizabeth I in restoring the True Reformed Church to its inheritance in England.

2. Duessa

Where Una's name points to the singleness of truth, Duessa's signifies the doubleness of falsehood and deceit. The reader is alerted to her significance in the Argument to canto ii (*'faire falshood'*), but like Una she is most fully identified by her appearance. Redcrosse, separated now from Una, meets Duessa accompanied by the Saracen Sansfoy and richly dressed in a manner which ought to be instantly recognizable:

> A goodly Lady clad in scarlot red,
> Purfled with gold and pearle of rich assay,
> And like a *Persian* mitre on her hed
> She wore, with crownes and owches garnished,
> The which her lavish lovers to her gave;
> Her wanton palfrey all was overspred
> With tinsell trappings, woven like a wave,
> Whose bridle rung with golden bels and bosses brave.   (ii.13)

The imagery of scarlet, gold and jewels is from the description in Revelation (12.4) of the Whore of Babylon, commonly interpreted by Protestants as the Papacy. The contrast to Una, Truth and the Reformed Church is developed point by point: the clothing, the mount, the companion. Similarly contrasted are their genealogies. Duessa is

> the sole daughter of an Emperour,
> He that the wide West under his rule has,
> And high hath set his throne, where *Tiberis* doth pas.   (ii.22)

Spenser is contrasting Roman Catholicism, whose authority was confined to Western Europe, with the universal rule of the True Primitive Church.

Redcrosse with his spoils, the shield of Faithlessness (Sansfoy) and false Duessa, seems to err grossly. Not even the story of an earlier victim of Duessa, in every detail parallel to his own (ii.30–43), illumines his blindness. The story of a man transformed into a speaking tree derives most immediately from Ariosto's *Orlando Furioso* (6.26–53). Sir John Harington's gloss on his English translation (1591) tells us that it signifies 'how men given over to sensualitie,

leese in the end the verie forme of man (which is reason) and so
become beastes or stockes'. Details of the incident described by
Spenser suggest, however, that the sensuality to which Duessa tempts
Fradubio and, increasingly, Redcrosse, should not be taken merely
literally. Fradubio tells Redcrosse that it is his 'nature weake' (ii.33)
that the witch has transformed to 'treen mould' (39); his lady
Fraelissa (frailty) suffers a similar fate. The only cure for these
degenerate frail natures is to be 'bathed in a living well' (43), which
suggests the sacrament of baptism. The absolution, of which baptism
is a sign, is for the sins of the flesh in the widest sense. The sixteenth-
century divine, William Perkins, gives lust its usual metaphorical
value when he tells us that 'lusting of the flesh . . . is to engender
evill motions and inclinations of selfe-love, envy, pride, unbeleefe,
anger, etc. . . . to hinder, and quench, and overwhelme all the good
motions of the spirit' (*The Combat of The Flesh and Spirit*, in *Workes* I,
470).

Duessa leads Redcrosse towards such spiritual, as much as carnal,
sin. Una will guide Redcrosse to the House of Holiness, whose low
door is locked and guarded by a porter, 'but when they knockt,/The
Porter opened unto them streight way' (x.5). The Porter is Humiltà,
and 'streight way' suggests both the speed with which the House is
opened to those who seek it (Matthew 7.7) and the strait and narrow
way into it (Matthew 7.14). By contrast Duessa conducts him along
a 'broad high way' (iv.2; cf. Matthew 7.13), through wide open gates
(iv.6), into the gaudy House of Pride. Duessa is well known in this
place (iv.15) and occupies a privileged position (iv.37). Her nature
is most fully developed, however, in the account of her association
with Night and her journey to Hell to revive Sansjoy (v.19–45). The
details of this nightmarish mission develop the contrast to Una's mission in the House of Holiness. Where Duessa goes for help to 'griesly
Night, with visage deadly sad,/That *Phoebus* chearefull face durst
never vew' (v.20), Una has recourse to Dame Caelia 'thought/From
heaven to come' (x.4). Dame Caelia's only joy is 'to relieve the
needes/Of wretched soules, and helpe the helpeless pore' (x.3),
whereas Night scarcely feels pity for her own progeny, 'for evermore
she hated, never loved' (v.24). Night claims relationship with Duessa
as the mother 'of falshood, and root of *Duessaes* race' (v.27), while
Dame Caelia joyfully knows Una 'to spring from heavenly race'
(x.8). The two episodes are systematically paralleled: the imagery of
light and ascent in one is set against that of darkness and descent in
the other; the clarity of Christian allegory is set against the murky
entanglement of pagan mythology. Central to both is a mission of

healing and regeneration: Duessa seeks bodily healing for Sansjoy from the damned Aesculapius, traditionally interpreted as a false Christ, who has blasphemously cobbled together a fleshly resurrection for Hippolytus (v.37–9; see Hamilton (1961) p. 71). Una seeks spiritual healing for Redcrosse, which takes the form of rigorous penitence and depends on the resurrection of the true Christ (x.24–8).

Like a persistently false version of Una, Duessa returns from her underworld visit to find herself, like Una before her, abandoned by Redcrosse (ii.7 and v.45), but where Una's pursuit is in vain owing to the speed with which Redcrosse's wrath pricks him on (ii.8), Duessa easily overtakes a Redcrosse grown 'dull and slow' through weariness, like the waters by which she finds him sitting, his armour discarded (vii.2–6). In this state he is taken captive by Duessa's seductions and Orgoglio's might. As Una's allegorical significance as the True Church is reiterated by Spenser at the crucial point of Arthur's intervention, so Duessa's significance as the false Roman Church is reiterated now at the moment of her triumph. Her new lover, Orgoglio, gives her

> gold and purple pall to weare,
> And triple crowne set on her head full hye,
> And her endowed with royall majestye.   (vii.16)

He also sets her on a blasphemous 'Beast with sevenfold head' (18). The imagery clearly points to its source in Revelation: 'I sawe a woman sit upon a scarlet coloured beast, full of names of blasphemie, which had seven heads and ten hornes. And the woman was arayed in purple and scarlet' (Revelation 17.3–4), 'and the Kings of the earth . . . have committed fornication, and lived in pleasure with her' (Revelation 18.9). The 'triple crowne' (vii.16) of the Papacy is Spenser's addition, designed to leave no doubt of the identity of beast or rider in the reader's mind. A marginal gloss to the Geneva Bible notes: 'the beast signifieth the ancient Rome: the woman that sitteth thereon, the new Rome which is the Papistry'. (For a more detailed discussion of Orgoglio, see pp. 37–40 below.) The detailed contrast between Una and Duessa is maintained to the end. Arthur's defeat of Orgoglio marks the end of Una's wandering in the wilderness and gives hope of her restoration to her kingdom, when she will put aside her veil and cloak and expose her full brightness (xii.23). By contrast, Duessa is stripped to reveal the monstrousness of her nature (viii.46–9). She in turn flees 'to the wastfull wildernesse' (50), but, unlike Una's, her flight is from 'heavens hated face' and from the world which now knows her too well.

I have suggested that Redcrosse is a type of the elect Christian, embodying in his adventures the spiritual drama of sinfulness, the intervention of Grace, and Regeneration. This is not to say Redcrosse is a mere cipher; Spenser attributes to him individual touches – his guilelessness, his youthful solemnity, his impetuosity – which allow us to feel a human sympathy, and affinity, with him. As is the case with Una and Duessa, Redcrosse's significance is elaborated in the details of his appearance long before he is named. In Redcrosse's case the appearance is deeply ambivalent:

> A Gentle Knight was pricking on the plaine,
>> Y cladd in mightie armes and silver shielde,
>> Wherein old dints of deepe wounds did remaine,
>> The cruell markes of many' a bloudy fielde;
>> Yet armes till that time did he never wield:
>> His angry steede did chide his foming bitt,
>> As much disdayning to the curbe to yield:
>> Full jolly knight he seemd, and faire did sitt,
> As one for knightly giusts and fierce encounters fitt.

> But on his brest a bloudie Crosse he bore,
>> The deare remembrance of his dying Lord,
>> For whose sweete sake that glorious badge he wore,
>> And dead as living ever him ador'd:
>> Upon his shield the like was also scor'd,
>> For soveraine hope, which in his helpe he had:
>> Right faithfull true he was in deede and word,
>> But of his cheere did seeme too solemne sad;
> Yet nothing did he dread, but ever was ydrad.   (i.1–2)

The 'yets' and 'buts' point to the contradictions: the armour is well used, but not by Redcrosse; he 'seemd' a 'jolly knight', fitted for the usual chivalric achievements, but his badge suggests a far more serious and significant undertaking; we are assured of his Christ-like qualities – 'Right faithfull true he was in deede and word' (cf. the description of Christ as 'faithfull and true' in Revelation 19.11) – but his demeanour suggests that he does not enjoy full assurance of those qualities. The 'bloudie Cross' on armour and shield suggests that Redcrosse wears the spiritual armour which St Paul tells us God provides for his children:

Take unto you the whole armour of God, that ye may be able to resist in the evill day . . . Stand therefore, and your loines gird about with veritie, and having on the brest-plate of righteousnesse. And your feete shod with the preparation of the Gospel of peace. Above all, take the shielde of faith, wherewith ye may quench all the fiery darts of the wicked. And take the helmet of salvation, and the sword of the Spirit, which is the word of God.

(Ephesians 6.13–17)

Thus armed and eager, but untried, Redcrosse rides forth. Spenser immediately embroils him in the actual ambivalence of experience. The heavens do not smile on the pair and they are forced to enter a wood where they find a confusion of paths (i.7). Their delight and innocence as they move through the wood are suggested by the variety and picturesqueness of the description of the trees, but the catalogue includes a sour note, 'the Maple seeldom inward sound' (i.9). The wood proves as deceptive as the tree and the 'little glooming light' (14) shed by Redcrosse's armour reveals to him what lies at its centre, the monster Error. The knight does win this encounter, though he gets entangled in '*Errours* endlesse traine' (18) and is almost choked by its vomit of books and blind frogs and toads (20). From these disgusting forms of error he is only rescued by the lady's timely reminder to 'add faith unto your force' (19) and by his fear of shame (24). The image of the vomiting monster seems to be modelled on two incidents in Revelation (12.15 and 16.13). Its significance is made clearer by Anthea Hume, who draws attention to the particular closeness of Spenser's language to that of the sixteenth-century reformer John Bale, who, commenting on these verses from Revelation, wrote of a 'vomit' of 'poison', a 'filthy flood' which signifies 'wavering superstitions, idolatry, and heathen ceremonies' which 'accumbreth' but do not overwhelm the faithful (Hume p. 78).

The episode to some extent prefaces Book 1, anticipating Redcrosse's continual susceptibility to error. It also points to the knight's identity as St George. The tableau of the knight with his red cross badge, the conquered monster and the lady with a lamb, is instantly recognizable. The effect at this point is partly ironic: this knight scarcely displays the decisive heroism we might expect of St George. Hardly has Redcrosse freed himself from the entanglements of Error, when he falls victim with Una to the deceptions of Archimago. Once again Spenser describes the appearance of a character in some detail before he is named, but in this case the early signs are misleading; we find ourselves as readers as deceived as Redcrosse and Una. The hermit appears to be the innocent and holy father he claims, praying as Christ taught we should with his eyes to the ground (Luke 18.13–14). Only belatedly is his true nature revealed:

34

Book 1

> For that old man of pleasing wordes had store,
> And well could file his tongue as smooth as glas;
> He told of Saintes and Popes, and evermore
> He strowd an *Ave-Mary* after and before.   (i.35)

The good old hermit, we discover, is a liar, a necromancer (36), indeed the arch- or chief magician, Archimago (43). Protestants commonly used the imagery of witchcraft and magic to vilify Roman Catholic priests,[5] but Archimago seems to have adopted his Roman Catholic guise merely for the purposes of the moment. His indefatigable persecution of Redcrosse, and particularly of Una, and his great power suggest rather that he is a manifestation of Satan, himself 'a liar, and the father thereof' (John 8.44), whose particular pleasure is to seek 'by all meanes to disquiet ye church of Christ, to disperse it, and to shake it from the true faith' (marginal gloss on Luke 22.31 in the Geneva Bible). This interpretation of Archimago seems confirmed when at the end of Book 1 he is bound with chains and put in a dungeon from which, nevertheless, he manages to escape (xii.36; and cf. 2.i.1). The punishment echoes that of Satan (Revelation 20.2–7), who is bound and cast into a bottomless pit, from which, however, after a thousand years, he is released 'for a little season' to continue his deceptions.

Archimago succeeds in disquieting and separating Redcrosse and Una by producing a false simulacrum of Una. Such falsification and slander of the True Church are typical of Satan: Calvin, writing of the signs by which we can recognize the True Church, warns that 'there is nothing on which Satan is more intent than . . . at one time to delete and abolish these marks, and thereby destroy the true and genuine distinction of the Church; at another, to bring them into contempt, and so hurry us into open revolt from the Church' (*Institutes* II, 290). As Redcrosse is shortly to be deceived by Duessa masquerading as Faith, so now he is deceived by a false Una behaving like the whoreish Duessa. Redcrosse's human frailty is evident from the episode: his faith wavers, his power to tell the true from the false is uncertain, and his fleshly lusts are easily stirred up. But equally the episode makes it clear that Redcrosse is no hardened reprobate: he does not willingly embrace the false Una but flees in a fury of misguided virtue. The inadequacy of the Christian's own powers to preserve him from sin is made ironically clear.

Redcrosse flies from Una 'pricked with wrath and fiery fierce disdaine' (ii.8). The line betrays the entanglement of errors by which the knight is increasingly trapped. The fierceness of his disdain suggests that his wrath may still owe something to the 'gealous fire' with

35

which the knight burned when he saw the false Una in bed with the
squire (ii.5); the sparks of concupiscence have begun to burn his
flesh. At the same time his wrath and disdain suggest Redcrosse's
sense of virtuous outrage at Una's apparent failure to live up to his
own deserts. He is 'much griev'd to thinke that gentle Dame so
light,/For whose defence he was to shed his blood' (i.55). Redcrosse
is no Christ. We note here that complex of sins which characterizes
fallen man. These were most commonly described as the lusts of the
flesh, but 'lust' was understood metaphorically as well as literally,
signifying not only man's sexual desires but more seriously that self-
assertion of the flesh under which Perkins listed 'self-love, envy,
pride, unbeleefe, anger' (see p. 31 above). Not until such pride and
confidence in self are broken and the humility that comes with
recognition of man's inherent helplessness and blindness is learned
can the work of regeneration begin.

Such flaws of the flesh become all too apparent in Redcrosse. The
seductions of Duessa embroil him increasingly deeply in the sins of
concupiscence, literally and metaphorically. At the same time he acts
with self-conscious virtue according to the inadequate rules of
chivalry and personal prowess. We are reminded of the apparent
contradiction in the first two stanzas of canto i:

> Full jolly knight he seemd, and faire did sitt,
> As one for knightly giusts and fierce encounters fitt.

> But on his brest a bloudie Crosse he bore . . .

The 'But' that begins the second stanza seems to suggest that the
code of gallant knighthood is not quite at one with the badge of the
cross, and this thought recurs again and again as we follow Redcrosse's adventures. To Duessa he acts as a knight should, but as
Redcrosse ought not:

> Faire Lady hart of flint would rew
> The undeserved woes and sorrowes, which ye shew.

> Henceforth in safe assuraunce may ye rest.   (ii.26–7)

Most clearly at odds with his Christian faith is the pride he takes
in the shield of Sansfoy (Faithlessness), which he values as a 'signe
of the conqueroure' (ii.20) and, even worse, a 'noble pray' (iv.39),
a reward for his knightly prowess which he disdains to lose. Spenser's
account of the spectacle of the Christian knight and Sansjoy fighting
in the lists of Pride for possession of Sansfoy's shield and of corrupt
Duessa reverberates with ironies. Redcrosse's affinity with his
Saracen adversary is suggested by the way in which Redcrosse's

knightly disapproval of the 'joyaunce vaine' of Lucifera's court coin-
cides with the arrival of the joyless Sansjoy (iv.37–8). Redcrosse's
joylessness is of a deeper kind than disdain of Lucifera's frivolity; he
and Sansjoy lack that joy which Paul describes as a fruit of the spirit,
as opposed to those works of the flesh which include 'hatred, debate,
emulations, wrath, contentions ' (Galatians 5.20 and 22). Spenser's
irony is evident in the narrator's introduction to canto v:

> The noble hart, that harbours vertuous thought,
>   And is with child of glorious great intent,
>   Can never rest, untill it forth have brought
>   Th'eternall brood of glorie excellent.   (v.1)

The great intentions and the 'glorie' of this enterprise belong rather
to the House of Pride than to the knight of Christ. In the midst of
the battle Sansjoy draws strength from a sight of Sansfoy's shield
hung up beside Duessa as the victor's prize (v.10). In the following
stanza Redcrosse draws strength from the same source, when in his
self-love he interprets Duessa's cry to Sansjoy, 'Thine the shield, and
I, and all' (v.11), as meant for himself. As a fitting climax to this
shameful contest, Redcrosse presents his prize with chivalric courtesy
to Lucifera, the Queen of Pride:

> Which she accepts, with thankes, and goodly gree,
>   Greatly advauncing his gay chevalree.
>   So marcheth home, and by her takes the knight.   (v.16)

Redcrosse is advanced to Duessa's place by Lucifera's side.

   Although tainted by its mores, Redcrosse is not seriously seduced
by the House of Pride. The vices over which Lucifera reigns are of
the most gross and worldly kind: the victims who lie in her dungeons
sought exclusively worldly power and gratification, while the six
beastly sins who draw her chariot are fleshly in the most literal sense.
Redcrosse is easily warned away from such obvious vice (v.52), but
he cannot escape so easily the sins of the flesh as they affect the spirit
– those 'evill motions and inclinations of selfe-love, envy, pride'
which 'hinder, and quench, and overwhelme all the good motions of
the spirit' (see p. 31 above). It is this spiritual pride, confidence in
his own virtue, that helps to bring Redcrosse low in Orgoglio's
dungeon.

THE ORGOGLIO AND DESPAIR EPISODES

A disdainful confidence in his own virtue and a weakness for the
rewards of the flesh have marked Redcrosse's behaviour since he left

Una. In canto vii his errors culminate; he casts aside his Christian armour and embraces Duessa, the Whore of Babylon, image of false religion. But Spenser is careful to emphasize the helplessness of Redcrosse even while he exposes his guilt:

> What man so wise, what earthly wit so ware,
>> As to descry the crafty cunning traine,
>> By which deceipt doth maske in visour faire,
>> And cast her colours dyed deepe in graine,
>> To seeme like Truth, whose shape she well can faine,
>> And fitting gestures to her purpose frame,
>> The guiltlesse man with guile to entertaine? (vii.1)

The narrator is sympathetic, but the words are ironic. Redcrosse has certainly not been 'wise' or 'ware', and he is far from guiltless; but if Duessa can trap such paragons, what chance has the merely ordinary Redcrosse? The frailty of man's natural condition, unaided by Grace, is suggested by Redcrosse's weariness, his sharing through the fountain the weakness of the nymph who 'sat downe to rest in middest of the race' (vii.5). Describing the helpless subservience of the Christian subject to the 'action of the flesh', Perkins describes him as 'like to one in a slumber . . . who thinkes that hee feeles something lying on his breast as heavie as a mountaine: and would faine have it away . . . but for his life cannot doe it' (*Workes* I, 470).

In this state Redcrosse is assailed by the giant Orgoglio. As usual Spenser gives us a detailed image of the giant before he fixes his identity with a name. In the case of Orgoglio, the portrait is more than usually rich in significant detail:

> at the last he heard a dreadfull sownd,
>> Which through the wood loud bellowing, did rebownd,
>> That all the earth for terrour seemd to shake,
>> And trees did tremble. Th'Elfe therewith astownd,
>> Upstarted lightly from his looser make,
> And his unready weapons gan in hand to take.

> But ere he could his armour on him dight,
>> Or get his shield, his monstrous enimy
>> With sturdie steps came stalking in his sight,
>> An hideous Geant horrible and hye,
>> That with his talnesse seemd to threat the skye,
>> The ground eke groned under him for dreed;
>> His living like saw never living eye,
>> Ne durst behold: his stature did exceed
> The hight of three the tallest sonnes of mortall seed.

> The greatest Earth his uncouth mother was,
>> And blustring *Æolus* his boasted sire,

> Who with his breath, which through the world doth pas,
> Her hollow womb did secretly inspire,
> And fild her hidden caves with stormie yre,
> That she conceiv'd; and trebling the dew time,
> In which the wombes of women do expire,
> Brought forth this monstrous masse of earthly slime,
> Puft up with emptie wind, and fild with sinfull crime.   (vii.7–9)

The association of giants with blasphemy and rebellion against heaven derives from the mythical story of the Titans who threatened Jove, told, for instance, by Ovid in the first book of the *Metamorphoses*. This giant, too, 'with his talnesse seemd to threat the skye' (8). Ovid's Titans were born of the earth, but Orgoglio's genesis 'of earthly slime, / Puft up with emptie wind' (9), and his death, when he evaporates 'like an emptie bladder' (viii.24), suggest that he represents particularly that prideful self-righteousness of fallen man 'rashly puft up with his fleshly minde' (Colossians 2.18) against which St Paul warns. Orgoglio is persistently associated with earthquakes, which were caused, so it was supposed, by 'great aboundance of wynde . . . emprysoned in the Caves, and Dungeons of the Earth' (cf. ix.2–5), and whose purpose was 'sometime . . . to testifie and denounce the secrete wrathe, and indignation of God . . . upon notorious malefactours' (Gabriel Harvey, in a letter to Spenser, printed in *Works* p. 616). Orgoglio seems not only to signify earthly rebelliousness, but also to act as an omen or a sign of God's wrath. Both apparently contradictory functions are present in the episode; Orgoglio represents the flesh, that earthly part of ourselves by which Redcrosse is now firmly imprisoned as evidenced by his embrace of Duessa, and he is the means by which Redcrosse's inward pride and self-conceit are broken in preparation for his regeneration. The Prottestant martyr John Bradford wrote of the battle between the flesh and the spirit, the 'old man' and the 'new man' within the Christian, as a battle between 'a mighty giant, such a one as was Goliath . . . [and] a little child, such a one as was David'. The terms in which Bradford describes this spiritual battle help us to understand the nature of Redcrosse's defeat and imprisonment and Arthur's eventual victory. Bradford tells us that the 'old man', Goliath, 'is more stronger, lusty, and stirring than is "the new man", because the birth of "the new man" is but begun now, and "the old man" is perfectly [i.e. completely] born . . . so is the nature of him clean contrary to the nature of "the new man", as being earthly and corrupt with Satan's seed'. The 'old man' so prevails in this fight that even the children of God themselves, think that they be nothing else but 'old', and that the Spirit and seed of God is lost and gone away: where yet notwithstanding the truth is otherwise, the Spirit and seed of God at the length appearing again, and dispelling away the clouds which cover 'the Sun' of God's seed from shining, as the clouds in the air do the corporal sun; so that sometime a man cannot tell by any sense that there is any sun, cloud and wind so hiding it from our sight: even so our caecity or blindness and corrupt affections do often shadow the sight of God's seed in God's children, as though they were plain reprobates.[6]

However, Bradford tells us that God 'holdeth his hand under his children in their falls'. Divine Grace intervenes to save Redcrosse from irremediable harm in the battle (vii.12) and then, with decisive, regenerative force, when Arthur's shield is unveiled, blinding Orgoglio with its more than sun-like brilliance: 'Such blazing brightnesse through the aier threw,/That eye mote not the same endure to vew' (viii.19).

The hopelessness and blindness of man overwhelmed by sin and imprisoned in his fleshly corruption is vividly described by Spenser as Arthur pushes past blind Ignorance and breaks into the hell-like depths of the knight's captivity to restore him to the light and to Una:

> But neither darkenesse fowle, nor filthy bands,
>   Nor noyous smell his purpose could withhold,
>   (Entire affection hateth nicer hands)
>   But that with constant zeale, and courage bold,
>   After long paines and labours manifold,
>   He found the meanes that Prisoner up to reare;
>   Whose feeble thighes, unhable to uphold
>   His pined corse, him scarse to light could beare,
> A ruefull spectacle of death and ghastly drere.
>
> His sad dull eyes, deepe sunck in hollow pits,
>   Could not endure th'unwonted sunne to view;
>   His bare thin cheekes for want of better bits,
>   And empty sides deceived of their dew,
>   Could make a stony hart his hap to rew;
>   His rawbone armes, whose mighty brawned bowrs
>   Were wont to rive steele plates, and helmets hew,
>   Were cleane consum'd, and all his vitall powres
> Decayd, and all his flesh shronk up like withered flowres.
>
>   (viii.40–1)

Redcrosse's exposure to the light is pathetically analogous to Orgoglio's evaporation (viii.24) and Duessa's stripping (viii.46–8). The pride of the flesh and its lusts are exposed for what they are: the lusts monstrous and deceitful, the pride empty, and the flesh subject to decay and death 'like withered flowres'.

With the unveiling of Arthur's shield and the destruction of Orgoglio, Redcrosse's regeneration begins. But first the illumination of Grace awakens in Redcrosse a corruscating sense of his own desperate sinfulness, and the damnation he has earned:

> Is not the measure of thy sinfull hire
> High heaped up with huge iniquitie,
> Against the day of wrath, to burden thee? (ix.46)

Despair, with his persistent, goading eloquence, is both the voice of Redcrosse's self-condemning conscience, and also the voice of the subtle tempter, Satan, enflaming with an expert touch the knight's weaknesses – his weariness, and his sense of failure and hopeless error:

> Is not enough thy evill life forespent?
> For he, that once hath missed the right way,
> The further he doth goe, the further he doth stray. (43)

Despair's technique is a familiar one of Satan's: to confuse Redcrosse by misusing the Bible, quoting God's judgement on the reprobate under the Old Covenant without reminding him of the promise of salvation to the elect under the New Covenant: 'Is not his law, Let every sinner die:/Die shall all flesh?' (47). Despair leaves out the second part of St Paul's promise to the Romans: 'the wages of sinne is death: but the gift of God is eternall life through Jesus Christ our Lord' (Romans 6.23). Its is appropriately Una, the True Church, who arouses in Redcrosse a saving faith in God's mercies by reminding him of the biblical promises Despair omits:

> In heavenly mercies hast thou not a part?
> Why shouldst thou then despeire, that chosen art?
> Where justice growes, there growes eke greater grace,
> The which doth quench the brond of hellish smart,
> And that accurst hand-writing doth deface. (ix.53)

THE HOUSE OF HOLINESS AND THE BATTLE WITH THE DRAGON

Where Duessa led a confident and self-righteous Redcrosse to the House of Pride, Una guides his shattered, and as yet but feeble, new self to the House of Holiness, where the process of his Sanctification is begun, first with his true Repentance, and then with his instruction in the life of true holiness (for these stages in the 'paradigm of salvation', see pp. 20–1 above). After the horrors, the confusion and the half-truths of the previous cantos, the clarity and calm of the House of Holiness are almost as restorative to the reader as to the knight. Even the grim surgical details of Redcrosse's penance (x.25–8) are placed in a settled and assured order which suggests the new spiritual comfort and certitude into which the Justified Redcrosse is initiated.

Redcrosse's growth in knowledge culminates in a vision of the heavenly Jerusalem and the promise of his own place there (x.57–61). The vision brings with it a final realization of the imperfection of even the best things of this world, whether 'great Cleopolis', the city of the 'Faerie Queene' (58), or 'deeds of armes' and the love of Una (62). But just at this point Redcrosse is given his new identity as St George, which carries with it both the promise of his own perfected Sanctification and also a reminder of his continuing duties in this world. The name Georgos, as Caxton noted, comes of 'erthe and . . . tilyenge/so george is to saye as tilyenge the erthe/that is his flesshe' (see p. 23 above). St George is still flesh and cannot yet escape that spiritual warfare with the Devil which is the condition of the elect Christian in the world (Ephesians 6.12). The knight's Justification and his instruction in the House of Holiness do not free him from temptation, though they assure him of his final victory.

With Redcrosse's assumption of the name St George, we are reminded, too, of the historical dimension of the English knight's long error, and the national significance of his imminent restoration of Una to her kingdom, suggesting as they do the restoration of a pure Reformed Church in England after the nation's long error in, or servitude to, Roman Catholicism. Nevertheless, the battle and the dragon of canto xi owe much of their imagery to Revelation, suggesting that beyond the personal and national significance of St George's fight lies the perspective of the continual struggle between Satan and God's elect throughout history, which will culminate at the end of time in the final defeat of Satan.

Spenser prepares himself for the battle by invoking his Muse, but not in the traditional epic manner:

> Come gently, but not with that mighty rage,
> Wherewith the martiall troupes thou doest infest,
> And harts of great Heroës doest enrage,
> That nought their kindled courage may aswage. (xi.6)

He asks her to

> let downe that haughtie string,
> And to my tunes thy second tenor rayse,
> That I this man of God his godly armes may blaze. (7)

Spenser both manages to rouse our blood by describing the effects of the Muse's haughtier string, and by nevertheless rejecting it reminds us that it is not human heroism that he is celebrating but the victory every elect Christian achieves in his weakness through Grace.

The dragon's appearance and the fight itself might seem to be entirely the product of the more fantastic reaches of Spenser's imagination, but in fact their details betray a close attention to significant detail. The size of the monster which threats the very heavens (xi.10) and its jaws which gape like Hell's mouth (xi.12) point to the cosmic dimensions of the evil St George faces. As St Paul warned, 'we wrestle not against flesh and blood, but against principalities . . . the princes of the darkness of this world' (Ephesians 6.12). The eyes of the beast are like 'two broad Beacons' set in the fields which 'warning give, that enemies conspyre,/With fire and sword the region to invade' (xi.14). To Elizabethans, such beacons warned particularly of the Roman Catholic enemy, the Spanish Armada, that instrument of Satan.

The part played by St George's armour illustrates the precision with which Spenser handles the details of the battle. On the first day the armour is heated by a 'flake of fire' till it sears with heat the body within (26). Spenser compares the pain to that suffered by Hercules from the shirt given him by his jealous mistress, a traditional image of the punishment of the lustful. The armour, put on for protection, in fact augments the heat: 'fyrie steele now burnt, that earst him arm'd,/That erst him goodly arm'd, now most of all him harm'd' (27). If we consult St Paul's description of the armour of the Christian man which St George has on, we find the piece that clothes St George's body, which therefore particularly burns him, is the 'breast-plate of righteousnesse' (Ephesians 6.14). We are here, I think, being reminded of the insufficiency of even the regenerate Christian's righteousness, of his attempt to live by the Law. The Law to the regenerate serves only to make him more than ever aware of his actual unrighteousness. Spenser has perhaps in mind St Paul's words, 'I knew not sinne, but by the Law: for I had not knowen lust, except the Law had sayd, Thou shalt not lust' and he adds '. . . sinne that it might appeare sinne, wrought death in me by that which is good' (Romans 7.7 and 13). The Genevan gloss notes that 'Sinne rage[s] more by reason' of the Law. St George's breastplate torments him by making him more than ever aware of his own sin, which is why he is tempted to put it off (26). He is saved from this torment only by falling into the Well of Life, in which he is revived by Grace.

On the second day it is St George's shield of faith and the sword of the spirit (Ephesians 6.16–17) that have a particularly significant role. The dragon stings the knight 'quite through his shield, and in his shoulder seasd' (38). When St George's sword severs the sting, the beast grips the shield with his claws. St George finds his own powers insufficient 'to reave by strength the gripped gage away' (41) and is saved again by 'his trustie sword' (42). Calvin uses St Paul's imagery in a similar fashion when he writes that faith 'is our shield, which receiving these darts [of unbelief], either wards them off entirely, or at least breaks their force, and prevents them from reaching the vitals' (*Institutes* I, 488). Fearful of again being scorched through his armour, the weary St George slips and is again saved by Grace, this time in the form of balm from the Tree of Life.

While it is clear that the Well of Life and the Tree of Life both represent the regenerative force of God's Grace, there is some debate about their precise significance.[7] Spenser's language of washing (30) and 'baptized hands' (36) and of balm trickling from the tree which can restore the dead to life (48) suggests the sacraments of baptism and the eucharist, but Redcrosse, as his badge suggests, must already have been baptized, and re-baptism was inconceivable to an ortho-dox Protestant. However, the sacraments, which in Protestant theology were a means by which God's promise of salvation to his elect is given an outward and visible form in order to support the natural feebleness of man's faith, do seem particularly appropriate to St George's needs in the fight. Actual baptism, it is true, was per-formed only once, but Calvin reminds us that it is 'for the whole of life. Wherefore, as often as we fall, we must recall the remembrance of our baptism; and thus fortify our minds, so as to feel certain and secure of the remission of sins' (*Institutes* II, 514). As visible signs of God's personal promise of salvation to him, the sacraments serve to support the elect Christian whom St George represents at the moments when his faith stumbles. Thus restored, George is able on the third day to imitate Christ's victory over death. Through Grace he is enabled to overthrow Satan to achieve the righteousness he lost at the Fall. On another level St George overthrows the forces of Satan in England and restores the True Church.

But Satan has many forms, and St George is not Christ. The dragon is killed and St George and Una are united, but for a time only. St George must return to serve Gloriana for six more years 'in warlike wize' (xii.18) before he can finally rest, and Archimago, another of Satan's forms, soon frees himself from the shackles which bind him (xii.36 and 2.i.1). Spenser thus leaves us with a reminder of the continual spiritual warfare which is the condition of the Chris-tian in this world.

Chapter 2

BOOK 2

INTRODUCTION

1. Temperance

That this Moderation of mind may be learned and practised, we must remember that two especiall meanes are to be used. First, we must labour to discerne between things that differ, Phil.1.10 . . . second . . . to consider that wee are in this world, as pilgrimes and strangers, 1.Pet.2.11.

(William Perkins, *Workes* II, 127)

Spenser wrote in his 'Letter to Raleigh' that Arthur was 'the image of a brave knight, perfected in the twelve private morall vertues, as Aristotle hath devised, the which is the purpose of these first twelve bookes'. This statement has caused difficulties: the virtues described by Aristotle in the *Ethics* are not twelve in number, and few of those he does describe bear the same names as Spenser's. Temperance is one of those few, but it does not follow that Spenser's treatment corresponds in all respects to Aristotle's. On the contrary, there are fundamental differences of emphasis between the pagan philosopher and the Protestant poet.

Central to Aristotle's discussion of the moral virtues is his concept of the 'mean'. Each virtue is described as occupying a mid-position between an excess of passion or appetite, and a deficiency (*Ethics* pp. 34–6). Temperance is the intermediate, or mean, state between self-indulgence and a deficiency (perhaps indifference?) for which Aristotle cannot find a name because he considers it so unusual (pp. 66–7). While themes of self-indulgence and moderation are clearly of importance in Book 2 of *The Faerie Queene*, the strict Aristotelian concept of virtue as a mean between excess and deficiency seems to have limited relevance beyond the Medina episode in canto ii. Such a definition of virtue in terms of stasis, or balance, is far from the questing militancy of Guyon, who seeks the Bower of Bliss in order to destroy it. Guyon's virtue consists in doing as well as being; he is the type of that militant Christian whom St Paul describes as taking arms 'against the assaults of the devill' (Ephesians 6.11).

In fact Aristotle's 'temperance' seems less illuminating for Book 2 than his 'incontinence' (Gk *akrasia*). According to Aristotle, the

temperate man is not attracted to the vices he rejects, while the continent man is pulled powerfully by his appetites but is able to restrain
them (p. 141). Aristotle's description of the incontinent man as 'in
a condition similar to that of men who are asleep, mad or drunk' (p.
144) seems to account for those victims of Acrasia who drink her Cup
of Excess (2.i.55, xii.56), or who, like Pyrochles, are overmastered
by a senseless passion. Only Guyon seems, like Aristotle's temperate
man, to have neither excessive nor bad appetites, though even he
must be restrained by the Palmer on occasion (xii.69).

Spenser's understanding of Aristotle must have been influenced by
the still-current medieval Christian tradition of the virtues: the 'war-
ranted truly-Greek Aristotle that a modern student tries to isolate
and read was neither a possibility nor a desirable possibility to
Spenser . . . Spenser was certainly unlikely to engage in a vast work
based on ideas so fundamental as the virtues without regarding the
living traditions, which explained what the ancients thought these
were' (Tuve p. 77). Rosemond Tuve draws particular attention to
two traditions which may have affected Spenser's view of
temperance: the four cardinal virtues, prudence, temperance, fortitude and justice, and a tradition in which the virtues were
developed as remedies for the seven vices.

Each of the four cardinal virtues had become associated with a
range of attendant virtues or facets. In the case of temperance, these
included continence, modesty, shamefastness, abstinence, moderation and sobriety (Tuve, Appendix). Thus we find continence as a
part of temperance without any of the precise distinctions between
the two which were so important for Aristotle. We also find moderation, or measure, and shamefastness, both important aspects of
temperance in Book 2 (e.g., Medina in canto ii, and ix.40–4).

The names and the order of the 'remedy' virtues were, apparently,
variable, but the account of temperance or 'evenhede' in the text
which Tuve describes as being amongst the most popular available
in print in the sixteenth century, Frere Lorens' *Somme le Roi*, contains
suggestive details for Book 2. Lorens links 'evenhede' with the third
gift of the Holy Spirit (Isaiah 11.2), that is 'cunnynge', or understanding, 'for it maketh man and womman cunnynge, wise, and
measurable in al thinge'.[1] The particular vice to which this gift is
opposed is, interestingly, anger, a key passion throughout Book 2.
The gift of 'cunnynge' teaches the reason to enquire into the truth
of things, to judge well, to consider carefully and to speak temperately (Tuve pp. 150–1), producing the virtue of equity or 'even-
nesse', which is 'propreliche that men maken bi juggement rightful

& trewe, nought to nyseliche ne to boistreous, without bowynge to that on side or to that other, whan a man goth forth evenliche and right as a lyne' (p. 152). So fundamental is this virtue that all other virtues are branches of it: 'with-out that vertue alle manere other vertues leseth the name of vertue and bicomen vices' (p. 159).

Tuve is not suggesting Lorens as a direct source for Book 2. His book is a version of a popular medieval tradition of describing the virtues, which survived into the sixteenth century (see Tuve pp. 79–85) and must have influenced Spenser's conception of temperance, confirming but also modifying his reading of Aristotle, particularly by its stress on a discerning wisdom, the gift of the Holy Spirit, as the ground of temperance. Interestingly, too, temperance is described by Lorens as the virtue which precedes and underpins all the others, perhaps helping to explain its position in *The Faerie Queene* – following holiness, of course, but preceding all the other virtues. It seems best, then, to understand Spenser's version of temperance as the product of an amalgam of traditions and sources, classical and 'living', and to avoid trying to explain its details in terms of a single system. Such eclecticism fits well with Spenser's methods elsewhere and with the Renaissance habit of weaving together the most useful features of a number of past traditions and reconciling them with the prevailing Christian ideology.

2. Spenser's use of speaking pictures in Book 2

When discussing Book 1, I noted Spenser's use of images which had accumulated for sixteenth-century Protestants a rich and fairly precise set of associations: the image of the Whore of Babylon from Revelation, with its connotations of Antichrist and Roman Catholicism, for example, or of the earthly giant, Orgoglio, whose stature inevitably drew into the poem thoughts of the classical Titans with all their associations of rebelliousness, pride and blasphemy. The sixteenth century was particularly fond of such traditional images – visual descriptions or details which had accumulated a specific set of moral connotations. Many of these were popularized in emblem books, in which typically each page contained an engraved picture with below verses explaining its significance. Frequently the same emblems turn up in different collections, thus testifying to their popularity. The most famous of the English emblem books, Geoffrey Whitney's *A Choice of Emblemes* (1586), contains many of the most frequently reproduced images with their conventional explanations. Spenser himself had earlier contributed to a type of emblem book, van der Noodt's *A Theatre . . . [for] voluptuous Worldlings* (1569). The popularity of the form was no doubt grounded in the fact that it contained the great moral commonplaces in a pithy, memorable and often a witty form. The impact of these books was delightful because it was visual and the images were often fantastic, or drawn from myth. They could also say much in little because their readers could be relied on to recognize many of the traditional connotations and implications. The store of such traditional images was greatly augmented by the medieval and Renaissance habit of glossing and moralizing classical texts. As the images of Revelation had accumulated a set of specific interpretations by the efforts of generations of commentators, so many of the incidents described in classical works, particularly the *Iliad*, the *Odyssey*, the *Aeneid* and the *Metamorphoses*, had long been overlaid with a tradition of moral explanation (see Seznec pp. 84–121).

Spenser uses such traditional images throughout *The Faerie Queene*, but they are particularly frequent and particularly important in Book 2, concentrating the narrative at moments or for whole episodes into forms that would have been rich with connotations to Spenser's contemporaries. Such images may be activated by a casual detail or developed in great detail; they may be isolated and dramatic, or part of the structural organization of the book. The variety and inventiveness of Spenser's use of them is very great. In canto xii, for example, the Palmer captures Acrasia and Verdant by throwing over them 'a subtile net, which onely for the same/The skilfull Palmer formally did frame' (xii.81). The detail is enough for the Renaissance reader to be able to link this incident with the capture with a golden net specially woven by her husband, Vulcan, of the adulterous Venus in the arms of her lover, Mars. Acrasia and her bower are themselves new and complex versions of a long tradition of seductive enchantresses and emasculating gardens to which Spenser alludes and which carried for the reader clear moral significance (see Giamatti (1966) esp. pp. 48–67).

Spenser's use of such traditional images almost always transforms them. An example is his description of the hag Occasion (iv.4–12). Like Acrasia and her bower, she is both familiar and strange, inventively composed of traditional elements in an entirely new combination yet immediately recognizable as a 'speaking picture' whose least detail carries moral significance. Spenser's description is dramatic and vigorous:

> And him behind, a wicked Hag did stalke,
> In ragged robes, and filthy disaray,
> Her other leg was lame, that she no'te walke,

> But on a staffe her feeble steps did stay;
> Her lockes, that loathly were and hoarie gray,
> Grew all afore, and loosely hong unrold,
> But all behind was bald, and worne away,
> That none thereof could ever taken hold,
> And eke her face ill favourd, full of wrinckles old.

> And ever as she went, her tongue did walke
> In foule reproch, and termes of vile despight,
> Provoking him by her outrageous talke,
> To heape more vengeance on that wretched wight;
> Sometimes she raught him stones, wherwith to smite,
> Sometimes her staffe, though it her one leg were,
> Withouten which she could not go upright;
> Ne any evill meanes she did forbeare,
> That might him move to wrath, and indignation reare.　(iv.4–5)

The locks that grow down her forehead leaving the back of her head bare come from traditional descriptions of Occasion, depicted by Whitney as a young woman with wings on her feet, balancing on a wheel in a rough sea. Her hair is shaven behind to show that occasion must be grasped as it approaches; once it is past, it is too late.[2] Spenser's Occasion retains nothing but the forelock and that is 'loathly . . . and hoarie gray'. This Occasion should be avoided rather than grasped. Nor does she fly away on winged feet. She remains goading and insulting. Spenser seems to have combined a detail from the iconography of Occasion with details from an almost equally familiar figure, Envy, whom Whitney, following Ovid, describes as an 'hideous hagge' whose tongue is a forked viper as befits her poisonous speech and whose 'feeble limmes' are supported by a staff which serves both as support and weapon (Whitney, p. 94; and cf. 2.iv.5). The details of Spenser's image are conventional, but their combination is original, giving him a double advantage: his image has the visual immediacy and memorability of an emblem (although the bedlam energy with which Spenser endows his Occasion is, of course, quite foreign to such static representations), and in this apparently simple form he is able to present his own highly idiosyncratic analysis of a malevolent Occasion.

Emblematic images may link widely separated episodes. Such, for example, is Spenser's adaptation of an emblem of temperance which recurs in Guyon's first adventure and in his last. In canto i, Amavia tells how she purged her erring husband, Mordant, of Acrasia's 'drugs of foule intemperance' (i.54), but that the witch deceived him with a cup engraved with a spell:

> Sad verse, give death to him that death does give,
> And losse of love, to her that loves to live,
> So soone as Bacchus with the Nymphe does lincke.　　(i.55)

The effect of the charm is to kill Mordant as soon as he drinks water from a chaste well. Spenser makes much of the virginal purity of the well, born as it is from the tears of one of Diana's nymphs as she fled from the passionate Faunus. So pure is the well that it will not let its waters be stained by the blood from Ruddymane's hands (ii.7–9).

The emblem of temperance that lies behind this episode is that of the mixing of wine and water, an image of moderation: 'the drunken god [Bacchus] should be tempered with sober nymphs'.[3] But Acrasia's spell perverts the emblem; by its means the linking of Bacchus with the nymph brings death and grief, not moderation. Nor will Spenser's chaste well dilute Acrasia's wine. As Nelson suggests, the notion of temperance as a mean seems here to be called into question: there can be no tempering of Acrasia's viciousness, just as there should be no tempering of the nymph's virtue; chastity and concupiscence are alternatives, they are not extremes between which a mean can be found. The uncompromising effect of the well antici-pates the uncompromising spilling of the wine of Excess (xii.57) and the destruction of Acrasia's Bower which ends Guyon's quest.

However traditional such images, Spenser re-uses or adapts them with freshness and originality. They bring to his poem clusters of associations, on which Spenser draws to enrich his own meaning. They may also lend a moral immediacy, presenting ideas to the reader in a particularly vivid and condensed form.

GUYON AND THE PALMER

Spenser links Guyon and Redcrosse with some care in the book's first incident. We find in Guyon 'great rule of Temp'raunce' (Proem 5), but, like Redcrosse, he is easily deceived and led astray by Archimago and Duessa, who lead him away from the Palmer and dupe him into attacking Redcrosse. Guyon's error is short-lived: confronted with 'the sacred badge of my Redeemers death' (i.27) on Redcrosse's shield, he is able to restrain his ill-timed wrath, and the wise Palmer arrives in time to establish the right relationship between the two knights. Guyon's quest is in some respects like that of Red-crosse, whom the Palmer first addresses:

> you a Saint with Saints your seat have wonne:
> But wretched we, where ye have left your marke,
> Must now anew begin, like race to runne;

Book 2

> God guide thee, *Guyon*, well to end thy warke,
> And to the wished haven bring thy weary barke.　　　(i.32)

The metaphor of the Christian life as a 'race' is often used in St Paul's epistles (e.g., Hebrews 12.1; see Hume p. 64). Guyon as a Christian warrior undertakes revenge on behalf of Ruddymane and his self-destroyed parents, representatives to some extent of erring and vulnerable humanity subject to those affections and perturbations of the body and mind that threaten the spirit. In his quest to defeat Acrasia, incontinence, Guyon is led and restrained by his holy Palmer and in his extreme need aided by direct divine intervention (viii. 3–8). Guyon's role is emphasized by his name, which may derive from *gyon*, which, according to Caxton in his version of the St George legend, means wrestler. Susan Snyder has suggested that such a derivation for Guyon's name recalls the description of the Christian warrior in Ephesians 6.12–13: 'For we wrestle not against flesh and blood, but against . . . spirituall wickednesses . . . For this cause take unto you the whole armour of God.'[4] Wrestling is an important motif throughout Book 2: Guyon wrestles with Furor (iv.14) and Occasion (iv.12), and Arthur with Maleger and Impatience (xi.29, 33–46).

Our first sight of Guyon tells us much about Spenser's conception of temperance:

> A goodly knight, all armd in harnesse meete,
> That from his head no place appeared to his feete.
>
> His carriage was full comely and upright,
> 　His countenaunce demure and temperate,
> 　But yet so sterne and terrible in sight,
> 　That cheard his friends, and did his foes amate:
> 　He was an Elfin borne of noble state,
> 　And mickle worship in his native land;
> 　Well could he tourney and in lists debate,
> 　And knighthood tooke of good Sir *Huons* hand,
> When with King *Oberon* he came to Faerie land.
>
> Him als accompanyd upon the way
> 　A comely Palmer, clad in blacke attire,
> 　Of ripest yeares, and haires all hoarie gray,
> 　That with a staffe his feeble steps did stire,
> 　Least his long way his aged limbes should tire:
> 　And if by lookes one may the mind aread,
> 　He seemd to be a sage and sober sire,
> 　And ever with slow pace the knight did lead,
> Who taught his trampling steed with equall steps to tread. (i.5–7)

The description emphasizes Guyon's warlike appearance and experience, his carriage and horsemanship, his genealogy, and his relationship with the Palmer. The significance of his Elfin birth will be discussed when we consider the chronicles of canto x, but the other details are of immediate importance. That Guyon is well armed and 'sterne' suggests his role as a Christian warrior but also raises the important question of anger and its right place. When Guyon rushes off 'with fierce ire/And zealous hast' (i.13) to attack Redcrosse, it is clear that his anger is misdirected. However, the place of righteous anger is an important motif throughout the book, and culminates in Guyon's 'tempest of . . . wrathfulness' in Acrasia's bower (xii.83; see p. 72 below).

Guyon's upright carriage and his horsemanship, bridling his fierce mount to keep pace with the aged Palmer, are clear signs of his virtue. The image of the passions as a horse to be bridled by reason derives from Plato's *Phaedrus* and had wide currency in the Renaissance. Guyon is able to bridle his horse, curbing it to the Palmer's pace, and indeed for much of the book he is horseless (ii.11–12). The Palmer is himself sometimes identified by commentators as Reason, but this seems inadequate. Guyon shows himself well able to restrain his steed in the absence of the Palmer when confronted by Redcrosse's shield, and his behaviour when again separated from the Palmer in cantos vi and vii, whatever its problems, scarcely represents that of a passionate man separated from reason. The aged Palmer whose pace holds Guyon back, and whose wisdom continually intervenes to explain and to distinguish the truth, certainly addresses Guyon's reason (e.g., i.34 and ii.11), but he seems to require a more complex identification. Perhaps most suggestive is Aristotle's account of 'practical wisdom', the essential companion of moral virtue but not to be identified with it (*Ethics* pp. 133–4). 'Practical wisdom', Aristotle tells us, is not a quality of the young, for the young lack experience. The particular qualities of 'practical wisdom' are sound deliberation, understanding and judgement, and these are associated with 'older and experienced men . . . because such people are clear-sighted thanks to the eye of experience' (p. 132).

Aristotle's 'practical wisdom', the guide and essential companion of virtue, is a secular concept, but the temperate man's need for wisdom and discernment is also emphasized by the Christian tradition. William Perkins refers to the need for discernment in the passage quoted at the head of this chapter, and Lorens associated temperance with the gift of 'cunnynge' or understanding (see p. 46 above). Guyon's guide 'that him guided still./Still he him guided' (i.34) is a Palmer, that is a pilgrim from the Holy Land whose undertaking and authority are Christian ('God guide thee, *Guyon*' (i.32)), though he has the experience and judgement of a man long versed in the ways of the world.

1. The Amavia episode

Amavia and Mordant are tragic figures. Spenser emphasizes the sense of waste: Mordant is a cropped blossom in the 'freshest flowre of lustie hed' (i.41), and the pathos of Amavia's death is underscored by the way Guyon is deeply moved by her (i.42 and 56). But the pathos should not blind us to their error, hinted at in Spenser's language. Amavia's response to her young husband's intemperance has been passionate but insufficient. Dressed as a palmer, she has tried to reproduce the role of Guyon's Palmer, guiding her husband away from Acrasia's bower 'through wise handling and faire governance' (i.54), but to no avail; Acrasia's poison proves more powerful. What seems to be lacking in Amavia's guidance of her husband, and even more of herself, is that faith in the higher guidance of God, and the patient endurance which are aspects of the Palmer's wisdom (i.7 and 32). When we first hear Amavia she is blaming the 'carelesse heavens' which 'take delight/To see sad pageants of mens miseries' (i.36), and later she stretches her 'feeble hands . . . on hye,/As heaven accusing guiltie of her death' (i.49). From her sense of being the victim of a malicious fate follow impatience, despair and her own suicide. Deeply human as Amavia's passion may be, it seems to fall short of the stern need for faith and endurance required of the Christian.

Guyon sees in the dead Amavia and Mordant an image of human nature ravaged by intemperate passions (i.57). Ruddymane, the child of these parents, seems to be an even more helpless image of human nature:

> Poore Orphane in the wide world scattered,
> As budding braunch rent from the native tree,
> And throwen forth, till it be withered:
> Such is the state of men: thus enter wee
> Into this life with woe, and end with miseree.   (ii.2)

His woeful human state seems dyed on to his hands, a symbol of the harm done to his parents (i.37). The ineradicable stain has been interpreted as that of original sin which we inherit from our first parents (e.g., Hamilton (1961) pp. 107–10). This seems entirely probable, though an interpretation of the pure well which will not let 'her waves with any filth be dyde' (ii.9) as baptism seems far less plausible. The well's primary function is as an image of uncompromising chastity (see p. 50 above). The petrified nymph from whom the stream flows is curiously similar to yet different from Amavia. Both the well and the bloody hands serve as monuments to 'all chast Dames' (ii.10), but from the nymph flows clean water and from Amavia blood. The difference lies perhaps in their faith: the nymph trusts the heavens and her chastity is preserved (ii.8), while Amavia thinks them 'carelesse' and malicious and commits suicide.

Amavia's guidance is not that of the Palmer, nor is her response to Acrasia that of Guyon. Understandably, her inclination is towards escape: she extricates her husband from Acrasia's Bower, though not, alas, from her influence, and on his death she seeks escape in her own death:

> Sharpe be thy wounds, but sweet the medicines bee,
> That long captived soules from wearie thraldome free.   (i.36)

Escape or flight is also her counsel to Guyon:

> Faire Sir, if ever there ye travell, shonne
> The cursed land where many wend amis,
> And know it by the name; it hight the *Bowre of blis*.   (i.51)

Guyon's response is quite different: he makes a vow over the dead couple's grave for both himself and their son to pursue vengeance 'Till guiltie bloud her guerdon doe obtaine' (i.61). Far from avoiding Acrasia, his quest is now towards her, impelled by a vow of revenge, but such righteous wrath must be grounded in temperance and judgement. Perkins tells us:

Just and lawfull anger must be kindled and stirred up by good and holy affections, as namely, by desire to maintaine the honour and praise of God, by the love of justice and vertue, by hatred and detestation of vice, and of all that is evill. One saith well to this purpose, that anger must attend upon vertue, and bee stirred up by it against sinne.   (*Workes* II, 121)

Before exercising such wrath wisely, Guyon, and the reader, must be perfected in the disciplines of temperance and wise judgement.

2. The Castle of Medina

The need of the temperate man for judgement, measure and self-restraint is spelt out by the Palmer:

> temperance (said he) with golden squire
> Betwixt them both can measure out a meane,
> Neither to melt in pleasures whot desire,
> Nor fry in hartlesse griefe and dolefull teene.
> Thrise happie man, who fares them both atweene. (i.58)

The golden set-square ('squire') was a common emblem of temperance and recalls the mathematical language of Aristotle's mean, although Spenser's extremes in the case of Amavia and Mordant are more dynamic than Aristotle's. In his excessive pleasure Mordant was deficient in a proper grief for his sin, and in her excessive grief Amavia was deficient in hope and endurance.

The well-judged mean, central to temperance, is most clearly dramatized by Spenser in the Castle of Medina. The tableau at dinner, in which the two sisters, Elissa (defect) and Perissa (excess), maintain a temporary truce through the mediations of Medina 'betwix them' is a perfect if fragile image of the Aristotelian mean: 'With equall measure she did moderate/The strong extremities of their outrage' (ii.38). The contest between Hudibras and Sansloy is more confusing and less easily resolved (ii. 19–26). The two knights are not opposite extremes but two forms of foolhardiness. Guyon's armed intervention to pacify the pair serves no other purpose than to redouble the fury of the knights who

> Against themselves turning their wrathfull spight,
> Gan with new rage their shields to hew and cut;
> But still when *Guyon* came to part their fight,
> With heavie load on him they freshly gan to smight. (23)

Not until Medina intervenes with her 'pitthy words and counsell sad' (28) is the mad cycle broken in an uneasy truce. Here we are given an image of intemperate anger, and an ineffective attempt to impose temperance by arms, to set against Guyon's undertaking of militant vengeance against Acrasia.

Spenser concludes the episode by linking Medina's rule with that of Gloriana who also sustains her domain in peace and order (40). But where Medina's efforts are wholly absorbed in maintaining a balance within her own house, Gloriana's power manifests itself in a more militant defence of virtue beyond the borders of her kingdom. Guyon describes her as 'My Soveraine,/Whose glory is in gracious deeds, and joyes/Throughout the world her mercy to maintaine' (43), and it is she, we now learn, who has sent out Guyon to redress the wrongs of Acrasia. This account of the origins of Guyon's quest differs from that in canto i, though it confirms the outline in the

'Letter to Raleigh'. The change perhaps reveals Spenser's desire to stress at this point the active militancy of the virtue which characterizes both Gloriana and Guyon.

3. Belphoebe and Braggadochio

Gloriana figures Elizabeth I in her public role, 'a most royall Queene or Empresse'; her private self, that of 'a most vertuous and beautifull Lady', is to be expressed in the person of Belphoebe ('Letter to Raleigh'). In canto iii, the language of public peace and a just militancy associated with Gloriana is laid aside for a more private vocabulary of balance and active virtue in the person of Belphoebe.

In her appearance and behaviour Belphoebe harmoniously mixes the attributes of two quite opposite goddesses, Venus and Diana (iii.22–31). She has Venus' beauty without her lustful wantonness, and she has the chastity and fearless virtue of Diana. Spenser's description of Belphoebe is as intricate and enamelled as the jewels which fasten her buskins (27), producing an extraordinarily rich icon in which Belphoebe/Elizabeth represents a dazzling balance: sensuousness tempered by chastity; physical beauty tempered by heavenly grace; softness tempered by fearlessness.

Against this icon of perfect balance is set the comically grotesque Braggadochio, a 'Scarcrow' (iii.7) amalgam of discordant elements decked out with the stolen horse and spear of Guyon. Belphoebe, like honour, dwells in the woods pursuing an active life:

> Before her gate high God did Sweat ordaine,
> And wakefull watches ever to abide:
> But easie is the way, and passage plaine
> To pleasures pallace. (41)

By contrast, Braggadochio makes for the Court, where he expects to find 'gay portaunce . . . /And gallant shew' (iii.5).

The absurd Braggadochio is a comic foil for Belphoebe, but he contrasts, too, with the foolhardy knights of Medina's castle and with Guyon himself. Where he represents an absolute opposite to Belphoebe – there can be no virtuous mediation between her fearless virtue and his cowardice – his relationship to the two foolhardy knights is rather that of Aristotelian extremes. He is deficient in courage, while they have a rash excess. The combination of courage and judgement which we find in Guyon and the Palmer marks the virtuous mean between such extremes. But Braggadochio and his companion, Trompart, also serve as a foil to that virtuous pair. Where the black Palmer restrains and guides Guyon with his wisdom, the 'peacocke' Trompart is 'wylie witted, and growne old/In cunning sleights' (iii.9) and eggs his foolish charge on. Where Guyon could control his horse, Braggadochio cannot, for he is untrained in 'chevalree' (iii.46, and cf. iv.1–2). Spenser's joke is extended to the parallel meetings with Archimago (i.8–12; iii. 11–13), though on the latter occasion it is the arch-deceiver who is most grossly deceived.

THE IRASCIBLE AND CONCUPISCIBLE BROTHERS: PYROCHLES AND CYMOCHLES

Appetite . . . is divided into two powers, or inclinations, concupiscible or irascible . . . Concupiscible covets always pleasant and delightsome things, and abhors that which is distasteful, harsh, and unpleasant. Irascible . . . avoid[s] it [i.e. the distasteful] with anger and indignation.[5]

The standard division of the passions or perturbations of the mind into the concupiscible and irascible (cf. i.58; vi.1) is clearly of great importance for the forms intemperance takes in Book 2. Amavia and Mordant rush to opposite extremes: Mordant becomes dominated by his concupiscible appetites, Amavia by the fury of grief. In canto ii, Perissa and Sansloy are concupiscent, while Elissa, Hudibras and also Sansloy are irascible and excessively prone to anger and discontent.

The two brothers Pyrochles and Cymochles most fully dramatize the irascible and concupiscible passions and their violent effects. The genealogy of the brothers suggests their cursed and imbalanced natures:

> The sonnes of old *Acrates* and *Despight*,
> *Acrates* sonne of *Phlegeton* and *Jarre*;
> But *Phlegeton* is sonne of *Herebus* and *Night*;
> But *Herebus* sonne of *Aeternitie* is hight. (iv.41)

Their father (Gk *akrateia*, incontinence) links them etymologically to Acrasia herself and genealogically to Duessa, who claimed Night as an ancestress (1.v.27). Phlegethon, one of the rivers of Hades, is described by Spenser in Book 1 as a 'fiery flood . . . /Whereas the damned ghosts in torments fry' (1.v.33). The names of the brothers suggest their own natures. Like his grandfather, Pyrochles burns (Gk *pyr*, fire, + *ochleo*, disturb, trouble), while Cymochles' name suggests the perturbations of water (Gk *kyma*, wave, + *ochleo*). Between them, they suggest not only the psychological imbalance of man's nature overthrown by passions but also a physical imbalance as understood by the Renaissance theory of the human body as a temperate mixture of humours. An excess of heat was the mark of a choleric humour and an excess of moisture of the phlegmatic humour. We shall explore the relevance of such theories to the brothers shortly.

Spenser deals first with the irascible passions (canto iv). Pyrochles is central to his grim account but by no means the only example of their power. We first meet Furor (iv.3), who both represents, and is consumed by, his passion. Spenser's description of Furor endows the personification with the mad dynamism of a man in a frenzy:

> And oft himselfe he chaunst to hurt unwares,
> Whilst reason blent through passion, nought descride,
> But as a blindfold Bull at randon fares,
> And where he hits, nought knowes, and whom he hurts, nought cares.
>
> (iv.7)

Furor is not an isolated passion; he is accompanied by Occasion, who includes many of the characteristics of Envy as conceived by the emblem writers (see my discussion p. 49 above). The part envy can play in providing the occasion for jealousy, which in turn produces anger, grief and the lust for revenge, is vividly illustrated by Phedon's story (iv.18–32). Unlike the version of this narrative which is used by Ariosto in *Orlando Furioso* (canto 5), or that used by Shakespeare as the Claudio/Hero plot of *Much Ado About Nothing*, Spenser's version does not end with the deceived and abused lovers reconciled. In a brief and violent fourteen stanzas, Phedon rushes from the joys of friendship and an imminent marriage through the full gamut of the irascible passions until he is in effect reduced to the dehumanized personification, Furor, who overtakes him in his pursuit of Pryene: 'I, breathing yre . . . with my heat kindled his cruell fyre;/Which kindled once, his mother did more rage inspyre' (32).

To such overmastering passion, Guyon offers the remedy of temperate restraint (33), but mere moderation will not do for such as Phedon (as it was not sufficient for Mordant):

> Then gan the Palmer thus, Most wretched man,
> That to affections does the bridle lend;
> In their beginning they are weake and wan,
> But soone through suff'rance grow to fearefull end.   (34)

The only remedy is total eradication of the passions:

> The sparks soone quench, the springing seed outweed,
> The drops dry up, and filth wipe cleane away:
> So shall wrath, gealosie, griefe, love dye and decay.   (35)

Militancy, not moderation, is needed at this stage.

Book 2

Fury dehumanizes Phedon, reducing him to the condition of the personification, Furor. Similarly reduced by a single passion are Pyrochles and his squire Atin (Gk *ate*, strife, discord), half personifications, half men. Pyrochles is suitably mounted: 'His steed was bloudy red, and fomed ire,/When with the maistring spur he did him roughly stire' (v.2). We are by now sufficiently familiar with the horse as a figure for man's passionate nature to be able to understand this detail quite easily. Appropriately, the first stroke of the Knight of Temperance unhorses Pyrochles, but it cannot halt him. Fury drives him on to an insane, self-lacerating violence:

> Ne thenceforth his approved skill, to ward,
> Or strike, or hurtle round in warlike gyre,
> Remembred he, ne car'd for his saufgard,
> But rudely rag'd, and like a cruell Tygre far'd. (v.8)

Guyon meets Pyrochles with exemplary virtue, mastering his violence temperately (v.13). When, however, he turns to helping and advising Pyrochles, he seems less successful; as in the case of Phedon, his remedy seems insufficient. His words 'Fly, O *Pyrochles*, fly the dreadfull warre,/That in thy selfe thy lesser parts do move' (v.16) echo Medina's advice (ii.30) but also remind us of Amavia's flight with Mordant. Such advice produced a temporary truce in Medina's castle, but it has little power over one as over-mastered by passion as Pyrochles, who wilfully chooses to unbind Occasion and Furor, with predictable results (v.19–23).

Pyrochles is reduced to one over-mastering passion, anger, and one over-mastering humour, the choleric. His brother, Cymochles, is similarly unbalanced, but his watery, unstable nature causes him to flit from one state to another. He is a lover of Acrasia, 'for he, by kind,/Was given all to lust and loose living' (v.28), although both in the Bower of Bliss where Atin first finds him and on Phaedria's isle his sensual appetite seems to manifest itself mainly in a kind of drugged sleep (v.30; vi.14). If Pyrochles has too much of the fiery choleric humour, Cymochles has too much of the moist phlegmatic humour. But while his preferred state is a sensuous drowsiness, he is easily moved, on the least whim, to intemperate anger (v.37; vi.27–8) and then as easily seduced again to a drowsy concupiscence (vi.8, 40).

PHAEDRIA AND MAMMON

Guyon is separated from the Palmer as he steps incautiously into Phaedria's craft (vi.19) and must face alone the blandishments of

Phaedria and Mammon (cantos vi and vii). While he may well lack a far-seeing and prudent wisdom in these episodes, Guyon by no means acts irrationally or intemperately; both Phaedria and Mammon make an effort to seduce the knight, but neither is able to move him. The two episodes are clearly linked both by the presence of the Palmer-less Guyon, and by their related but different perversions of Christ's Sermon on the Mount (Matthew 6.24–9):

> No man can serve two masters: for either hee shall hate the one, and love the other, or else he shall leane to the one, and despise the other. Yee cannot serve God and riches [Mammon]. Therefore I say unto you, Bee not carefull for your life, what yee shall eate, or what ye shall drinke: nor yet for your bodie, what yee shall put on . . . Behold the foules of the heaven: for they sowe not, neither reape, nor carrie into the barns: yet your heavenly Father feedeth them . . . And why care ye for raiment? Learne, how the lilies of the field doe growe: they labour not, neither spin: Yet I say unto you, that even Solomon in all his glory was not arayd like one of these.

1. Phaedria

Phaedria echoes the Sermon in her song to Cymochles:

> The lily, Ladie of the flowring field,
>   The Flowre-deluce, her lovely Paramoure,
>   Bid thee to them thy fruitlesse labours yield,
>   And soone leave off this toylesome wearie stoure;
>   Loe loe how brave she decks her bounteous boure,
>   With silken curtens and gold coverlets,
>   Therein to shroud her sumptuous Belamoure,
>   Yet neither spinnes nor cardes, ne cares nor frets,
> But to her mother Nature all her care she lets.
>
> Why then dost thou, O man, that of them all
>   Art Lord, and eke of nature Soveraine,
>   Wilfully make thy selfe a wretched thrall,
>   And wast thy joyous houres in needlesse paine,
>   Seeking for daunger and adventures vaine?   (vi.16–17)

The differences are obvious: Phaedria's is an invitation not to trust in God, but to live an easy life of pleasure. If Pyrochles' fieriness suggests an excess of the choleric humour, and Cymochles' moist drowsiness of the phlegmatic, Phaedria, 'fresh and faire' (vi.3), devoted to idle mirth and 'amours' (vi.35), seems to represent an excess of the sanguine humour. Her light and wanton nature, diverting, and on the look-out for diversion, is epitomized by the 'little Gondelay' (vi.2) in which she sits. It is a shallow, painted craft (vi.4–5) without oar or pilot or sail, guided only by Phaedria's whim. With Cymochles as her victim, willingly led astray, we hear only of her merry tales and laughter and the lapping water (vi.6–11), but when Guyon becomes her reluctant passenger we are given an insight into the actual filth and stagnation of the element which supports her:

> Through the dull billowes thicke as troubled mire,
> Whom neither wind out of their seat could forse,
> Nor timely tides did drive out of their sluggish sourse.   (vi.20)

This sluggish lake gives us a repellent image of the murkiness of Phaedria's moral nature below the merry lightness. So sluggish is Phaedria's lake that it will not cool Pyrochles' furious burning (vi.41–6), providing us with yet another example of an ineffective attempt to moderate passion. An emblem of temperance features the quenching, or tempering, of a red-hot iron in water,[6] but Pyrochles' extreme choler will not be quenched by the means he uses.

2. The Cave of Mammon and its sequel

Mammon more seriously challenges the teaching of the Sermon on the Mount, inviting Guyon to serve riches rather than God (cf. Matthew 6.24). He scorns Guyon's description of the first 'golden' age of the world, in which man was content with what God had given him and 'with glad thankes, and unreproved truth,/The gifts of soveraigne bountie did embrace' (vii.16). To Mammon, such bounty is mere primitive poverty:

> leave the rudenesse of that antique age
> To them, that liv'd therein in state forlorne;
> Thou that doest live in later times, must wage
> Thy workes for wealth, and life for gold engage.   (vii.18)

The ironies are not confined to the differing understanding of a 'golden' age. Mammon's view of the first age of the world as a time of barbarity from which men have grown to civility and the exchange of money is put into the mouth of 'an uncouth, salvage and uncivile wight' (vii.3) who lives in 'desert wildernesse' (vii.2) far from the society of men. Spenser firmly links Mammon's kind of 'golden' age to barbarity. Such features of a 'developed' society as mining, the luxuries of wealth and an excessively sophisticated Court are in this episode signs of degeneration, of a slippage from a truly 'golden' to an iron age.

Mammon first offers his wealth and its rewards to Guyon and then takes the Knight of Temperance down to his hellish realm. His

House has three parts: the rooms where his bullion is stored and refined (30–9), the great hall where Philotime holds her golden chain (43–9), and the Garden of Proserpina (51–64). The first two present us with fantastic, but relatively clear, images of the nature of worldly wealth and ambition. Everywhere there is a horrible and frenzied activity, whether it be of the deformed devils who work the great smelting furnaces (35), or of the courtiers on ambition's chain who tread each other in their greed for advancement (47). The significance of the Garden of Proserpina is more vexed. The vegetation of the garden is poisonous and black except for the golden apples that hang from the central tree. In the middle of the garden is a silver seat, and in the black river Cocytus that flows round it are the half-drowned, tortured spirits of Tantalus and Pilate. Mammon tempts the now weary and hungry Guyon to taste the golden fruit and rest on the silver stool.

Various attempts have been made to link the features of the Garden and to explain the nature of the evil it embodies.[7] The Garden seems to represent an aspect of Mammon's power less crude than wealth or worldly ambition. In the Sermon on the Mount, Christ sets Mammon in opposition to God: 'No man can serve two masters . . . Yee cannot serve God and riches.' Mammon represents not merely riches but, more widely, the things of this world; he calls himself 'god of the world and worldlings' (8). Many of the details of the Garden seem to depend on an illicit or disastrous mingling of the divine and the human: the golden apples refer us to four stories from Greek mythology (54–5), one a theft of the divine apples of the Hesperides, and three in which goddesses have intervened in human affairs, in the case of Paris with disastrous results.[8] Spenser tell us that Tantalus, 'Of whom high *Joue* wont whilome feasted bee' (59), lies tormented by hunger and thirst. The reference may be to either of two versions of Tantalus' feasting, both involving transgression of the divine by a human (see note in Hamilton's edition on stanza 59). Pilate, of course, falsely judged the divine Christ. Proserpina herself, though not human, belonged to the upper world until she ate the seeds of a pomegranate which condemned her to spend half her life in the Underworld. If, as seems probable, there is a hint of the Tree of Knowledge in the dark tree whose golden fruit Mammon tempts Guyon to eat, then the episode refers us to the most serious of all transgression of the divine by a human, the eating of the fruit in Eden. Even the silver seat seems best explained as a reference to the seat to which Theseus grew when he, a worldling, entered the forbidden Underworld (see note in Hamilton's edition on stanza 63). The

Garden, then, seems to give us images of the illicit intervention of pagan divinities in the affairs of men, and the transgression of the divine by worldlings. It acts as a warning to Guyon to recognize his condition – 'of the earth, earthly' (1 Corinthians 15.47) – but, at the same time, owing service to God not Mammon.

Guyon remains resolutely an 'earthly wight' (50) in the face of Mammon's falsely divine temptations: he courteously refuses the 'immortal' Philotime and will not eat of the golden fruit, or sit on the silver seat. Guyon's earthly condition is essential to the episode. His replies to Mammon's temptations throughout, although virtuous, have been earthly in perspective: 'Faire shields, gay steedes, bright armes be my delight:/Those be the riches fit for an advent'rous knight' (10). Most important, Guyon's confidence at the beginning of the episode, when he congratulates himself on his self-sufficiency – 'And evermore himselfe with comfort feedes,/Of his owne vertues, and prayse-worthy deedes' (2) – is developed at the end of this episode when Guyon's mortal nature can no longer withstand his long sleepless fast and he faints (66), making himself vulnerable to Pyrochles and Cymochles (viii.11ff.).

Guyon's over-confidence and earthly perspective reveal his need for the Palmer's guidance. Guyon, too, represents a perversion of the Sermon on the Mount. Christ taught 'Bee not carefull for your life, what yee shall eate, or what ye shall drinke' (Matthew 6.25). Guyon's carelessness amounts to rashness, a foolhardiness which is rather an over-confidence in his own powers than a trustfulness in God's. Nevertheless, the promise of God's care (Matthew 6.33) is dramatically fulfilled for Guyon. The narrator's question as Guyon lies in a dead faint on the ground –

> And is there care in heaven? and is there love
> In heavenly spirits to these creatures bace,
> That may compassion of their evils move? –   (viii.1)

is answered by the astonishing intervention of an angel (viii. 3–8). The illicit and fictional examples of divine interference in human affairs in Proserpina's garden are capped by an example of 'th'exceeding grace/Of highest God' (viii.1), the only true intervention of the divine in the human.

God's merciful care for Guyon not only brings the Palmer to his side; it, more practically, brings Prince Arthur to combat the two brothers Cymochles and Pyrochles. Their physical and bloody battle, ending when the prince wrestles Pyrochles to the ground and cuts off his head, presents a striking contrast to the inaction of the previous canto with its oppressive darkness and its exclusively verbal duelling. But the language of physical battle directs us to more insidious and internal battles. Arthur destroys two intemperate knights whose bodies have been 'Distempred through misrule and passions bace' (ix.1), while Guyon, on the ground, wrestles successfully with another bodily distemper, his faint: 'Life having maistered her sencelesse foe' (viii.53). The word 'maistered' draws on the long and vigorous description of Arthur's struggle to suggest the internal struggle within Guyon's body. The phrase 'sencelesse foe' is particularly striking: it describes Guyon's faint, of course, but it also suggests a ghostly adversary, impervious to fleshly wounds because senseless. Just such a struggle between the healthy, temperate body and its sickly, intemperate adversary is developed at length in the account of the House of Alma and her enemies in the next three cantos.

THE HOUSE OF ALMA

The House of Alma (Ital. *alma*, soul) images the emphatically mortal, human body but celebrates it as a 'worke divine' (ix.22), God's masterpiece 'that all this other worlds worke doth excell' (ix.47). The account of the House itself in canto ix proceeds with a stately clarity reminiscent of the description of the House of Holiness in Book 1, but with rather more humour. Spenser translates the parts of the human body, even its most intimate functions, into the language of a busy and well-ordered household with its stomach kitchen, its belching chimney and its 'back gate' from whence the waste is 'throwne out privily' (32). Less well ordered is the turret of the mind, where the imagination is encumbered by flies and painted '*Hippodames*' (50-1), and the amnesiac memory must be assisted in its chaotic archives by a youthful Anamnestes (Reminder) (58).

In Alma's House, Guyon and Arthur find reflections of themselves. In the 'goodly Parlour' of the heart, they are confronted with passionate aspects of their own virtues whose painful intensity disconcerts them (33-44) – Arthur's '*Prays-desire*' and Guyon's '*Shamefastenesse*', the latter a traditional aspect of temperance (see p. 46 above). More welcome are the tomes of history they find in Memory's library (59-60).

1. The chronicles

The British History recounted at such length in canto x may well seem dry and difficult to twentieth-century readers, but the elevated

tone in which Spenser introduces the canto should warn us of the
importance of the topic for sixteenth-century readers:

> More ample spirit, then hitherto was wount,
> Here needes me, whiles the famous auncestries
> Of my most dreaded Soveraigne I recount,
> By which all earthly Princes she doth farre surmount.   (x.1)

The Tudors' descent from ancient legendary kings of Britain and
from Arthur himself was taken very seriously and actively promul-
gated as part of the Tudor monarchy's propaganda. The long line of
descent gave status to the female and Protestant Elizabeth, and to the
nation a sense of antiquity and continuity. The names and deeds of
those British rulers who precede Arthur are recounted in the volume
of '*Briton moniments*' found in Alma's House. Those who succeed Arthur, as far as Elizabeth herself, are revealed to Britomart and to us
in a more prophetic tone by Merlin in 3.iii.

This half-legendary, half-mythical matter may seem almost entirely spurious to us now, but to the sixteenth century much of it
seemed historical, or at least to have a basis in fact, and it was recounted in numerous chronicles which derived their material in part
or in whole from Geoffrey of Monmouth's *Historia Regum Britanniae*
(twelfth century). Spenser has sifted a number of these chronicles to
produce a single, composite history.

The conscientious enumeration of often painful facts in the '*Briton
moniments*' is very different from the method of the '*Antiquitie of
Faerie*', the volume Guyon takes to read. Here the detail is vague and
fabulous:

> His sonne was *Elfinell*, who overcame
>   The wicked *Gobbelines* in bloudy field:
>   But *Elfant* was of most renowmed fame,
>   Who all of Christall did *Panthea* build:
>   Then *Elfar*, who two brethren gyants kild,
>   The one of which had two heads, th'other three.   (x.73)

The chronicle culminates in the reigns of Elficleos, Oberon and
Gloriana, who seem both to prefigure and, in an idealized way, to
represent the reigns of the three key figures of the Tudor dynasty,
Henry VII, Henry VIII and Elizabeth.

The distinction between British and Faery is one upon which
Spenser insists throughout the poem, and it is clearly of special importance in this canto. Its significance is best grasped if we refer to
the distinction between history and poetry made by Sir Philip Sidney
in *An Apologie for Poetrie*. The poet, he tells us, is unique because he
is not bound to imitate the world as it is, but

disdaining to be tied to any such subjection, lifted up with the vigour of his own invention, doth grow in effect another nature, in making things either better than Nature bringeth forth, or, quite anew . . . [Nature's] world is brazen, the poets only deliver a golden.   (p. 100)

The historian, on the other hand,

is so tied, not to what should be but to what is, to the particular truth of things and not to the general reason of things, that his example draweth no necessary consequence, and therefore a less fruitful doctrine.   (p. 107)

The two chronicles juxtapose the methods of the historian and the poet. Dear as the British History might be to Arthur, it is nevertheless a tale of treachery and misfortune, of intemperance in the body of the state, as much as of courage and triumph. The Elfin chronicle, by contrast, tells only of the great and the good; it is a golden and clearly fictional record, providing

> famous moniments,
> And brave ensample, both of martiall,
> And civill rule to kings and states imperiall.   (74)

2. Maleger

As the body politic of Britain has been wracked by wars, so the human body has its enemies and must be ruled wisely. Spenser marks the transition from the chronicle histories to the account of Maleger by drawing on the familiar analogy between the state and the body:

> What warre so cruell, or what siege so sore,
>   As that, which strong affections do apply
>   Against the fort of reason evermore
>   To bring the soule into captivitie
>   . . .

> But in a body, which doth freely yeeld
>   His partes to reasons rule obedient,
>   And letteth her that ought the scepter weeld,
>   All happy peace and goodly government
>   Is setled there in sure establishment;
>   There *Alma* like a virgin Queene most bright,
>   Doth florish . . .   (xi.1–2)

As the metaphor transfers us from the state to the body, so the reference to the 'goodly government' of a virgin queen transfers us back to the state and that other virgin queen, Elizabeth, in whose

Book 2

well-ordered and temperate rule we are to see the providential culmination of the turbulent British History.

Fortified by the temperate hospitality of Alma and the 'brave ensamples' of the *'Antiquitie of Faerie'*, Guyon departs with the Palmer to fulfil his quest (xi.4). Arthur's task is to stay with Alma to do battle against Maleger and his cohorts. There are twelve troops: seven, the number of the deadly sins, batter the main gate of Alma's castle, while the other five assail the bulwarks of the five senses. The initial appearance of military organization belies the actual nightmarish chaos of the 'rablement', in which the corrupt appetites and their temptations are imaged by disjointed bits of bestial bodies thrown together in grotesque disorder. Such, for instance, are those who attack the bulwark of taste:

> a grysie rablement,
> Some mouth'd like greedy Oystriges, some fast [faced]
> Like loathly Toades, some fashioned in the wast
> Like swine; for so deformd is luxury,
> Surfeat, misdiet, and unthriftie wast,
> Vaine feasts, and idle superfluity.   (xi.12)

The rapid listing gives an effect of an overwhelming horde, though the ills these monsters represent are weak and idle indulgences. Their mixture of power and weakness is stressed by Spenser's imagery: their 'fluttring arrowes' are 'thicke as flakes of snow' (18) and like 'heaped hayle' (19) which Arthur has no difficulty warding off with his shield; in their onrush they are 'Like a great water flood' threatening the fertile plain (18), but before Arthur's sword they scatter 'As withered leaves drop from their dried stockes' (19). The images are of sterility and blight, betraying the 'rablement's' real weakness beneath an initial appearance of force.

The nature of their captain, Maleger, is similarly ambivalent. He is big-boned yet insubstantial (20); he rides upon a fierce tiger whose chief attribute is speed in flight (26); he seems close to death (22), yet he is difficult to kill; and he is accompanied by Impatience and Impotence, suggesting in himself the same mixture of apparent ferocity and actual debility that characterizes his hordes. Spenser gives us a vivid description of this emaciated monster before naming him in stanza 23. His name (Lat. *mal*, evil, + *aeger*, disease) suggests the intimate relation between moral and physical weakness that he embodies. Stanza 22 describes him as 'pale and wan as ashes', trembling and 'cold and drery as a Snake'. The description suggests an excess of the fourth humour, cold, black melancholy, the most dangerous for the moral as well as the physical health of the body:

67

[Melancholy] is a kind of earthy and blacke blood . . . [that] by his corrupt substance and contagious qualitie, and partly by corrupt spirits, annoyeth both heart and braine, being the seates and instruments of reason and affections. (Perkins, *Workes* II, 46)

So 'strange, and often fearefull' are the effects of this disease that Perkins reports it was called 'the *Divels baite*'.

Maleger appears 'like a ghost . . . whose grave-clothes were un-bound' (20) and wears a dead man's skull on his head (22). With his ash-like paleness he seems an embodiment of death itself, but he is 'a mortal wight'. Spenser's description of his paradoxical nature, 'Flesh without bloud, a person without spright . . . /That was most strong in most infirmitee' (40) echoes the imagery of St Paul's description of man's fallen nature, against which the regenerate must continually struggle: 'O wretched man that I am, who shall deliver mee from the body of this death?' (Romans 7.24). Like Guyon, but more sinisterly, Maleger is 'of the earth, earthly' (1 Corinthians 15.47); his genesis is from his mother, Earth, who continually revives him when he falls on her (45).

Maleger's evil then is physical, moral and spiritual. Arthur's vic-tory over such an enemy is achieved by means which stress the spiritual significance of the struggle. His first strategy, to exhaust Maleger (27) is frustrated by Impotence and Impatience, who wrestle Arthur to the ground (29). From these he is rescued by his squire, clearly an agent of Grace on this occasion: 'had not grace thee blest, thou shouldest not survive' (30). Finding that his weapons are inef-fective against this adversary, Arthur wrestles with him, recalling St Paul's admonition to the regenerate Christian to 'wrestle . . . against spirituall wickednesses' (Ephesians 6.12).

Arthur's fight with Maleger is modelled on the mythical battle between Hercules and Antaeus. Each time Hercules wrestled Antaeus to his mother, Earth, he revived. Hercules finally killed him by throttling him and holding his body aloft till he died. For Renaissance mythographers, the contest allegorized the defeat of the lusts of the body (Lotspeich p. 37). Unlike Antaeus, Maleger again revives when his crushed body is thrown to the ground. Arthur can only rid himself of his adversary by throwing his body into a 'stan-ding lake' (46), an image of baptism, or, more logically, of Arthur's remembrance of the promise given at baptism of the washing away of sin (Hume pp. 125–6).

By washing away the foul Maleger and drowning Impatience and her 'burning fier brands' (47), this lake is more effective than those earlier significant waters: the chaste, pure well which would not mix

with Acrasia's poison (i.55) or be defiled with the blood on Ruddymane's hands (ii.9), and the idle lake which would not quench the
inwardly burning Pyrochles (vi.44). But it is no image of temperance
as moderation; it does not dilute, it destroys those lusts and passions
which it touches.

THE BOWER OF BLISS

We move from the baptismal lake to the turbulent seas of canto xii
through which Guyon must pass to accomplish his quest of
vengeance on Acrasia (Gk *akrasia*, ill-temperature,. bad mixture –
Aristotle's incontinence). Guyon travels in a 'well rigged boate'
(xi.4), with a 'wary' boatman appointed by Alma rowing steadily forwards, and the Palmer at the helm, an image of the temperate man's
continual need for vigilance, support and counsel. We recall the
aimless Phaedria, whose 'shallow ship' slides over the water without
oars or pilot (vi.5), and who reappears in a frivolous attempt to draw
Guyon's boat off course in canto xii (14–17). Acrasia clearly
represents more powerful and dangerous appetites.

The dangers that surround the Bower of Bliss are closely related
to it, showing the reader, clearly and horrifically, the vices and
disasters that beset those who pursue Acrasia's illusory gratifications.
Spenser models Guyon's journey on Odysseus' voyage through such
dangers as Scylla and Charybdis, the Wandering Islands and the
Sirens (*Odyssey* 12; cf. Tasso, *Gerusalemme Liberata* 15). Odysseus was,
for the Renaissance, the type of the wise and temperate man vir-
tuously resisting the moral dangers that tempt him on his journey
(see. e.g., Sidney, *Apology* p. 108). Spenser's travellers pass through
an animate landscape that attempts to threaten and deceive by turns,
and against which they seem small and vulnerable:

> On th'other side, they saw that perilous Rocke,
>   Threatning it selfe on them to ruinate,
>   On whose sharpe clifts the ribs of vessels broke,
>   And shivered ships, which had bene wrecked late,
>   Yet stuck, with carkasses exanimate. (xii.7)

The shivered ribs of the vessels suggest the shattered bones of the
men who have been driven, or who have driven themselves, on to this
'*Rocke of* vile *Reproch*'. But, as was the case with Maleger and his
hordes, the appearance of threatening power proves impotent in the
face of steadfast virtue. The travellers row untouched amongst the
dangers, and the monstrous sea-creatures and wild beasts tremble

before the Palmer's staff (26 and 40). It is Guyon and the Palmer who have real power, more threatening to the Bower of Bliss than the force of the beasts that surround it:

> Nought feard their force, the fortilage to win,
> But wisedomes powre, and temperaunces might,
> By which the mightiest things efforced bin. (43)

Spenser's account of the Bower itself draws on one of the Odyssean dangers, the witch Circe's island (*Odyssey* 10), as well as on Renaissance versions, most notably Tasso's description of the enchantress Armida who in her sensual paradise saps the virtue of the Christian champion Rinaldo (*Gerusalemme Liberata* 15–16). On Circe's island men are transformed into beasts by drinking her bewitched wine (cf. the cups of Agdistes and Excess, ix.49 and 56–7). Homer's episode was commonly allegorized to illustrate the bestializing effects of lust on men (e.g., Whitney's emblem '*Homines voluptatibus trans-formantur*'). Odysseus resists Circe's magic with the help of a herb given him by Mercury. In Spenser's poem, the Palmer's staff is given Mercurial powers:

> Of that same wood it fram'd was cunningly,
>   Of which *Caduceus* whilome was made,
>   *Caduceus* the rod of *Mercury*,
>   With which he wonts the *Stygian* realmes invade
>   . . .
>   And rule the *Furyes*, when they most do rage:
> Such vertue in his staffe had eke this Palmer sage. (41)

The pattern of the temperate Odysseus protected by divine aid lies behind Guyon guided by the wise and holy Palmer. Such emphasis on the help Guyon needs, and is given, contributes to our sense of the dangers of the Bower, as do the arduous and fearful approach to it and the evidence of Acrasia's potent witchcraft, which is able to summon up 'thousand thousands' sea-monsters (25) and, like Circe's, to change men to beasts (39).

The danger of the Bower is compounded by its exquisite beauty. It is 'the most daintie Paradise on ground' (58). Spenser dwells on its loveliness, the perfection of its details, the sweetness of its sounds and sights:

> The painted flowres, the trees upshooting hye,
> The dales for shade, the hilles for breathing space,
> The trembling groves, the Christall running by. (58)

Where the Cave of Mammon was as unattractive to the reader as to Guyon, the Bower of Bliss appeals powerfully to the senses, but everywhere a corrupt art is visible to 'decke . . . and too lavishly adorne' (50) what was naturally good. The art of the Bower is at the opposite pole from the 'goodly workemanship' of God (ix.21) which built Alma's House. Spenser carefully and repeatedly hints at its evils in the very language he uses to evoke the skill of the art. The outer gate, for instance, is a piece of rare workmanship but it is made of ivory, recalling the Virgilian gate of Hades, through which pass false dreams (*Aeneid* 6.893–6, and *Faerie Queene* 1.i.40). It is engraved with the story of Medea, an enchantress closely related to Circe and Acrasia, who in pursuit of her passion for Jason betrayed her father, killed her brother and, after Jason's betrayal of her, burned his new love, Creüsa, with a bewitched garment. This hideous tale of crime and lust is engraved in the gate with the utmost beauty. The tone of Spenser's verse is one of wonder and admiration at the art, but the details recall the most destructive parts of the story:

> Ye might have seene the frothy billowes fry
> Under the ship, as thorough them she went,
> That seemd the waves were into yvory,
> Or yvory into the waves were sent;
> And other where the snowy substaunce sprent
> With vermell, like the boyes bloud therein shed,
> A piteous spectacle did represent,
> And otherwhiles with gold besprinkeled;
> Yt seemd th'enchaunted flame, which did *Creüsa* wed.   (45)

The Genius who sits at this marvellous gate is there 'to entize' strangers (46), and his nature is made clear to us: 'The foe of life, that good envyes to all,/That secretly doth us procure to fall' (48). Loveliest and most dangerous of all is Acrasia, veiling her alabaster body in a 'subtile web' woven beyond the skill of the spider Arachne (77). Spider-like, she is found hovering over her latest lover, through whose eyes she 'did sucke his spright' (73).

So outwardly lovely is Acrasia's Bower that commentators have often baulked at its destruction (e.g., Berger p. 218, and Alpers pp. 305–6). Certainly Spenser's language emphasizes the pity of Guyon's act:

> But all those pleasant bowres and Pallace brave,
> *Guyon* broke downe, with rigour pittilesse;
> Ne ought their goodly workmanship might save
> Them from the tempest of his wrathfulnesse,
> But that their blisse he turn'd to balefulnesse:
> Their groves he feld, their gardins did deface,
> Their arbers spoyle, their Cabinets suppresse,

> Their banket houses burne, their buildings race,
> And of the fairest late, now made the fowlest place.   (83)

The sad waste of it is emphasized, but the whole episode has made
clear that the delinquency is Acrasia's: she it is who has perverted
nature and art, making of their beauty a web to trap men's souls.
Guyon's 'wrathfulnesse' is that 'just and lawfull anger' of which
Perkins wrote (see p. 54 above). The idea is commonplace; another
sixteenth-century Protestant authority wrote: 'There is an holy kind
of anger, which the scripture disalloweth not . . . For a good man
hath a zeal of God, and in that godly zeal he is angry at the iniquity
and naughtiness of mankind.'[9] Moderation and self-restraint are
qualities we have come to expect from a temperate Guyon, but a
tempering response to incontinence and its seductions is inap-
propriate. As we saw in canto i, Acrasia's wine cannot be safely
diluted, it must be spilt.

The Palmer's final act is to turn the beast victims of Acrasia's
magic back into men. But while Acrasia's garden has drawn and
seduced the weak and unwary, there are also those who willingly seek
it out. It is a sign of Spenser's realism that the destruction of the
Bower and the action of the Palmer's staff will not free these men
from themselves. We are left with the determinedly unregenerate
Grill,

> That hath so soone forgot the excellence
> Of his creation, when he life began,
> That now he chooseth, with vile difference,
> To be a beast, and lacke intelligence.   (87)

Chapter 3

BOOK 3

INTRODUCTION

1. The virtue of chastity

I call not that *Virginity a vertue*, which resideth only in the *Bodies integrity*
. . . But I call that *Virginity a vertue* which is willing and desirous to yeeld it
selfe upon honest and lawfull terms, when just reason requireth; and until
then, is kept with a modest chastity of Body and Mind.

(John Donne, *Paradoxes and Problemes* xii)[1]

Spenser's celebration of chastity in Book 3 should be put in the
same context of Protestant praise for married love that informs
Donne's apparent paradox. Chastity in this view is as much an aspect
of marriage as it is of virginity; indeed many Protestants gave marriage precedence over virginity as the natural and blessed calling of
men and women. Milton wrote of the love for which marriage was
instituted:

What is it then but that desire which God put into *Adam* in Paradise before
he knew the sin of incontinence; that desire which God saw it was not good
that man should be left alone to burn in; the desire and longing to put off
an unkindly solitarines by uniting another body, but not without a fit soule
to his in the cheerfull society of wedlock?

(*The Doctrine of Divorce* Book I, chap. 4)[2]

Chastity in Book 3, in spite of the preoccupation of the Proem with
the example of Queen Elizabeth, is emphatically conceived in terms
of the chaste and God-given desire which Milton describes. Milton
puts emphasis on the desire for marriage as a 'longing to put off an
unkindly solitarines' and the 1559 Prayer Book similarly lists 'mutual
societie, helpe, and comfort' as reasons for the institution of
marriage.

For the sixteenth century, marriage was not the private affair of
the nuclear family which it has become in the twentieth century.
Marriage was a public act and it had public significance; the social
bonds forged in marriage were at the centre of analogous bonds
within society at large, within nations, and even within the
framework of nature, based like the bonds of marriage on love and
obedience, desire and the restraint of law. Spenser's treatment of

chaste love continually makes us aware of such far-reaching reverberations. The full symbolic significance of chaste love as a binding force central to social, national and indeed universal concord will be developed in Book 4, but some of that significance is already apparent in Book 3, as we shall see when we discuss the Britomart and the Marinell/Florimell narratives.

Many of the ideas at work in Book 3 are developed more directly in the *Hymne of Love*, published in 1596 though written earlier. In this poem Spenser describes love's power in the elemental as well as the human spheres. Love it is that binds the elements and releases the potential fertility of matter: 'Ayre hated earth, and water hated fyre,/Till Love relented their rebellious yre' (ll. 83–4), and love it is that infuses all living things with the secret spark of fire by which they all

> moved are
> To multiply the likenesse of their kynd,
> Whilest they seeke onely, without further care,
> To quench the flame, which they in burning fynd.
> (ll. 99–102)

Such is the power of the 'Great God of might' among elemental and natural things. The human experience of love is more problematic, being composed, in its earlier stages at least, primarily of pain and frustration. This, according to the *Hymne of Love*, is how it should be:

> Yet herein eke thy glory seemeth more,
> By so hard handling those which best thee serve,
> That ere thou doest them vnto grace restore,
> Thou mayest well trie if they will ever swerve.   (ll. 162–5)

Love distinguishes between virtuous and brutish minds, spurring the first on to noble deeds and revealing the bestiality of the base (ll. 169–89). This distinction is crucial to Book 3 of *The Faerie Queene*, in which love and lust are sharply differentiated:

> Not that same, which doth base affections move
> In brutish minds, and filthy lust inflame,
> But that sweet fit, that doth true beautie love,
> And choseth vertue for his dearest Dame,
> Whence spring all noble deeds and never dying fame   (iii.1)

To emphasize the bestiality of lust Spenser associates it throughout Book 3 with grotesque, sub-human figures: the 'griesly Foster' (i.17); the sluggish churl and his mother's agent, the hyena that 'feeds on womens flesh' (vii.12 and 22); the fisherman whose sperm is associated with the dead, congealed scales of fish that fill his boat (viii.26), and the monstrous giants, Argante and Olyphant, who committed incest in the womb and have indulged in every abomination since (vii.7–9).

Love is sharply distinguished from such bestial impulses, but it by no means always inspires and illuminates even the minds of the virtuous. In the *Hymne of Love* Spenser describes some of the mental torments induced by love in the 'fayning fancie' of the lover:

> Sights never seene, and thousand shadowes vaine,
> To breake his sleepe, and waste his ydle braine;
> Thou that hast never lov'd canst not beleeve,
> Least part of th'evils which poore lovers greeve.   (ll. 255–8)

In Book 3, Spenser shows himself to be particularly sensitive to this aspect of the human experience of love, whether it be Britomart's sleeplessness (canto ii), or the bizarre house of erotic delusions created by Busirane (cantos xi and xii). Chaste love is undoubtedly for Spenser a God-given impulse, blessed and innocent, but it is also a sexual impulse and hence subject to all the pains, uncertainties and frustrations that attend the human experience of Cupid's powers.

2. Narrative modes

The range of Spenser's treatment of the topic of love, as a force for binding the elements and governing the fertility of nature, its perversion as lust, its pains and delusions, is reflected by the variety and flexibility of the narrative methods he uses in this book. Spenser is more than usually eclectic, interweaving Ariostan romance narrative with the language and imagery of Petrarchanism, the landscapes and beings of myth, and the castles and houses of medieval love-allegory. Each narrative mode brings with it associations and techniques which Spenser exploits to develop his complex account of the workings of love.

a. Ariostan romance

After the relative austerity of the narratives of Books 1 and 2, Book 3 presents us with what may seem at first a bewildering variety and richness. This is partly due to the multiple narrative strands which interlace throughout this book. We follow the quite separate adventures of Britomart, Marinell and Florimell, Belphoebe and Timias, and Amoret and Scudamour, as well as a number of more minor figures. The narrative of each of these figures emerges into the foreground for one or two cantos before receding, to re-emerge perhaps later in Book 3, or perhaps not until Book 4.

Spenser's model for the multiple interlacing narratives of Book 3 is Ariosto's *Orlando Furioso* (*OF*). A number of the incidents in Book 3 owe a specific debt to similar incidents in *OF*: Florimell's flight (viii.1–2) imitates that of Angelica pursued by lovers from whom she wishes to escape (e.g., *OF* 1.13), and Britomart is a close literary relation to Ariosto's female warrior Bradamante: both pursue their future husbands through the obstacles of separation, and both learn of their dynastic destinies from Merlin (*OF* 3). The sense which Ariosto's poem gives of the obstacles fate puts in the way of fulfilment and of the impelling power of passion are effects perfectly suited to Spenser's conception of love. From Ariosto, too, Spenser often borrows a tone of humorous sympathy for the all-too-human doubts and pangs of love of his otherwise invulnerable heroine (cf. *OF* 32.11–25 and, e.g., *The Faerie Queene* 3.ii.27–39). Spenser increases the comedy of Britomart's love-stricken girlishness by adding the sympathetic but garrulous Glauce. In a bawdier vein, Spenser's tale of Malbecco and Hellenore among the satyrs (canto x) gives us a view of inexhaustible female sexual appetite to parallel the notorious tale of the host (*OF* 28).

Spenser's technique of interweaving multiple narratives helps to create effects which are central to Book 3. The first of these is the sense we have of our being in a more populous and socially complex world than was true of Books 1 and 2. Many different individuals, both Faery and British, pursuing quite independent quests, pass across the landscape, most in search of a partner from whom they are separated. The book emphasizes men and women as social animals, living among diverse fellows, and subject to the bonds and desires that draw one individual to another. As we shall see, the social repercussions of love are a central concern of Spenser in Books 3 and 4.

The second point to make is that the multiple interweaving narratives of Book 3 help to create, even more than in Book 1, the sense of our being in the midst of a puzzling world in which people and places are often not what they seem and where it is often difficult to interpret events fully or accurately until they are passed. This is an effect experienced by the characters themselves: Britomart's identity is commonly mistaken; Florimell misinterprets Arthur's intentions; False Florimell deceives all beholders; Cymoent misunderstands Proteus; and to some extent the narratives, fragmented by interweaving, give the reader a similar experience. The problematic nature of the

world of Book 3 is perhaps best expressed by the narrator's comment
on Proteus' ambiguous prophecy:

> So tickle be the termes of mortall state,
> And full of subtile sophismes, which do play
> With double senses, and with false debate,
> T'approve the unknowen purpose of eternall fate.   (iv.28)

Such an experience seems central to Spenser's conception of love in
its early stages. It is a force which drives individuals on willy-nilly,
to unknown ends, into dangers, and often against reason.

A third effect of the multiple interweaving narratives is the oppor-
tunity for variety they give to Spenser. Each narrative and each
episode, as the stories interrupt one another, can be used to develop
a different but complementary aspect of the central virtue. In Book
3 we do not find a single exemplar of the titular virtue, though
Britomart is its most powerful embodiment. Our understanding of
chastity develops as we observe its various aspects in the independent
narrative strands.

b. Myth

The techniques of myth play a crucial part in Book 3. The chivalric
romance narrative of Marinell's fight with Britomart shifts into myth
on the appearance of Marinell's mother, the sea-nymph Cymoent,
who hastens to the scene in a marvellous chariot drawn by dolphins,
and canto vi is taken up entirely with the squabble of the goddesses
Venus and Diana, the Danae-like impregnation of Chrysogonee by
the sun, and the mythical Garden of Adonis. The transition from
chivalric romance to such myths of Spenser's own invention denotes
a subtle shift in meaning: we move from the human to the elemental
sphere, from the operation of love in individuals to its more universal
laws and repercussions. For instance, the confrontation of Venus
and Diana in canto vi serves to suggest two aspects of Venus' nature
and thus of the love she represents. The two aspects of her nature are
differentiated, as was traditional in Renaissance iconography, by the
different attributes with which she is associated. Linked with her
lover Mars (vi.24) and the armed Cupid she denotes the dangerous
and disruptive effects of sexual desire, too often experienced as pain,
frustration and mere appetite. Without Cupid and his arrows, and
in the company of a temporarily reconciled Diana, as in canto vi, she
denotes a more positive and approved aspect of love's power – the
generative, procreative love which functions within the bounds of

nature's laws. It is this aspect of love's power that is developed in the mythical stories of Chrysogonee's conception and the fertile Garden of Adonis. Similarly, as we shall see, the shift into myth in the Marinell narrative in canto iv signals a shift in significance from the human and social repercussions of love and its denial, to their repercussions in the natural world. As their names suggest, Florimell (Lat. *flos*, flower, hence the land) and Marinell (Lat. *mare*, sea) take on, over the course of their narrative through Books 3 and 4, elemental significance.

c. Courtly codes of love

Spenser's invented myths point to the elemental and cosmic spheres of love's influence. In contrast, his use of the sophisticated vocabularies of literary codes of love points to a distorting human view of love, especially of its terrors. Britomart's temporary despair by the seashore when she thinks of love as cruel and spiteful (iv.8–10) is expressed in the language of a Petrarchan sonnet, 'Passa la nave mia colma d'oblio' (*Rime* 189). Later the language of Petrarchanism helps to generate the False Florimell (viii.5–9), made, like innumerable sonneteers' mistresses, of snow and wax and golden wire. The 'wicked Spright' (viii.8) who moves this artificial idol is Spenser's addition and tells us much about his perception of the dangers of such deification of externals. A more predatory and cynical code of love is that of Ovid's *Ars Amatoria*, a handbook on the art of seduction which both Paridell and the adulterous Hellenore have conned well (ix. 28–31). Grimmest of all are the Houses of Malecasta and Busirane, in which we find not love but elaborate rituals for seduction. The artful hangings and entertainments display desire as an unpleasant codified game in which the object of lust is a prey to be caught. Both houses use the language of medieval love-allegory, found, for example, in the *Roman de la Rose*, with its personifications of the steps of courtship and of the fears and desires of passion. The tapestries that decorate the walls draw their matter from the notorious versions of sexual passion and the sexual antics of the gods found in Ovid's *Metamorphoses*. Spenser returns throughout Book 3 to the false fears and perversions of love, which derive from such literary representations of the passion as a painful and predatory ritual, representations which are at the opposite extreme to the vocabulary of natural sensuous abundance that characterizes the Garden of Adonis.

Book 3

BRITOMART'S NARRATIVE

If not the only exemplar of chastity in Book 3, Britomart is undoubtedly its major champion. She is a distinctive heroine, quite unlike any of the other titular knights of *The Faerie Queene*. Her difference derives in part from the degree of idiosyncratic characterization Spenser gives her. Redcrosse was characterized by his sadness (1.i.2), and Calidore feels a human longing for the delight of the shepherd's life (6.x.3), but Britomart's humanness is handled with a degree of detail and humour which is unusual. Unusual too is her role, a woman disguised as a man in search of a lover she has merely glimpsed in a magic mirror. There is none of the status and clarity of a commission from Gloriana or a mission of virtuous revenge such as initiate the quests of the knights of other books. Disguise, a sign of deceit in Book 1, becomes in Britomart's case a sign of the combination of militancy and wariness with which she pursues her destiny, qualities which stand her in good stead amongst the uncertainties and unexpected dangers that beset her.

Britomart's encounter with Malecasta and her six knights in canto i establishes with clarity and symmetry Britomart's role in opposition to unchastity. Where Malecasta forces herself on all who pass by whether they defeat or are defeated by her six knights (26–7), Britomart, with Redcrosse, stands for singleness and faithfulness in love (24–5). The contrast between the two women is developed with the humour characteristic of this book. Malecasta's shameless invitations are met by Britomart's polite dissemblance (48–50), the latter's armed innocence (52–4) confronts the former's showy wantonness (52–5). The two finally confront each other in their shifts, the one outraged with sword drawn, the other frustrated and swooning (63).

The six knights who serve Malecasta personify the steps of love in a courtly game of seduction (44–5), from the relative innocence of eye-glances, through which, traditional physiology taught, love first entered the heart, through talk and pleasantries, to kissing, wine and finally the pleasures of the night. It is significant that Britomart is wounded only by Gardante (eye-glances; Ital. *guardante*, looking) (65), indicating her susceptibility to Artegall's image glimpsed in the glass, but is impervious to the five more predatory brothers.

Castle Joyeus is decorated with a tapestry made by a 'cunning hand' (34) in which the story of Venus and Adonis is depicted. The emphasis on Venus' voyeurism (36), on the luxuriousness and idleness of the life they lead, on Venus' timorousness (37) and on the final tragedy in which Adonis is transformed into a 'dainty flowre'

(38) contributes to the particular character of Castle Joyeus and the sort of love, idle and fatal, that it represents. This boudoir version of the Venus and Adonis myth contrasts sharply with the powerful, generative Garden of Adonis of canto vi, but it anticipates, as a paler and slighter version, the artful and disturbing hangings on the walls of Busirane's House in canto xi.

The sympathy with which Spenser handles the humanness and deviousness of his heroine is most fully developed in canto ii. In the first few stanzas, Britomart lies to Redcrosse first about her upbring-ing (cf. ii.6–7 and iii.53) and then about her motives in searching for Artegall. Disguise and deviousness are for Britomart necessary and forgivable strategies to protect her feminine vulnerability. In the description of her first pangs of love, her feminine frailty is emphasiz-ed, sympathetically but conventionally by Spenser: her curiosity about who her husband will be prompts the image of Artegall in the first place (ii.23), and after the first glance there are the fancies and sleepless nights that troubled all Renaissance lovers (27–9). But con-ventional as Britomart's pangs may be, they are described sym-pathetically and vividly by Spenser. Her huge Aetna (32) of passion contrasts with the unsteady 'sparkes of fire' (i.47) of Malecasta's casual lust. Spenser draws the reader into Britomart's own ex-perience of the overwhelming force of genuine passion, irresistible and wholly disorientating. Only subsequently does he assure both Britomart and the reader of the passion's virtuous and providential nature.

Spenser's development of Britomart's significance in canto iii is unexpected and bold. She is transformed from a love-sick 'silly Mayd' (ii. 27) to a figure of dynastic and national importance. Britomart's British progeny represents Elizabeth Tudor's ancestry. In the 'royall virgin . . . which shall/Stretch her white rod over the *Belgicke* shore,/And the great Castle smite' (iii.49) we are to see the culmination of the ancient British race in the person of Artegall and Britomart's most illustrious descendant. The linking of the British and Saxon nations that will take place, in Merlin's prophecy, under Elizabeth – 'Thenceforth eternall union shall be made /Betweene the nations different afore' (49) – is anticipated in the British Britomart's action in borrowing the Saxon Angela's armour, though combining it with a magic British lance (58–60), in order to fit herself for her quest to find the husband who will bring this prophetic future to pass.

In the person of Britomart, Spenser takes us from the human ex-perience of love with all its fancies and fears to love as the source and bond of nations and dynasties. The full significance of Spenser's conception of love as concord, in which the binding together of individuals by love is seen as both the cause and the symbol of the wider bonds of society and of nations, is not developed until Book 4. Nevertheless, through Merlin's prophecies we are already able to see the vast scope of virtuous love, begun in the private pangs of erotic desire and culminating in the new golden age of Elizabethan prosperity and peace.

THE FLORIMELL AND MARINELL NARRATIVES

Florimell is fleetingly glimpsed in canto i as she flees in terror from friends and foes, a brief image of feminine vulnerability to set against Britomart's 'stout hardiment' (i.19). In canto iv we first meet Marinell, although it is not until the following canto that the connection between Marinell's fate and Florimell's flight is made (v.8–10). As in the case of Britomart, we find a story of love between individuals acquiring wider social and, in this case, elemental significance.

Marinell's narrative begins with images of waste. He lives alone by the sea-shore defending from all comers a treasure which lies scattered, unused, among the sand and which has itself been thrown up by the sea:

> And him enriched through the overthrow
> And wreckes of many wretches, which did weepe,
> And often waile their wealth, which he from them did keepe.
>
> (iv.22)

The unused treasures thrown up by the sea which Marinell keeps from their rightful owners are paralleled by the treasures of his love and manhood which he keeps from use:

> Yet many Ladies faire did oft complaine,
> That they for love of him would algates dy:
> Dy, who so list for him, he was loves enimy.   (iv.26)

Marinell's chastity is false, a form of selfish and fearful sterility. The unnaturalness of his denial is suggested by the interlaced 'love . . . dy:/Dy . . . loves', a verbal effect Spenser uses again in Book 4 to describe the logic of love and death forced upon Florimell by Marinell's action (4.xii.9).

The sterility of the sea links Britomart and Marinell in canto iv. Britomart turns from her complaint, in which the sea becomes an image of her own sense of pain and indirection (6–10), to confront

Marinell, the cause, through his refusal of love, of pain and indirection to others.[3] Britomart's despair is a brief indulgence and she sets herself again in active pursuit of fulfilled love by defeating Marinell. The contrast between the two is compounded by their differing responses to the future. Merlin's prophecies inspire Britomart's 'generous stout courage' (iii.57) to meet her destiny by exposing herself to the uncertainties and dangers of an active quest. Marinell and his mother, on the other hand, misinterpret Proteus' ambiguous prophecies (iv.25) and respond with fear, attempting to cheat destiny by cheating nature:

> For thy she gave him warning every day,
> > The love of women not to entertaine;
> > A lesson too too hard for living clay,
> > From love in course of nature to refraine.   (iv.26)

For Spenser the uncertainties of human fate and the feeble power of mankind to avert its effects are matter for elegy (iv.28) but also a challenge giving heroic spirits like Britomart a chance to prove their full worth. Love is a primary agent of this uncertain, but ultimately ordered, fate:

> > The fatall purpose of divine foresight,
> > Thou doest effect in destined descents,
> > Through deepe impression of thy secret might,
> > And stirredst up th'Heroes high intents,
> Which the late world admyres for wondrous moniments.   (iii.2)

The disordering effects of Marinell's attempt to avert his fate are more fully grasped when we come to Florimell's story. Her love for Marinell spurs her on to seek him out (v.10), but Marinell's refusal of that love and his apparent death leave her exposed to the lawlessness of force and lust: the wild 'Foster' (i.17); the unsocial witch, her beast-like son and their rapacious hyena (vii.6–23); the obscene fisherman (viii.22–7); and the sea-god Proteus, who changes his nature at will (viii.39–41) and finally imprisons Florimell beneath the sea (viii.41–2).

Florimell's panic-stricken flight from one danger to another is a direct consequence of Marinell's refusal to love. A more indirect consequence is the creation of False Florimell, an agent of yet more disorder. The full extent of her capacity to provoke discord and dissension only becomes apparent in Book 4, but her potential is already visible in 3.viii. She substitutes for the faithfulness and chastity of the displaced Florimell the rolling eyes and 'wicked Spright' (viii.8) of unchastity. She circulates from one possessor to another, causing each one to 'thinke him selfe in heaven, that was in hell' (viii.19). Thus a concatenation of events links this false image of woman as an object of love and the disorder she wreaks in society with Marinell's initial attempt to evade love and the 'course of nature' (iv.26).

If the effects of Marinell's inaction are dire within the society of Faeryland, the symbolic implications of Florimell's imprisonment by Proteus are still worse. I noted in my discussion of narrative modes (pp. 77–8 above) that the shift from a romance to a mythic narrative mode tends to denote a shift in significance from love's social and human effects, to love as an elemental force. The shift from romance to myth in canto iv alerts us to the significance of Marinell's association with the sea. At present in his narrative Marinell seems to embody the more destructive aspects of the sea (iv. 22–3), but to the Elizabethans the sea was a place of great fertility. Venus was born from the foam of the sea, suggesting its importance as a source of generation and abundance (cf.4.xii.1–2). The potential, but wasted, fruitfulness of Marinell is further suggested by his connection with Florimell. Roche (p. 190) has linked the names Florimell and Marinell, which, as we have seen (p. 78 above), etymologically derive from flower and sea, with a sixteenth-century emblem which shows Cupid holding in one hand a flower and in the other a fish, illustrating love's power over land and sea. We have to wait until Book 4 for such a union to be effected between Marinell and Florimell, but the symbolism of their names already suggests their potential elemental significance.

Responding to the mythic nature of so much of the Florimell/ Marinell narrative some commentators have suggested that the story follows the pattern of the Proserpina myth, in which Proserpina, the daughter of Ceres, goddess of fruitfulness, is imprisoned below the ground in the house of Hades for the winter months of each year, to emerge again in spring as a sign of renewed seasonal life (see, e.g., Hamilton (1961) pp. 148–52). If such a pattern is at work in the Florimell/Marinell narrative then it reaffirms the elemental dimension to the story suggested by Spenser's myth-like narrative techniques and the implications of the names.

Such an interpretation is strengthened by the function of Proteus. His dungeon beneath the sea is described at 4.xi.4 as being like 'the balefull house of lowest hell', washed by the Styx, the place of Proserpina's incarceration. The unbound, shape-shifting Proteus had a rich range of significances for Renaissance mythographers.[4] Foremost among these were two meanings which are particularly suggestive in the Florimell/Marinell narrative: Proteus as lawlessness, and Proteus as First Matter.

Proteus as a figure of lawlessness is present in *OF*, in which he is a force of sexual and civil violence. He rapes the daughter of the king of Ebuda and then, when the king severely punishes his daughter with death, he avenges himself on the people of the island by demanding a tribute of virgins for his rapacious sea-monster. Ariosto's emphasis is on the violation of all laws by Proteus who 'per grand'ira, rompe ordine e legge' (8.54: 'through fury he broke all order and law'). Spenser's Proteus offers less physical violence than Ariosto's, but in his bewildering shape-shifting and his assaults on Florimell's chastity he reflects in a concentrated form the unrestrained lawlessness and aggression Florimell has experienced since she left Gloriana's court in search of Marinell.

Most familiarly for Renaissance thinkers, Proteus represented First Matter, the material from which all things are made. Sir Francis Bacon tells us that 'the sense of this fable relates, it would seem, to the secrets of nature and the conditions of matter. For under the person of Proteus, matter – the most ancient of all things next to God – is meant to be represented.'[5] Such primary matter should be a perpetual generative source; Proteus is another figure for the chaos that lies beneath the Garden of Adonis and 'supplyes/The substance of natures fruitful progenyes' (vi.36). Unlike the Garden of Adonis, however, the Florimell/Marinell narrative in Book 3 is a story of sterility and of nature's laws disrupted. Not until Book 4 is the full generative potential of Proteus revealed. In 3.viii Proteus' capacity for transformation is unproductively devoted to seducing Florimell. Finally he imprisons her and the spring-like flowering which her name suggests in a dark, death-like dungeon.

The myth-like techniques of the narrative and the mythological associations of the material Spenser uses extend the story of Marinell's misguided refusal of love far beyond its local significance as part of the love-story of two individuals. In Britomart's case, the private bond of marriage is to be the source of wider social and national orders. In the case of Florimell and Marinell, the disrupted bond of love becomes the symbolic source of wider disruptions, both in society and in nature.

BELPHOEBE: CANTOS v–vi

In Britomart and Florimell we are given images of loving chastity, the virtuous and faithful desire that leads them on to unite themselves with the objects of their love. In Belphoebe we have a rather different image of chastity – as virginity. We have seen that the ideal no longer enjoyed the status in Protestant thought that it had under Roman Catholicism (see pp. 73–4 above). For Elizabethan Protestants, however, the situation was tricky; Protestant idealization of marriage conflicted with the virginal image that by the late 1580s had become the established form of praise for Queen Elizabeth. In both popular and courtly writing she was Diana, Cynthia, Phoebe, the virginal moon goddess.

At the beginning of Book 3, Spenser clearly indicates that we are to interpret Belphoebe as a complement to one aspect of Elizabeth:

> Ne let his fairest *Cynthia* refuse,
> In mirrours more then one her selfe to see,
> But either *Gloriana* let her chuse,
> Or in *Belphoebe* fashioned to bee:
> In th'one her rule, in th'other her rare chastitee.   (Proem 5)

Spenser's means of praising the virginal queen in a book devoted to the celebration of chaste sexual love as a central bond of both society and nature is to emphasize the exceptional qualities of Belphoebe. In this he is in fact following orthodox Protestant thought, in which virginity was an exceptional, undoubtedly saintly calling for the perfect few. Calvin wrote that 'it is not in every man's power to live chaste in celibacy . . . it is a special grace which the Lord bestows only on certain individuals, in order that they may be less encumbered in his service' (*Institutes*, I, 349). Spenser insists on Belphoebe's exceptional qualities. She is an 'ensample' to all women 'To whom in perfect love, and spotlesse fame/Of chastitie, none living may compaire' (v.54). She is likened to the rose, most perfect of flowers (we are perhaps invited to think of the Tudor rose), which God transferred from paradise to earth 'To make ensample of his heavenly grace' (52).

Belphoebe is the 'perfect complement' (v.55) of chastity and courtesy, the virtues of Diana and of Venus (see my discussion p. 56 above). Although impervious to sexual love herself (50) she can nevertheless create havoc in lesser mortals. Timias, wounded in the thigh by a brother of the forester who lustfully pursued Florimell (v.20), clearly represents a man wounded by sexual appetite, though by killing the forester who inflicted the wound he defeats its more outrageous manifestation. Under Belphoebe's care, Timias' 'foule sore' (v.41) in his thigh becomes a less physical wound to his heart: 'She his hurt thigh to him recur'd againe,/But hurt his hart, the

85

which before was sound' (42). There is a progression here from mere physical desire to a love that chooses rather 'to dye for sorrow great, /Then with dishonorable terms her to entreat' (49). But there the ascent seems to halt. There is no apparent further progress up the Neoplatonic stair which should take the lover from adoration of one particular woman to the flight of the soul 'kindled in the most holy fire of true heavenly love . . . to couple herselfe with the nature of Angels'[6]. Belphoebe, though perfect, is earthly: 'Nor Goddesse I, nor Angell, but the Mayd,/And daughter of a woody Nymphe' (36). The verbal interlacing of 'love' and 'death' which was a sign of unnaturalness and waste in the Florimell/Marinell story in canto iv (see p. 81 above) recurs again in canto vi as a sign of Timias' irresoluble dilemma as the honourable but human lover of an earthly but unattainable love:

> Dye rather, dye, and dying do her serve,
> Dying her serve, and living her adore;
> Thy life she gave, thy life she doth deserve:
> Dye rather, dye, then ever from her service swerve. (46)

Timias' love for Belphoebe is to frustrate and deflect him from his truly honourable calling as Arthur's companion for the course of the next three books.

AMORET AND THE GARDEN OF ADONIS

Belphoebe's twin, Amoret, is developed in very different terms. Their miraculous birth from the action of the sun's beams on Chrysogonee's 'pregnant flesh' (vi.7), in Belphoebe's case suggests her super-human and regal origins, but in Amoret's forms part of the imagery of fertility which surrounds her and which suggests that her role, unlike that of the exceptional and solitary Belphoebe, is to embody an ideal of marriageable womanhood. Venus entrusts her to the care of Psyche,

> yfostered to bee,
> And trained up in true feminitee:
> Who no lesse carefully her tendered,
> Then her owne daughter *Pleasure*, to whom shee
> Made her companion, and her lessoned
> In all the lore of love, and goodly womanhead. (vi.51)

Amoret absorbs by education and no doubt by association some of the ideals embodied in the surrounding Garden of Adonis, but that mythical paradise gives us a version of love's power which is more basic and universal than the specifically human experience.

Spenser prefaces his account of the Garden of Adonis with two mythical narratives of his own invention: the miraculous impregnation and parturition of Chrysogonee (vi.5–10, 26–7), and the humorous encounter of Venus and Diana as Venus searches for the missing Cupid (vi.11–25). The reader's attention is guided and focused with a lightness of touch before we turn to the grander and more resonant mythical description of the Garden itself. The myth of Chrysogonee (Gk *chrysos*, gold, + *gone*, birth), with its emphasis on her naturalness – 'She bath'd with roses red, and violets blew,/And all the sweetest flowres, that in the forrest grew' (6) – is a version of the myth of the natural fertility of matter which follows, though it introduces the divine agency of the sun, whose role is not directly mentioned in the Garden itself:

> Great father he of generation
>> Is rightly cald, th'author of life and light;
>> And his faire sister for creation
>> Ministreth matter fit, which tempred right
>> With heate and humour, breedes the living wight.   (vi.9)

The Garden is preceded by a reminder, couched in the language of a myth of nature, of the primacy of the divine impulse needed to impregnate what would otherwise be inert.

The sun, Phoebus, works with his sister Phoebe, or Diana, or the moon, who tempers matter for creation (9); the stanza alludes to the moon's menstrual influence over the cycle of fertility. This aspect of Diana is not one which at first seems relevant to the virginal goddess, enemy of sexual love, who squabbles with Venus in the following stanzas, but Spenser has carefully designed the confrontation of Venus and Diana, an apparent meeting of opposites, in order to emphasize those elements in each which will eventually lead to their temporary reconciliation. Diana, as we are reminded, through her association with the moon presides over women's fertility, and she was commonly invoked at childbirth (cf. *Epithalamion* ll. 383–7). When Venus meets her in canto vi she is unarmed and unbound, looking more like the traditional image of Venus:

> And her lancke loynes ungirt, and brests unbraste,
> After her heat the breathing cold to taste;
> Her golden lockes, that late in tresses bright
> Embreaded were for hindring of her haste,
> Now loose about her shoulders hong undight,
> And were with sweet *Ambrosia* all besprinckled light.   (18)

Similarly Venus is unarmed, for she is without her wanton son Cupid and his sharp arrows. As Cupid's arrows are a familiar Renaissance emblem for the randomness and immorality of sexual lust, so Venus without the armed Cupid is a sign of a chaster, more responsible form of sexual love.

Such iconographic hints in the descriptions of the two goddesses make symbolic sense of their reconciliation, temporary though it be. Their peace presides over the finding of the two children of Chrysogonee, suggesting that on each child is bestowed the blessing of a more amenable Diana and a chaster Venus. It acts too as a preface to the description of the Garden, in which Venus reigns as a goddess of generative love and not as the meretricious patroness of human lust.

The Garden itself is a complex metaphor for the endless, creative cycle of matter from the chaos of first matter, through its formation into specific forms, animal and vegetable, which gradually decay and are transformed again through death back into the basic materials of life. Gardens themselves are potent symbols bringing with them suggestions of feminine sexuality and of paradisial perfection (see Giamatti (1966) pp. 49–56 and 289). The innocence and generosity of this Garden sharply distinguish it from that depraved paradise, the devious and selfish Bower of Bliss.

The difficulty of the Garden of Adonis for scholars is the extent of Spenser's eclecticism. He draws his ideas, images and vocabulary from a wide range of sources to create his own composite metaphor of the generative impulse of matter. However philosophically inconsistent details of this metaphor may be, or however puzzling their source, the main emphases are clear. The Garden is one place and emphatically earthly (29), but the description focuses on three special aspects of its nature. The first of these describes the relationship of the Garden to the world beyond its gates. It is a seminary in which grow both the vegetative souls, the potential for life and growth in each created thing, and the fleshly forms that will clothe them. Genius, the porter of the two gates of life and death (31), officiates over their birth into the world and their replanting in the Garden after death (32–3). We are not here dealing with the divine soul in man, which is unique and not reusable, but with the 'soul' of matter, its capacity for individual growth and change. Spenser emphasizes both the permanence and the continual change of matter. Underlying the constant movement of forms and souls in and out of the Garden is the essentially unchanging nature of matter itself and the orderliness of nature's disposition in contrast with the undifferentiated chaos of matter's primal source:

Infinite shapes of creatures there are bred,
    And uncouth formes, which none yet ever knew,
    And every sort is in a sundry bed
    Set by it selfe, and ranckt in comely rew:
    Some fit for reasonable soules t'indew,
    Some made for beasts, some made for birds to weare,
    And all the fruitfull spawne of fishes hew
    In endlesse rancks along enraunged were,
That seem'd the *Ocean* could not containe them there.

Daily they grow, and daily forth are sent
    Into the world, it to replenish more;
    Yet is the stocke not lessened, nor spent,
    But still remaines in everlasting store,
    As it at first created was of yore.
    For in the wide wombe of the world there lyes,
    In hatefull darkenesse and in deepe horrore,
    An huge eternall *Chaos*, which supplyes
The substances of natures fruitfull progenyes.   (35–6)

Matter is permanent, but the forms it continually creates are subject to time and change. As always with this topic, Spenser's treatment is half elegiac, half celebratory. Through time the boundless fertility of creation is revealed, but through time too comes transience and loss. This is the second aspect of the Garden which Spenser emphasizes. The vegetative souls which return to the Garden 'grow afresh, as they had never seene/Fleshly corruption, nor mortall paine' (33). Although not subject to death, the vegetative souls grow and are therefore subject to time. The forms with which the souls are clothed are, however, subject to death, mown down by Time, who with his scythe is Death but also a harvester:

                wicked *Time*, who with his scyth addrest,
                Does mow the flowring herbes and goodly things,
                And all their glory to the ground downe flings,
                Where they doe wither, and are fowly mard.   (39)

The flowers and grasses wither, but the mowing makes way for new growth. In spite of Spenser's elegiac tone, his imagery points to the necessity and ultimate fruitfulness of Time as Death.

The third aspect of the Garden is developed as we approach the 'stately Mount' in the 'middest of that Paradise' (43). The sexuality of Venus' Garden, which has so far been subdued, now becomes central. The metaphors for the generative centre of the Garden are richly and overtly sexual: on the *mons veneris* is an uncut grove of myrtle trees from which drops a 'sweet gum' producing 'most dainty odours, and most sweet delight' (43). In this private and shaded place

Adonis lies 'Lapped in flowres and pretious spycery', and here Venus 'Possesseth him, and of his sweetnesse takes her fill' (46). This, then, is a place of sexual delight and abundance, but it is also a place of transformation. The flowers which grow in this secret grove are the bodies of unhappy lovers transformed to growing things, free from human pain (45). Adonis is appropriately placed among such metamorphosed lovers, for, in the version of the myth depicted in Malecasta's tapestry, he too was transformed into a flower (i.38). This grove of the generative Venus is a place where the tragic human experience of love can be transformed into new forms of growth and beauty. Adonis is not transformed into a flower in this Garden; he has a more important function as 'the Father of all formes' (47). His sexual union with Venus is both another metaphor for the creation of transient forms from eternal matter and also the generative centre of the Garden, a sexual image for the very source of nature's fertility, the means by which the jarring elements are transformed into the infinite variety of the visible world.

At the end of his description of the Garden, as at the beginning, Spenser emphasizes that here we have to do with a good Venus, a legitimate sexual love, rather than one of its wanton and irresponsible versions. Cupid when he comes to the Garden lays his dangerous arrows aside (49). This unarmed Cupid is linked with Psyche, traditionally interpreted as the human soul (see note in Hamilton's edition to stanza 50). Their child, Pleasure, suggests the fruitfulness and joy of such a union. It is appropriate that Amoret should be given into Psyche's care, learning from her 'the lore of love, and goodly womanhead' (51) but also perhaps something of the trials and pains which the human soul has often to experience before it achieves the joys of love's satisfaction (50).

MALECCO: CANTOS ix–x

At the beginning of canto ix a group (Satyrane, Paridell, Britomart and the Squire of Dames) gathers outside Malbecco's gates. All have been brought there by a professed fidelity in love, but in each fidelity produces markedly different effects. In the service of his mistress, the Squire of Dames must first seduce as many as he can (vii.54) and then cap 'the spoiles of [his] victorious games' (54) by finding an equal number of chaste ladies (56), a task he finds hopeless. Satyrane attempts to do faithful service to Florimell. Finding the witch's hyena feeding on Florimell's abandoned horse (vii.30), he defeats and binds it with the 'golden girdle' (31) also abandoned by Florimell in her flight. But Satyrane is not fortunate enough to accomplish anything of significance. While Florimell flees further and further from those who professedly seek to help her, to be rescued by the dangerously unbound Proteus (viii.30–42), Satyrane's binding of the lesser beast, the hyena, is soon undone. Seeking to free the bound Squire of Dames from the lustful giantess Argante, he finds himself bound in the Squire's place (vii.37–43). Generous and well meaning as Satyrane's interventions are, he lacks the force or virtue to carry them through and they prove misdirected.

Satyrane saves the Squire from Argante, but he must himself be rescued by the virgin knight Sir Palladine (vii.52), another manifestation of that chaste militancy that characterizes Britomart (cf.xii.3–6). Britomart is brought to Malbecco's gate by her faithful quest for Artegall. There she meets and at once falls out with Paridell (ix.14–16), who claims to be one of those 'noble knights of Maydenhead' (vii.47) who pursue Florimell 'to savegard her' (viii.46). Paridell's loyalty to Florimell is short-lived once Malbecco's house is entered. He is the polar opposite of Britomart. Where she is chaste, faithful and straightforward, he is faithless and devious, dallying with Malbecco's young wife Hellenore by means of speaking looks and spilt wine, a cynical language of seduction culled from Ovid's *Ars Amatoria*:

> For all that art he learned had of yore.
> Ne was she ignoraunt of that lewd lore,
> But in his eye his meaning wisely red,
> And with the like him answerd evermore:
> She sent at him one firie dart, whose hed
> Empoisned was with privy lust, and gealous dred. (ix.28)

The antithesis of Paridell and Britomart is further pointed by their ancestries. Britomart's quest for Artegall is also a quest for her historical destiny as descendant of the 'auncient *Trojan* blood' (iii.22) of Brute, an ancestor of the Tudors (iii.21–49; ix.44–51). Paridell also derives from Trojan stock – from Paris, whose theft of Helen 'kindled' the Trojan war and 'Brought unto balefull ruine' (ix.34) his and Britomart's ancestral city. The achievement of Britomart's ancestor Brute, was to found, not destroy, a city (46).

Paridell's re-enactment of his ancestor's theft does not burn a city, but it destroys Malbecco's house:

> This second *Hellene*, faire Dame *Hellenore*,
> The whiles her husband ranne with sory haste,
> To quench the flames, which she had tyn'd before,
> Laught at his foolish labour spent in waste;
> And ranne into her lovers armes right fast. (x.13)

Malbecco's love for his libidinous wife, second only to his love of money (x.15), is the most perverse and sterile form of faithfulness in the book. In an absurd parody of the knights of Maidenhead on their quest for Florimell, he sets out after his wife 'To search her forth, where so she might be fond' (x.19). Where Florimell is imprisoned for her faithfulness by the loose Proteus, Malbecco finds his loose wife (x.50) enjoying an apparently boundless sexual freedom with the satyrs (x.48). What he sees drives him to that place of sterility and despair throughout Book 3, the sea-shore:

> There dwels he ever, miserable swaine,
> Hatefull both to him selfe, and every wight;
> Where he through privy griefe, and horrour vaine, ·
> Is woxen so deform'd, that he has quight
> Forgot he was a man, and *Gealosie* is hight.   (x.60)

AMORET AND BUSIRANE'S HOUSE

The House of Busirane is at the opposite extreme to the Garden of Adonis, a place of delusion and art in which the natural and passionate impulses of chaste love are transformed to fears and false imaginations. The reasons for Amoret's imprisonment are left ambiguous. At the end of canto vi we are told that Amoret suffered for Scudamour's sake

> Sore trouble of an hainous enimy;
> Who her would forced have to have forlore
> Her former love, and stedfast loialty.   (vi.53)

Scudamour in his 'bitter plaintes' (xi.9) before Busirane's House gives a similar version:

> My Lady and my love is cruelly pend
> In dolefull darkenesse from the vew of day,
> Whilest deadly torments do her chast brest rend,
> And the sharpe steele doth rive her hart in tway,
> All for she *Scudamore* will not denay.   (xi.11)

We do not discover in Book 3, however, how Amoret has been carried off by Busirane (see 4.i.2–4).

There are hints that Scudamour and even Amoret herself may be partially responsible for her imprisonment. Britomart comes across Scudamour in a posture of despair and of unknightly abandon (xi.7). When he sees Britomart enter the House through the screen of fire and sulphur, he attempts the flames with 'greedy will, and envious desire' and 'threatfull pride' (26). The vocabulary suggests rashness and disorder; it is not entirely surprising that, unlike the Knight of Chastity, Scudamour is 'all scorcht and pitifully brent' (26).

Scudamour, then, apparently for faults of his own, cannot rescue Amoret. But there are hints that the traps which ensnare Amoret are partly of her own making. The 'two grysie villeins' who hold Amoret are Cruelty and Despight (xii.19), traditional personifications of a lady's imperious behaviour towards her lover. Such a reading seems to be confirmed by the suggestion that the 'rude confused rout' (xii.25) of personified states of mind that pursue Amoret represent, among other things, the myriad 'phantasies/In wavering wemens wit' (xii.26).

The ambiguities that surround the reasons for Amoret's incarceration are merely some of the many that assail us, as they assail Britomart, on entering this place of nightmares and illusions. Our responses are to some extent suggested by Britomart's: 'she oft and oft it over-red,/Yet could not find what sence it figured' (xi.50). Britomart neither understands the devious images of the House nor pays attention to its warnings. She enters the House in spite of fears of sacrilege (xi.22–3) and she enters the iron wicket (xii.29) in spite of its warning *Be not too bold* (xi.54). It is, apparently, by means of such a combination of innocence and boldness that Busirane's House and the delusions it represents can be destroyed.

Britomart's wonder and incomprehension suggest to us the fabulous but false nature of the House. The reader, however, less innocent than Britomart, might be expected to understand the nature of its delusions in a little more detail. Their combination of the artful and the diabolical is evident in the first room of the House, hung with tapestries skilfully, but deceptively, worked:

> For round about, the wals yclothed were
>   With goodly arras of great majesty,
>   Woven with gold and silke so close and nere,
>   That the rich metall lurked privily,
>   As faining to be hid from envious eye;
>   Yet here, and there, and every where unwares
>   It shewd it selfe, and shone unwillingly;
>   Like a discolourd Snake, whose hidden snares
> Through the greene gras his long bright burnisht backe declares.
>
>   (xi.28)

The snake in the grass was a familiar emblem of lurking evil.

The tapestries tell 'all of love, and all of lusty-hed' (29). These images are of a love that is lawless, violent, deceitful and very often destructive. While Jove transforms himself into bestial shapes for his rapes on earth, Cupid thrusts into his throne (x.35) and wreaks yet more havoc among gods and men. This Cupid makes beasts of gods, tumbles kings and queens with the 'raskall rablement' (46), breaks the laws of heaven and earth and destroys the innocent. But, as the artificial environment of Busirane's House should remind us, such stories are untrue. They are dazzling, but monstrous figments of the human imagination, that abundantly creative, but perilous faculty. It is no coincidence that the source for Busirane's tapestries is Ovid's *Metamorphoses*, a book that was at the heart of the Elizabethan controversy on the dangers of art. The Humanist Vives expressed a widespread Renaissance awareness of the potential harmfulness of art:

If that very picture which we are gazing at, is obscene, does that not contaminate our minds, especially if it be subtly and artistically depicted? Not undeservedly did wise men wish to banish from the state such artists together with their pictures.[7]

Ovid is cited as one of those poets who 'openly approve' such disgraceful subjects. Unlike Vives, Spenser would not banish poets from the commonwealth because their art is subject to abuse, but he is aware of the dangers as well as the achievements of art. Busirane's tapestry is ravishing but evil; it is part of the apparatus by means of which Busirane can crucify the natural and chaste love which Amoret represents.

In the middle of the night, to the sounds of trumpets and thunder, the masque of Cupid appears (xii.3ff.). The night, when lovers are most tormented either by delusionary dreams or by waking pains, is a suitable time for these apparitions. The masque itself is a nightmare thing. Its oddest quality is the ambiguity of its mode of being. We seem to see a procession of literary personifications of psychological states of mind, but Spenser is insistent that these are in fact actors in a masque dressed in the ritualized attributes of such personifications. When we look closer, we find they are not really actors at all but merely behave like actors:

> And forth issewd, as on the ready flore
> Of some Theatre, a grave personage
>
> . . .
>
> And to the vulgar beckning with his hand,
> In signe of silence, as to heare a play . . .   (xii.3–4)

The other personifications follow 'in manner of a maske' (5). The rapidity with which the masquers vanish when Britomart enters the iron wicket (30) establishes them as in fact visions or spirits, 'idle shewes' and 'false charmes' (29) having no substance in truth.

The personifications the masquers represent seem to belong both to literary convention and to the language of love psychology. They are part of a literary tradition that had codified the slightest nuance of love into an elaborate game or duel in which the lover attempted to gain the heart of his mistress while the lady defended her honour with such weapons as *'Daunger'*, *'Displeasure'*, *'Despight'* and *'Cruelty'*. In the *Court of Love*, for instance, mistakenly printed throughout the sixteenth century in editions of Chaucer, the lover in his dream sees such personifications as Displeasure, Despair, Delight, Liar and Dissemblance. The masque is part of the fabric of false art out of which Busirane's House is constructed, art used to distort and pervert chaste love and sexual passion.

However, the masque is more disturbing than the Ovidian tapestries because the personifications cannot be entirely dismissed as a literary distortion of love. The states of mind, *'Fancy'*, *'Desyre'*, *'Doubt'*, *'Feare'*, *'Hope'*, *'Suspect'*, *'Griefe*, and *Fury'* (7–16), and the disordered rout of passions that follows (25) are those which contemporary psychologists described in their analyses of the ills of love. Erotic passion was considered 'very dangerous unto him that suffereth himselfe to be carried by it, For what becomes of him? He is no more himselfe, his bodie endureth a thousand labours in search of his pleasure, his minde a thousand hells to satisfie his desires.'[8] This psychologist describes the mental torments from the male point of view, but the personifications of the masque of Cupid are ambiguous, representing a woman's fears and regrets about such love as well as the male experience of unrestrained desire and its consequences. With characteristic ambiguity Spenser links his rout of maladies to the innumerable 'phantasies/In wavering wemens wit . . . /Or paines in love, or punishments in hell' (26) without equating them with any of these. The experience can be male, female or diabolic, or all three at once.

The ambiguity of the masque itself is extended to Amoret's part in it. She is held by Despight and Cruelty (19), traditional signs of the pride of ladies who scorn love, but her appearance between these two is rather as a victim than as a perpetrator. Similarly her heart is 'Quite through transfixed with a deadly dart' (21), but the traditional sign of the heart wounded by love seems in this case a sign of Amoret's torture by Busirane. When Britomart forces the magician to undo his spells Amoret's heart is healed, though her love for Scudamour remains. We may see Amoret as the victim of her own false delusions about the nature of love, trapped perhaps by the false lessons of pain and disdain derived from artificial literary convention; or as a more abstract embodiment of the innocence of 'goodly womanhead' and 'chaste affectione' (vi. 51 and 52) which the whole House of Busirane, with its diabolic magic, its false art and its corrupt imagination, is designed to destroy.

Britomart's bold chastity makes her largely impervious to the delusive dangers of Busirane's House. In Castle Joyeus she was scratched by the weapon of Gardante, and here she receives a superficial wound from the dart with which Busirane was torturing Amoret. Britomart is in love and not wholly unsusceptible to its mental fears and pains. But the wound is superficial, and confronted with her bold chastity Busirane's dangerous House proves insubstantial, vanishing completely. Busirane is bound with chains, reminding us of the still unbound Proteus who holds Florimell prisoner. The 1590 edition of *The Faerie Queene*, which consisted of the first three books only, ended with a passionate image of marriage, Amoret and Scudamour losing their separateness in an hermaphroditic unity. The 1596 edition leaves Amoret's story, like those of Florimell and Britomart, unresolved. The book ends with all three faithful lovers still exposed to the trials and tribulations by means of which love tests and proves their worth.

Chapter 4

BOOK 4

INTRODUCTION

1. Friendship and concord

Tully defineth friendship in this manner, saying that it is none other thing but a perfect consent of all things appertaining as well to God as to man, with benevolence and charity; and that he knoweth nothing given of God (except sapience) to man more commodious. Which definition is excellent and very true. For in God, and all thing that cometh of God, nothing is of more great estimation than love, called in Latin *amor*, whereof *amicitia* cometh, named in English friendship or amity; the which taken away from the life of man, no house shall abide standing, no field be in culture. And that is lightly perceived, if a man do remember what cometh of dissension and discord.

(Sir Thomas Elyot, *The Governor* (1531) pp. 132–3)

Elyot quotes Cicero's definition of friendship from *De Amicitia*, the standard source-book for ideas about friendship in the sixteenth century, and elaborates it to stress the close relationship of friendship to love and concord. This is essentially Spenser's understanding. *Amicitia*'s derivation from *amor* helps to explain the close links between Books 3 and 4. For Spenser friendship is an inclusive term for mutual virtuous love in whatever form it appears: between lovers or brothers, as much as between man and man, or woman and woman. Where Book 3 dealt with the effects of sexual love upon individuals, Book 4 is concerned with the various kinds of alliance, worthy and unworthy, wrought by love. From such alliances grows society, and Elyot places friendship at the heart of civil concord: 'friendship . . . taken away from the life of man, no house shall abide standing, no field shall be in culture'. The relationship of friendship and justice is emphasized by another Renaissance source-book on the virtue, Aristotle's *Ethics*: 'friendship appears to hold city-states together, and lawgivers esteem it more highly than justice . . . indeed justice in the fullest sense is considered to be a friendly quality' (p. 167). We can see then the aptness of Spenser's placing of Book 4 between the Books of Chastity and of Justice.

Concord in Book 4 is not confined to the 'perfect consent' (Elyot's phrase) of men and women. In the sixteenth century, when analogies could easily be drawn between the microcosmic world of man and the wider macrocosms of nation and universe, friendship could be an image of vaster bonds. The power of love to draw together the elements as well as men is a favourite theme of Spenser's. In *Colin Clouts Come Home Againe*, he describes this cosmic concord in terms of friendship. By Love's power,

> the world was made of yore,
> And all that therein wondrous doth appeare.
> For how should else things so far from attone
> And so great enemies as of them bee,
> Be ever drawne together into one,
> And taught in such accordance to agree?
> Through him the cold began to covet heat,
> And water fire; the light to mount on hie,
> And th'heavie downe to peize; the hungry t'eat
> And voydnesse to seeke full satietie.
> So being former foes, they wexed friends. · (ll. 841–51)

In Book 4 of *The Faerie Queene*, Concord's power is described in very similar terms:

> By her the heaven is in his course contained,
> And all the world in state unmoved stands,
> As their Almightie maker first ordained,
> And bound them with inviolable bands;
> Else would the waters overflow the lands,
> And fire devoure the ayre, and hell them quight,
> But that she holds them with her blessed hands. (x.35)

Her power to create harmony amongst discordant elements, *discordia concors*, extends equally to the cosmos and to the relationships of men and women: 'Of little much, of foes she maketh frends,/And to afflicted minds sweet rest and quiet sends' (x.34). While Book 4 is primarily concerned with the relationships between men and women, we are reminded of the wider significance of friendship, particularly in the closing episodes of the book. Here Spenser gives us a rich and complex image of elemental concord in the marriage of the rivers Thames and Medway and in the betrothal of Florimell and Marinell, whose names suggest the elements of earth and water (see p. 83 above).

Appropriately for a book whose theme is friendship, there are two titular heroes, friends who are in turn 'allide with bands of mutuall couplement' (iii.52) in a network of relationships as lovers, brothers and allies. Cambel and Triamond's narrative of discord resolved in a perfectly symmetrical concord in which each is lover, brother and friend (cantos ii and iii) forms the book's central paradigm, but it is significant that unlike Spenser's other titular heroes their story does not dominate Book 4. Instead Ate, goddess of discord, 'mother of debate,/And all dissention' (i.19) is let loose throughout its central cantos. But her dominance is temporary; Concord, the heavenly 'mother of blessed *Peace*, and *Friendship* trew' (x.34), although a marginal figure in the narrative, has the moral and final victory. The patterns of mutual love exemplified by the Cambel/Triamond/Canacee/Cambina grouping are repeated again and again in the second half of the book as we see concord's power to join separated lovers and friends and reaffirm the wider bonds of society.

2. Book 4 and Chaucer

Book 4 borrows two of its characters from Chaucer's *Squire's Tale*, in which it is proposed to tell the tale of the brother and sister Cambalo and Canacee:

> And after wol I speke of Cambalo,
> That faught in lystes with the bretheren two
> For Canacee er that he myghte hire wynne.   (ll. 667–9)

The story is never told, for the *Squire's Tale* is unfinished. Spenser uses this fact to develop the theme of time's destruction of the written wisdom of the past:

> But wicked Time that all good thoughts doth waste,
> And workes of noblest wits to nought out weare,
> That famous moniment hath quite defaste,
> And robd the world of threasure endlesse deare,
> The which mote have enriched all us heare.   (ii.33)

The manner in which such works might enrich us is made clear in the first two stanzas of canto ii, in which Spenser celebrates the power of poetry to dispel discord: 'Such Musicke is wise words with time concented,/To moderate stiffe minds, disposd to strive' (ii.2).

In order that such soothing wisdom should not be lost in Chaucer's case, Spenser intervenes, attempting to 'follow here the footing of thy feete,/That with thy meaning so I may the rather meete' (ii.34), thus enacting in his different medium a similar act of friendship to that we later witness between the knights Cambel and Triamond, each of whom is willing to adopt the appearance of the other to restore the reputation of his friend (iv.26–33). Such an act of literary friendship is only possible, Spenser tells Chaucer, 'through infusion sweete/Of thine owne spirit, which doth in me survive' (ii.34). Once again, Spenser's description of his relationship to the earlier poet anticipates the narrative of Book 4, in this case the relationship between the three brothers Priamond, Diamond and Triamond, each of whose spirit passes to the next brother to strengthen and renew him (ii.52). Spenser acknowledges that his style, and in this book some of his narratives, imitate Chaucer, but such imitation is an act of literary friendship, which, like all acts of true friendship, deals a blow against discord. In restoring Chaucer's lost words, Spenser affirms his faith in the civilizing power of poetry and defeats the destructiveness of time.

In *The Parliament of Fowls*, Chaucer himself gives a similar view of literary friendship and continuity. The poem begins with Chaucer reading Cicero's *Dream of Scipio*, whose message is one of amity as the basis of social concord:

> loke ay besyly thow werche and wysse
> To commune profit, and thow shalt not mysse
> To comen swiftly to that place deere
> That ful of blysse is and of soules cleere. (ll. 74–7)

Pondering this 'olde bok totorn' (l. 110), Chaucer falls asleep and dreams that Cicero's Scipio leads him to the 'parliament of fowls'. In turn Spenser ponders Chaucer's book, like Cicero's 'write with lettres olde' (l. 19), and transforms its imagery and motifs into his own Temple of Venus (canto x). In his dream Chaucer is taken to a temple in a paradisaical garden (ll. 171–210). The Venus who disports herself in the temple brings both suffering and pleasure. In one half of the gate to the garden are 'Disdayn and Daunger' (l. 136), who guide some lovers to pain and despair. Those more fortunate are led 'unto the welle of grace,/There grene and lusty May shal evere endure' (ll. 129–30). Before Venus' temple door sits 'Dame Pees' (l. 240), and within are heard the sighs of lovers burning with desire and jealousy. Outside, amongst the birds, Nature arbitrates each one's choice of mate, leaving the crucial desision between suitors for the female eagle's hand not to battle but to the lady's own choice: 'she hireself shal han hir eleccioun/Of whom hire lest' (ll. 621–2). When the female eagle's timidity leads her to ask for a year's grace before making her choice, that, too, is granted (ll. 647–8). A brief glance at Spenser's Temple of Venus will show how thoroughly he is reworking Chaucer's *Parliament*, though with his own emphases and significant alterations (see my discussion of the Temple, pp. 115–17 below). Spenser's moral imagination is formed by Chaucer's as Chaucer's dreamer's was by Cicero's book.

Nature's defence of the lady's 'choys al fre' (l. 649) is a motif that re-echoes through Book 4, developed in part through another debt to Chaucer. He begins his story of Cambel and Canacee with the opening words of the *Knight's Tale*, 'Whylome as antique stories tellen us' (ii.32), which in turn acknowledge Chaucer's own debt to his storytelling predecessors; writing continually remakes and repeats what has been written in the past. The *Knight's Tale* itself lends its themes and its wisdom to Book 4. It tells of the conflict between virtuous friendship and sexual love. Two cousins, Palamon and Arcite, call each other 'brother' as a sign of their love for each other. Imprisoned together, they see the same lady from the window and both fall in love with her. Their friendship is changed to bitter rivalry which culminates in an elaborate tournament between the two cousins and their supporters, with Emily, the lady, as the prize. As with Satyrane's tournament, in canto iv, the result is not as straightforward as the organizers hoped; the best man does not win the fairest lady by his own might. In the *Knight's Tale*, as in Book 4, pairings are brought about by the workings of providence in spite of, not because of, men's efforts to settle such matters by force.

THE CAUSES OF DISCORD

1. 'The prize of beautie'

Book 4 is so arranged that we, like the characters, experience the discord that divides before the friendly love that binds. We focus first on Amoret's distresses, which began when Scudamour claimed her as his prize: 'For from the time that *Scudamour* her bought/In perilous fight, she never joyed day' (i.2). Now, rescued from Busirane by the disguised Britomart, she again finds herself a prize of conquest, bound by chivalric rules:

> For well she wist, as true it was indeed,
> > That her lives Lord and patrone of her health
> > Right well deserved as his duefull meed,
> > Her love, her service, and her utmost wealth.   (6)

Amoret is painfully aware that such dues are in conflict with her honour and her inclinations as Scudamour's 'virgine wife' (6). Spenser develops Amoret's dilemma with humour; after all, we know Britomart, in spite of her lustful talk (7), is a woman and no threat to Amoret's chastity. But the issue of strength's claim to beauty is a serious one in Book 4. It is restated in the opening adventure, in which Amoret once again finds herself a prize of battle, forced into

the role by the customs of a castle which require 'that hee/Which had
no love nor lemman there in store,/Should either winne him one, or
lye without the dore' (9). In this instance concord is established by
the Knight of Chastity, who, a lady herself, both wins Amoret and
offers herself as prize to the knight she defeats, making nonsense of
the castle's rules and healing the discord they cause through friendship: 'So did they all their former strife accord' (15).

Here, in the opening canto, Spenser is shaping with a light touch
issues that will reverberate throughout the book, causing much of its
discord: Does strength have a claim to beauty? Can mutual love be
achieved by right of conquest? In the midst of Satyrane's tournaments of strength and beauty, Spenser's narrator states a chivalric
ideal:

> It hath bene through all ages ever seene,
> That with the praise of armes and chevalrie,
> The prize of beautie still hath joyned beene;
> And that for reasons speciall privitie:
> For either doth on other much relie.
> ·For he me seemes most fit the faire to serve,
> That can her best defend from villenie;
> And she most fit his service doth deserve,
> That fairest is and from her faith will never swerve.   (v.1)

But the same narrator later laments that with the degeneracy of the
world, beauty 'which wont to vanquish God and man,/Was made the
vassall of the victors might' (viii.32). There are many examples in the
book of attempts by strength to claim beauty as a prize. Most are ill-
fated, and in none is the relationship unproblematic. Nevertheless
the failure of so many attempts does not invalidate the chivalric
ideal. Throughout the book we find that not by their own means, but
providentially, the truly strong, those who deserve 'the praise of
arms', have gained the 'fairest', those who are inwardly fair, while
the speciously strong have gained only the speciously beautiful.
Human attempts, however well-intentioned, to resolve matters of
love by force seem doomed, likely, as Amoret fears in canto i, to bind
together the wrong couples in the wrong way and to keep those who
should be bound apart.

2. Ate

Britomart changes her appearance from that of knight to that of
lady to bring about a friendly accord. She does not so much change
her form as reveal different aspects of her nature, militant chastity

and virginal beauty. A few stanzas later we encounter the shape-changing Duessa, whose disguises reveal the essential doubleness of her nature:

> For she could d'on so manie shapes in sight,
> As ever could Cameleon colours new;
> So could she forge all colours, save the trew.   (i.18)

Duessa's companion is Ate, Homer's goddess of Discord (*Iliad* 19.91–4, 126–31). Ate's significance seems at first to be at odds with her apparently marginal position as Duessa's serving-woman and bawd (31), but the squalidness of her social role is apt; she works 'privily' (ii.11 or iv.11), egging others on.

Spenser's vivid description of Ate makes her real power and significance plain. She dwells 'hard by the gates of hell' (i.20), the walls decorated with the relics of shattered civilizations and cities (21–2), of groups of men once bound by loyalty or kinship (23), and of individual friends, brothers and lovers who proved unnatural and forsworn (24). The nature of discord itself, growing from small beginnings to a climax of fury and contradiction, is vividly evoked by the crescendo of Spenser's description. In the 'barren ground' around her house she sows 'little seedes':

> The seedes of evill wordes, and factious deedes;
> Which when to ripenesse due they growen arre,
> Bring foorth an infinite increase, that breedes
> Tumultuous trouble and contentious jarre,
> The which most often end in bloudshed and in warre.   (25)

As the seeds themselves grow from weeds to bloodshed and war, so Ate feeds at first on the 'cursed seedes' which 'serve/To her for bread' and then on men themselves 'That she may sucke their life, and drinke their blood' (26). The monstrousness of the image is developed in the monstrousness of Ate's appearance;

> With squinted eyes contrarie wayes intended,
> And loathly mouth, unmeete a mouth to bee,
> That nought but gall and venim comprehended,   (27)

until Ate becomes a frenzied embodiment of conflict and contradiction:

> unequal were her handes twaine,
> That one did reach, the other pusht away,
> That one did make, the other mard againe,
> And sought to bring all things unto decay.   (29)

Alongside Duessa and her ugly bawd ride Blandamour and Paridell, a parody pair of friends whose actions at first bear a glancing resemblance to the actions of true friends. Blandamour gives Paridell his paramour, Duessa, and undertakes to fight Britomart in his stead (i.35). Paridell fights Scudamour at Blandamour's request (40). We find here distorted echoes of the commonplaces of true friendship, that goods should be shared in common, and that each should be willing to risk his life for the other. But the alliance of Blandamour and Paridell is formed for the pursuit of injustice and is motivated by self-seeking: 'the left hand rubs the right' (40). They confirm Aristotle's opinion that true friendship between bad men is impossible: 'Wicked men . . . have no firmness, and are not consistent even with themselves; they become friends for a little while because they rejoice in one another's wickedness' (p. 179). The short season of Blandamour and Paridell's friendship is soon over, shortened yet further by failure in battle and jealousy over False Florimell. Their real malice breaks through the 'fayned friendship' (ii.18), and they attack one another 'like two mad mastiffes' (ii.17).

Our first view of this group seemed to present us with an image of order and amity:

> Two armed Knights, that toward them did pace,
> And ech of them had ryding by his side
> A Ladie   (i.17)

This appearance is false, and before long they form an image of discord: the two knights fighting ferociously and the ladies egging them on (ii.18–19). Their anger is cooled and their specious friendship patched by the Squire of Dames (ii.20–8), whom we last met in Book 3 canto vii serving his tyrannical mistress by tempting the virtue of others. Appropriately the concord achieved by such a figure is imperfect. The group again presents an outwardly plausible image of order and amity, but we are in no doubt as to its speciousness: 'So well accorded forth they rode together/In friendly sort, that lasted but a while' (ii.29).

CAMBEL AND TRIAMOND

Spenser juxtaposes the specious concord of the fair-weather friends with an image of genuine order and amity:

> Two knights, that lincked rode in lovely wise,
> As if they secret counsels did partake;
> And each not farre behinde him had his make,
> To weete, two Ladies of most goodly hew,
> That twixt themselves did gentle purpose make.   (ii.30)

In the narrative that follows Spenser unfolds this group of four, with attention to numerical orderliness, into one group of three (the brothers who are subsumed into Triamond), and a number of groups of two (the sister/brother pairs Cambel and Canacee, Triamond and Cambina; the lovers Cambel and Cambina, and Triamond and Canacee; and the friends, Cambel and Triamond, and Cambina and Canacee). The quartet of amity becomes a figure of completeness containing within itself an example of every kind of friendly alliance.

The narratives of Cambel and Triamond and their relationships enact a number of traditional formulae about friendship. Most important is the commonplace that true friends are like brothers.[1] This is particularly apparent in the story of Agape's three sons (ii.41–54). *Agape* is the Greek word for charitable love; it is particularly associated with the brotherly love advocated by St Paul: 'But as touching brotherly love, yee neede not that I write unto you: for yee are taught of God to love one another' (1 Thessalonians 4.9). This is the lesson Agape teaches her sons: to 'love each other deare, what ever them befell' (53); this they learn well, 'And never discord did amongst them fall' (54). So firm is their affection 'As if but one soule in them all did dwell' (43), reiterating the commonplace that friends share a single soul that was already traditional when Aristotle was writing (*Ethics* p. 202). These brothers seem able to share the same life, or live in each other's bodies (52). Aristotle describes brothers as identifying with one another: 'they are therefore in a sense the same thing, though in separate individuals' (p. 185). Shakespeare uses the same formula when he has the Duchess of Gloucester speak to Gaunt of his dead brother: 'though thou livest and breathest,/Yet art thou slain in him' (*Richard II* I.ii.24–5).

A striking Renaissance formula embedded in Spenser's allegory of Agape's three sons is the emblem '*Concordia Insuperabilis*', first illustrated in Alciatus' *Emblemata* (1550), and depicting a warrior with three heads, six arms and six legs (Roche p. 18). Alciatus' verses explain that the image represents three brothers who lived in 'such concord, along with mutual justice and one love, that unconquered they held ample reigns by means of human strength' (Nohrnberg pp. 610–11). A sixteenth-century commentary on Alciatus' emblem extends its significance: 'By this we learn that those who live in unanimity and good accord make themselves invincible' (Roche p. 18).

The names of the three brothers have tantalized commentators. Priamond, Diamond and Triamond mean first, second and third

world, and it may be that Spenser is referring to no more than the
notion that man is a world in little (Hume pp. 179–81). However,
Renaissance thought did divide creation into three worlds 'the
sublunary, the fallen world in which we live, subject to change and
decay; the *celestial*, the unchanging world of the planets and stars; the
supercelestial, the dwelling of angels and the Godhead' (Roche p. 7).
Within the little world of man, there is another triad, that of the three
souls, vegetative, animal and rational (Nohrnberg pp. 612–13).
Again the triad is hierarchical, with the rational soul endowed with
immortality. On their mutual concord the good order of the body
depends. It may be that Spenser's allegory glances at one or both of
these triads. We might note that, in the case of Triamond (ii. 52),
Spenser has transformed the commonplace of friendship, the sharing
of a single soul, into three souls in a single body, giving support to
a reading in terms of man's three souls. The name, Telamond (Gk
telos, perfect or complete, + Lat. *mundus*, world) which appears on
the title-page of the book instead of Triamond, suggest that Spenser
saw the third brother as an image of wholeness, joining three parts
in one. If such allusions are present, they are there, I believe, as
analogies, merely hinted at, to remind us that friendship is an essential principle of creation on all levels, amongst brothers, more widely
within society, within the body and binding the whole universe.

Agape's descent to Demogorgon's realms to learn her sons' fates
(ii.47) contrasts with Cymoent's similar enquiry in Book 3 (iv.25).
Where Cymoent misunderstood the nature of her son's fate and
taught him to despise love, Agape accepts what the Fates tell her but
seeks to mitigate it by teaching her sons to love (ii.53). Spenser's
language makes it clear that the apparently mysterious transmigra-
tion of spirit from one brother to another in battle (iii.13–22) is a
metaphor for the effect of their deep love for one another:

> that same soule, which therein dwelt,
> Streight entring into *Triamond*, him fild
> With double life, and griefe, which when he felt,
> As one whose inner parts had bene ythrild
> With point of steele, that close his hartbloud splid.   (22)

Equally potent is Agape's love, mediated through her daughter,
Cambina. Cambel's tournament degenerates into a slaughterous
stalemate (iii.36) in spite of his good intentions that it should resolve
the discord amongst Canacee's suitors and establish order (ii.37–8).
It is at this point that the strange and powerful figure of Cambina
appears in a chariot, 'like a storme' (38), curbing 'two grim lyons,

taken from the wood' (39; see my discussion of these stanzas, pp. 16–19 above). Her instruments of concord, the 'rod of peace' (42) and cup of Nepenthe, 'Devized by the Gods, for to asswage/Harts grief, and bitter gall away to chace' (43) have divine power which of force binds 'with mightier band' (48) Cambel and Triamond's fury, converting it to peace and love (49). The love Cambina embodies is a powerful force, but where she fails to use its restraining power among the 'unruly preace' of spectators at the tournament, confusion is let loose:

> Some fearing shriekt, some being harmed hould,
> Some laught for sport, some did for wonder shout,
> And some that would seeme wise, their wonder turnd to dout.
>
> (41)

By contrast Spenser concludes the battle between Cambel and Triamond with a tableau in keeping with his formulaic treatment of their narrative:

> Instead of strokes, each other kissed glad,
> And lovely haulst from feare of treason free,
> And plighted hands for ever friends to be.   (49)

Roche (p. 28) has shown how close this is to another of Alciatus' emblems, '*Concordia*', which shows two warriors shaking hands in the midst of a battlefield. In the final stanza of the canto, Spenser weaves a complex four-square figure around Cambel and Triamond, Canacee and Cambina, in which each of love's possible forms, love of kin, friendship and sexual love, so intertwine that 'all alike did love, and loved were' (52). Together they form so perfect an example of the concord of mutual love that they become its consummate pattern: 'since their days such lovers were not found elswhere' (52).

SATYRANE'S TOURNAMENT AND ITS SEQUEL

Cambell's attempt to resolve the conflicts of Canacee's suitors produces discord which is only finally resolved by Cambina's intervention. Satyrane's similar attempt to put a stop to the feuding over Florimell's lost girdle (ii.26) likewise multiplies the discord and resolves nothing, but this time no semi-divine figure intervenes to bring peace.

Spenser's account of Satyrane's 'publike turneying' (ii.26) to establish the stoutest knight and fairest lady is fraught with ironies. They begin before the tournament itself with an incident involving Braggadochio that acts as a prelude to what is to follow. Braggadochio, meeting with Blandamour and his group of false friends, lays claim to the False Florimell 'as his owne prize,/Whom formerly he had in battell wonne' (iv.8). For Blandamour she is also a prize, seized by force from Ferraugh (ii.4–7), so it is with a certain consistency that he agrees she should continue to be a trophy of battle: 'who so winnes her, may her have by right' (iv.9). False Florimell's soiled currency, passing from the hand of one impudent challenger to another, suits her nature but inevitably casts doubt on the validity of the more ceremonious battling that is to follow under Satyrane's management, at which False Florimell once again becomes the trophy. Blandamour complicates his challenge to Braggadochio by adding Ate to their contest as the loser's prize (iv.9). Predictably Braggadochio does not like this arrangement:

> But *Braggadochio* said, he never thought
> For such an Hag, that seemed worse then nought,
> His person to emperill so in fight.   (iv.10)

All the knights present enjoy the joke of Braggadochio's cowardice, but we can see that there is a joke, too, at their expense. False Florimell is more like Ate than anyone realizes. Whoever wins her has in fact won something 'worse then nought', a source of discord whose fairness and brightness are a mere superficial illusion. Those who mock Braggadochio are all, in fact, about to imperil their persons in a battle whose ultimate prize is such a hag. At this stage no one can anticipate that the final victor of Satyrane's contest, the winner of False Florimell and the cestus, will be none other than this Braggadochio, indeed her most fitting mate, but whose claim, by the standards and perception of the knights, seems the most absurd.

Spenser drops a hint of misplaced values in his description of the opening ceremonies of the tournament:

> Then first of all forth came Sir *Satyrane*,
>   Bearing that precious relicke in an arke
>   Of gold, that bad eyes might it not prophane:
>   Which drawing softly forth out of the darke,
>   He open shewd, that all men it mote marke.
>   A gorgeous girdle, curiously embost
>   With pearle and precious stone, worth many a marke. (iv.15)

The language of relics and mysteries suggests what in Protestant eyes was the worship of graven images associated with Roman Catholicism. Such idolatry made the mistake which is fundamental to Satyrane's tournament, of substituting an image for the thing itself: in this case the substitution of the mark of chastity and a false simulacrum of beauty for true chastity and true, that is inner, beauty. Florimell's girdle is valued for its glittering appearance and not for its power 'to bind lascivious desire,/And loose affections streightly to restraine' (v.4).

Not all the participants are dishonourable. Cambel and Triamond, particularly, perform memorable acts of friendship and courage (iv.27–36), but the tournament as a whole seems to degenerate as each day passes. The first day is described with a certain formality and little emphasis on the ferocity of the participants. On the second day passions are aroused and imagery of wild boars and captive lions culminates in a description of Cambel and Triamond as 'two greedy wolves' who

> breake by force
> Into an heard, farre from the husband farme,
> They spoile and ravine without all remorse. (35)

On the third day the fighting is dominated by a knight whose savage nature is indicated by the wildness of his appearance and his motto '*Salvagesse sans finesse*' (39). The two named adversaries of this savage knight are Sir Sangliere (the boar) and Sir Brianor (the bear). It seems as though Satyrane's tournament has become a battle between wild beasts beyond the boundaries of civilization, a grim image of discord from which we are rescued by Britomart, whose enchanted spear, with minimum ferocity, defeats without destroying (43–8). But even our satisfaction with Britomart's victory is undercut by irony. The savage knight, we learn (42), is the much-sought Artegall. Defending the Order of Maidenhead, Britomart has overthrown her destined husband and excited his hatred (v.9). The disguised Artegall may deserve such an overthrow, but the discordant effects of Satyrane's tournament are confirmed.

We have already noted the irony of introducing canto v by a statement of an ideal relation of strength and beauty which bears little relation to the event it prefaces (see p. 102 above). Whatever the ideal, in the man-made ordering of Satyrane's tournament, False Florimell wins the beauty contest: 'so forged things do fairest shew' (v.15). Spenser prefaces her triumph with a reminder of her origins in contrast to those of the true Florimell. The latter was fostered by the Graces in the absence of the lascivious Venus (v.5), learning, we may assume, their loving generosity of spirit and their guilelessness (see 6.x.23–4). By contrast, Spenser's imagery reminds us of False Florimell's manufactured origins:

As guilefull Goldsmith that by secret skill,
  With golden foyle doth finely over spred
  Some baser metall, which commend he will
  Unto the vulgar for good gold insted,
  He much more goodly glosse thereon doth shed,
  To hide his falshood, then if it were trew:
  So hard, this Idole was to be ared.   (v.15; cf. 3.viii.5–9)

With her triumph, the contest dwindles rapidly to farce. First the cestus passes from waist to waist, demonstrating the incontinence of each lady to the loud laughter of the Squire of Dames (18), then False Florimell passes from hand to hand, first to Britomart, whose 'dew right' (20) she is but who does not want her and who is anyway a woman, then to Artegall, 'but he was gone/In great displeasure, that he could not get her' (21), and then to Satyrane, who finds himself back where he began, besieged by feuding knights, though now it is not the true Florimell's belt which is at issue but False Florimell. This time Satyrane's attempt to 'accord them all' (25) more wisely leaves the choice to False Florimell herself. Once again Satyrane establishes rules and the contest is stated in idealized terms (25), and again the result confounds the design: False Florimell fittingly chooses the cowardly Braggadochio 'of her accord' (26).

No accord results from False Florimell's choice. Her suitors

chaft and rag'd,
And woxe nigh mad for very harts despight,
That from revenge their willes they scarse asswag'd.   (27)

We discover the sequel in canto ix, when we come across four of these rejected suitors endlessly and jealously skirmishing amongst themselves for a prize none of the four possesses (20–31). Stirred up by Ate and Duessa (ix.24), they make of themselves an emblem of the contentiousness into which false friendship degenerates:

Such mortall malice, wonder was to see
In friends profest, and so great outrage donne:
But sooth is said, and tride in each degree,
Faint friends when they fall out, most cruell fomen bee.   (27)

More seriously, the tournament leaves its mark on Sir Artegall, the savage knight, whom the legacy of discord from Satyrane's tournament transforms into a figure of passionate hatred, consumed with 'despiteous ire,/That nought but spoyle and vengeance did require' (vi.11). Fittingly for a sequel to Satyrane's tournament, the fight between Artegall and Britomart is described in terms that make clear just how wrong-headed and perverse human judgement can be:

> Certes some hellish furie, or some feend
> This mischiefe framd, for their first loves defeature,
> To bath their hands in bloud of dearest freend,
> Thereby to make their loves beginning, their lives end. (17)

Happily, destiny cuts through the Gordian knot tied up by human effort. With the revelation of Britomart's beauty, Artegall is deprived of will and his arm falls powerless (vi.21). In Britomart, too, nature asserts its power in spite of will:

> She arm'd her tongue, and thought at him to scold;
> Nathlesse her tongue not to her will obayd,
> But brought forth speeches myld, when she would have missayd.
> (27)

Spenser handles the reconciliation of the pair with sympathetic humour. The central canto of Book 4 moves us from a bleak vision of human error, obstinacy and ferocity to a kindlier one of the conquering power of love. Artegall and Britomart resolve their differences in a true and mutual accord which is characterized by the binding of oaths and the recognition of wider, public ceremonies and hierarchies:

> At last through many vowes which forth he pour'd,
> And many othes, she yeelded her consent
> To be his love, and take him for her Lord,
> Till they with mariage meet might finish that accord. (41)

LUST'S VICTIMS

Having been exposed to lust in its most sophisticated form in Busirane's House (3.xi and xii), Amoret is now exposed to it in its crudest form. Out of the forest, while Britomart sleeps, rushes 'a wilde and salvage man' (vii.5) whose monstrous physical features represent a brutal version of the male genitalia (5–6). The incident recapitulates in a different key and with different results Britomart's confrontation with the savage knight, Sir Artegall, who lay in waiting for her 'under a forrest side' (vi.2). Britomart gains a peaceful victory over Artegall, who willingly binds himself within the ceremonies of civilization (vi.41). But brutal Lust is not susceptible to the influence of another; it is the very antithesis of mutual love, living 'farre from all peoples hearing' (vii.8), alone even in the brutish satisfaction of its lust (20). Such a destructive extremity of appetite must be destroyed by its extreme opposite, the militant virginity of Belphoebe (vii.31).

1. Timias

Timias' encounter with Lust seems to reflect the subtle difficulties that he faces in his relationship with Belphoebe. For him, to destroy Lust is to wound or destroy Amoret, whom the monster holds before him 'as a buckler' (26). Amoret, as we saw when we considered canto vi of Book 3, represents the promise of marriageable beauty, as opposed to her sister, Belphoebe, who denies to all such sexual satisfaction (see p. 86 above). Timias is bound to Belphoebe by a love that must deny sexual desire, a dilemma which threatens to kill him in Book 3 (v.49). Belphoebe's effect on Timias' more normal sexual desire threatens to be as destructive as her effect on unrestrained Lust. Mismanaging his dilemma in Book 4, Timias manages to damage Lust, but also Amoret (vii. 27 and 35), and to lose Belphoebe. Letting Lust go loose, he lingers over the wounded Amoret (35), desirable image of a beauty formed to return love, thereby incurring the stern Belphoebe's wrath: 'Is this the faith, she said, and said no more,/But turnd her face, and fled away for evermore' (36).

Timias' response is to turn himself into a romantic version of Lust:

> Unto those woods he turned back againe,
> Full of sad anguish, and in heavy case:
> And finding there fit solitary place
> For wofull wight, chose out a gloomy glade,
> Where hardly eye mote see bright heavens face,
> For mossy trees, which covered all with shade
> And sad melancholy: there he his cabin made. (38)

He has none of Lust's brutal energy, but he is similarly rendered savage by his passion. Spenser makes his degeneration painfully evident by bringing Arthur to his cabin (42). In a book which holds before us friendship as the ideal bond, Timias' choice of passionate despair rather than virtuous activity as Arthur's companion must be condemned, though Spenser handles his story with sympathy.[2] Timias' restoration to Belphoebe's favour by means of a turtle dove is told with delightful fantasy (viii.3–17), but their new accord leaves him still in the woods 'all mindlesse of his owne deare Lord/The noble Prince' (viii.18).

Where Timias and Belphoebe abandoned the friendless Amoret and Aemylia to pursue the drama of their paradoxical passion (vii.36–7), Arthur succours in the most humble fashion the two distressed ladies (viii.22). Where Timias, restored to favour, lives happily in the forest 'Fearlesse of fortunes chaunge or envies dread' (18), Arthur, Amoret and Aemylia must leave the forest and face Slander's venom (viii.23–36). It is worth noting that Timias does not remain happy for long. In Book 6 he is attacked by the Blatant Beast, a more ferocious manifestation of Slander. From this encounter Timias is rescued by Prince Arthur, who restores him from the role of Belphoebe's servant to the nobler calling of active virtue in the world (see p. 162 below).

2. Aemylia and the Squire of Low Degree

In order to emphasize the innocence of Arthur, Amoret and Aemylia in the face of Slander's calumnies, Spenser contrasts the present with an idealized past:

> But antique age yet in the infancie
> Of time, did live then like an innocent,
> In simple truth and blameless chastitie. (30)

With the degeneration of the world, values are turned topsy-turvy:

> Then faire grew foule, and foule grew faire in sight,
> And that which wont to vanquish God and man,
> Was made the vassall of the victors might. (32)

But that is what happened in Satyrane's tournament. The passage serves the purpose of emphasizing the virtue of Arthur and his companions, but it is also ironic; the world of Book 4 seems often as 'warre old' (31; Spenser's fanciful etymology for 'world') as our own. Indeed Aemylia herself is no perfect example of that golden age innocence when 'each unto his lust did make a lawe,/From all forbidden things his liking to withdraw' (30).

Aemylia, we learn, puts sexual love before any other bond of affection. Having chosen her lover in spite of her father, she is determined 'Both sire, and friends, and all for ever to forgo' (vii.16). This is not the virtuous choice advocated by the narrator:

> Hard is the doubt, and difficult to deeme,
> When all three kinds of love together meet,
> And doe dispart the hart with powre extreme,
> Whether shall weigh the balance downe; to weet
> The deare affection unto kindred sweet,
> Or raging fire of love to woman kind,
> Or zeale of friends combynd with vertues meet.
> But of them all the band of vertuous mind
> Me seemes the gentle hart should most assured bind. (ix.1)

Aemylia chooses desire rather than friendship. Predictably, at the place and time appointed for her elopement with the Squire of Low

Degree, Aemylia is carried off by Lust (vii.18), and her lover is caught and bound by Corflambo (viii.51). Where Lust is brutishly physical, Corflambo's violence is to the heart and the mind:

> For most of strength and beautie his desire
> Was spoyle to make, and wast them unto nought,
> By casting secret flakes of lustfull fire
> From his false eyes, into their harts and parts entire.   (viii.48)

Both lovers are victims of their sexual appetites grown monstrous at precisely the point where they break the bounds of social and parental law.

Corflambo's daughter, Poeana, who attempts to seduce Aemylia's lover, the Squire, is not unlike Aemylia herself. Both are wilful and aggressive in pursuit of their passion (vii.17; viii.52) and put their lovers before their fathers (vii.16; ix.3). Their parallelism complements that of the Squire and his friend Placidas. So similar are these two that 'never two so like did living creature see' (viii.55). Their physical likeness images their friendship for each other, which each values more than the love of women (vii.57 and 60). Amongst these four, Arthur creates concord by killing Corflambo (viii.45) and binding his daughter (ix.6):

> From that day forth in peace and joyous blis,
> They liv'd together long without debate,
> Ne private jarre, ne spite of enemis
> Could shake the safe assuraunce of their state.   (ix.16)

Spenser's handling of this narrative seems deliberately abbreviated. It is not the personalities that are important, but their faults and virtues and their relationships. In schematic form we have the hierarchy of parental, sexual and amicable love dramatized and resolved in an emblem of four-square love and friendship which echoes the Cambel/Triamond group (iii.52) and contrasts with the discordant false friends whose strife continues for the rest of the canto (ix.20–37), also to be halted by Arthur, though, we may suspect, less conclusively (37).

SCUDAMOUR'S STORY

1. Scudamour in the House of Care

In cantos x and xi of Book 3, the story of Malbecco's sufferings were juxtaposed to those of Scudamour. Malbecco was the type of jealousy, sleepless, emaciated, self-consuming:

> Fowle Gealosie, that turnest love divine
> To joylesse dread, and mak'st the loving hart
> With hatefull thoughts to languish and to pine,
> And feed it selfe with selfe-consuming smart.
> Of all the passions in the mind thou vilest art. (3.xi.1)

Unlike Malbecco's wanton Hellenore, Amoret remains chaste and
faithful. Whatever else Scudamour suffers in Book 3, he is free from
jealousy. Ironically, by canto v of Book 4 Scudamour is himself
wracked by jealousy, brought to this state by Ate's and Duessa's
poisonous insinuations (i.46–9). His mental state is dramatically
evoked by his hard night on the floor of Care's 'little cottage' (v.32).
This mean and comfortless place clearly parallels the 'little cotage'
(viii.23) of Slander, equally mean and comfortless, in which his love
Amoret and her companions seek rest at nightfall. The two episodes
serve to bring home to us the discord through which the separated
lovers must pass before achieving the final concord of union, but they
also contrast with one another.

Slander attacks Amoret and her companions from without and is
unable seriously to disturb them. They hear her with patience and
are able to sleep. Scudamour finds no such peace: he is pinched by
Care's burning tongs (v.44) and must listen to the rhythms of his
beating jealousy echoed by the blacksmiths' hammers (36 and 41),
which cacophonously parody the supposed discovery of musical harmony by the smith Tubalcain when he listened to a sequence of six
notes in numerical proportion (Genesis 4.22).[3] Earlier, when
Scudamour had first been goaded by Ate, we were told that only
music could slake the fire she sets burning: 'Such Musicke is wise
words with time concented' (ii.2). No such harmony is heard in
Care's house, the image of Scudamour's inner discord.

2. The Temple of Venus

Although it is not made explicit, we assume the reunion of
Scudamour and Amoret takes place at the end of canto ix by Arthur's
means and in Britomart's presence. In canto x we have, in the
narrative of Scudamour's first conquest of Amoret, a rich and complex version of Book 4's central theme of *discordia concors* (Roche p.
129). But the narrative is mediated through the understanding and
emotions of Scudamour, whose expectations of the Temple seem
oversimple and for whom its rewards prove painful. The episode is,
at least in part, about the difficulties that beset human judgement and
action in matters of love.

Scudamour's confusion is compounded by the arrangement of the Temple and its landscape. He gains entrance by means of the chivalric virtues of valour and boldness, defeating the twenty knights who defend the shield of Cupid (x.7–10) and refusing to be abashed by those mental fears, Doubt, Delay and Daunger, which traditionally beset the lover (12–20). It seems natural for him to expect in his own case that time-honoured pattern of achievement and reward which makes beauty the 'prize' of 'armes and chevalrie' (v.1). Indeed Cupid's shield seems to promise as much: ' *Whose ever be the shield, faire Amoret be his*' (x.8). But once within the Temple, the reader, if not Scudamour, perceives how much must still be endured. We enter first the wonderful gardens in which harmony has already been achieved. Art and nature have resolved their differences in mutual collaboration (21–2), opposites are reconciled in the various landscape of shadow and sunlight, hills and dales, bowers and labyrinths (24), and lovers and friends enjoy a bliss which is no longer susceptible to discord (25–7).

Such achieved bliss is not yet Scudamour's, and he passes eagerly forwards, but in fact backwards to an earlier stage, that of opposites still held in lively tension. In the porch of the Temple is Concord forcing the antagonistic brothers Love and Hate 'hand to joyne in hand' (33). The Venus who presides over the Temple holds opposites together in a mysterious unity (41), but she presides over a passion which her worshippers experience as discord (43). She is celebrated as the source of nature's abundant fertility (44–5) but also of the fury and pain of sexual desire:

> The Lyons rore, the Tygres loudly bray,
> The raging Buls rebellow through the wood,
> And breaking forth, dare tempt the deepest flood,
> To come where thou doest draw them with desire:
> So all things else, that nourish vitall blood,
> Soone as with fury thou doest them inspire,
> In generation seeke to quench their inward fire.　　　(46)

Scudamour's advance takes him a further step backwards, to the first sight of his beloved from which all the pain, and ultimately the bliss, seen in reverse in canto x, and experienced over the course of Books 3 and 4, will derive. The meeting of the bold knight, fresh from battle, with the timid Amoret seated amidst a bevy of the retiring womanly virtues (49–51) is itself a collision of opposites. In this enterprise, Scudamour had no model for action:

> For sacrilege me seem'd the Church to rob,
> And folly seem'd to leave the thing undonne,
> Which with so strong attempt I had begonne.　　　(53)

In his dilemma, Scudamour had recourse to the strength and boldness which conquered the Temple's outer defences, 'And nought for nicenesse nor for envy sparing,/In presence of them all forth led her thence' (56), and so his troubles begin.

To some extent the meeting of Scudamour and Amoret enacts an inevitable conflict between opposites which is at the heart of Venus' power and whose resolution will lead to a richer bliss: 'Much dearer be the things, which come through hard distresse' (28). In spite of its difficulties, their match seems destined, blessed by Venus and Concord (56–7). But the episode also looks back to Amoret's abduction on her wedding day to Busirane's House (i.3), that place of imaginary female terrors about love (3.xii.26). The shield which is the sign of Amoret as prize warns its possessor *'Blessed the man that well can use his blis'* (8). The relationship of strength and beauty needs perhaps to be restated in the terms Arthur uses when describing the rights of women a few stanzas before Scudamour's narrative begins: 'That of their loves choise they might freedom clame,/And in that right should by all knights be shielded' (ix.37).

THE MARRIAGE OF MEDWAY AND THAMES

The opening of canto xi, describing Florimell's continuing captivity to Proteus, seems to invite us to recall Amoret's sufferings at the House of Busirane. The parallels are striking: like Amoret, Florimell is kept bound, subject to the tyranny of a powerful and magical oppressor; where Amoret's prison is walled with fire (3.xi.21), Florimell's is 'wall'd . . . with waves' (4.xi. 3), and both suffer their captivity for seven months (3.xi.10; 4.i.4 and xi.4). Both Amoret and Florimell are examples of chaste and constant love triumphant over the oppression of tyrannical lust, but their stories point to allegories of different aspects of love. The Florimell story, echoing the myth of Proserpina who spent the winter months in Hades to rise again to the light in spring (see p. 83 above), points to an allegory of the flowering beauty and fertility of nature which is stifled and imprisoned by the lawless Proteus.

Having introduced the Florimell narrative in canto xi, Spenser then suspends it until canto xii, to follow his account of the wedding of the Medway and Thames. The two are linked by place – the wedding takes place in Proteus' hall in the dungeons of which Florimell is imprisoned – they are also linked by theme. In his account of the wedding, Spenser states his theme of friendship as a fundamental principle binding all created things in a vision of joyful harmony and order. The canto is richly elaborate, a stately celebration, but it is static, like an emblem or a pageant. In the conclusion of the Florimell narrative in canto xii, Spenser restates the same theme but in a different mode, stressing the struggle and tension that lie below the pageant's stately vision.

In my discussion of Proteus' significance (see pp. 83–4 above), I noted that Proteus was most commonly allegorized as First Matter, the raw material from which creation emerges. But such raw matter must be bound and ordered to produce form; in lawless pursuit of Florimell, Proteus is rendered impotent and oppressive. In canto xi, we see him not as Florimell's oppressor, but as host to the Medway and Thames and their guests, the many rivers and waters of life. In this legitimate role, he becomes the patron of the ceremony's order and joy and its promise of fertility.

The marriage of the rivers involves both water and land in Spenser's vision of concord. The rivers are kin to the gods of the ocean and share their immense fertility:

> O what an endlesse worke have I in hand,
>   To count the seas abundant progeny,
>   Whose fruitfull seede farre passeth those in land,
>   And also those which wonne in th'azure sky?
>   For much more eath to tell the starres on hy,
>   Albe they endlesse seeme in estimation,
>   Then to recount the Seas posterity:
>   So fertile be the flouds in generation,
> So huge their numbers, and so numberlesse their nation.   (xii.1)

The sea, so often a sign of sterile or frustrated love in Book 3, is now a sign of fertility, the parent of Venus (xii.2). But the marriage represents a binding of that fertile energy. The sons of Neptune are powerful and often unruly, giants and bringers of tempests (xi.13–16), but at this ceremony they march decorously and in order.

The same order and ceremonious accord are apparent in the myriad rivers. Whatever its attribute, slow or tempestuous, deep or shallow, each one has its right place. With the English rivers which attend on Thames, Spenser extends the range of his myth to give us a vision of national as well as natural concord. As Spenser names the rivers, he describes the country and cities through which they flow and reminds us of past strife which stained the waters (xi.37). In Proteus' hall all these rivers, peaceable or strifeful, march together (39), willing on this day to 'doe their duefull service' (44) to Thames. The acknowledgement of service is significant as Thames bears as his crown Gloriana's capital city, Troynovaunt, the 'kingdomes throne'

(28). On this day, in which love and order triumph, all the diverse and divergent parts of England, and even Ireland (40–4), come together peacefully to pay homage to the Thames and to London, source of Tudor power.

While, in Proteus' hall, Medway is bound to Thames in joyful marriage and the diverse water gods bind themselves in their orderly and hierarchical procession, Florimell is 'bound' in Proteus' dungeon. Spenser emphasizes the word, repeating it in various forms four times in the first three stanzas of canto xi. Florimell's illegitimate binding stems from disorderly looseness in Proteus and in Marinell. Proteus, the shape-shifter, must be bound by the law before he can be of value. Marinell too is unbound, or bound in the wrong way; he follows his mother 'like her thrall' (xi.7), kept free by her from the natural bonds of marriage. The intricate word-play on love, life and death and on freedom and thraldom which interlaces Florimell's lament to the gods, in Proteus' dungeon (xii.7–11), suggests both the beating circularity of her thoughts, and also the puzzling paradoxes which entrap her. Marinell's love would make prison a place of freedom, but for Marinell love is a prison:

> let mee live, as lovers ought to do,
> And of my lifes deare love beloved be:
> And if he shall through pride your doome undo,
> Do you by duresse him compell thereto,
> And in this prison put him here with me:
> One prison fittest is to hold us two:
> So had I rather to be thrall, then free;
> Such thraldome or such freedome let it surely be.   (xii.10)

From this impasse Florimell is rescued by the influence of pity and love on Marinell (13) and by Neptune's warrant 'straight t'enlarge the mayd' (32). Florimell is led to Marinell as his bride (33), and her effect on him is described in the imagery of spring:

> As withered weed through cruell winters tine,
> That feeles the warmth of sunny beames reflection,
> Liftes up his head, that did before decline
> And gins to spread his leafe before the faire sunshine.   (34)

Spenser leaves us with this last image of the joy of friendship. It is a delicately private image, catching the shyness of Marinell's and Florimell's love and awakened hope, but it carries with it resonances that lead our thoughts to the grandeur of Spenser's celebration of friendship as a bond releasing the vast creativity of nature. Such bonds are established through love, but also through law which must bind the transgressors. Neptune's role takes our thoughts forward to Book 5, in which the loves of Marinell and Florimell will be 'perfected' (35).

Chapter 5

BOOK 5

INTRODUCTION

1. Justice

The just, therefore, is nothing other than the *proportionate*; the unjust is what violates proportion.   (Aristotle, *Ethics* p. 98)

Take away Kings, Princes, Rulers, Magistrates, Judges and such estates of GODS order, no man shall ride or goe by the high way unrobbed, no man shall sleep in his owne house or bedde unkilled, no man shall keepe his wife, children, and possession in quietnesse, all things shall bee common, and there must needes follow all mischiefe, and utter destruction both of soules, bodies, goodes, and common wealthes.
            (From the Homily *Concerning good Order, and obedience to Rulers and Magistrates* (1547))[1]

Traditionally representations of Justice have two attributes, a drawn sword and a pair of scales. The scales are a sign of the impartiality of justice, the giving to each of what is due. This is the first skill Astraea teaches Artegall, Spenser's Knight of Justice: 'There she him taught to weigh both right and wrong/In equall ballance with due recompence' (5.i.7). The sword ascribes a more dynamic embattled role to Justice, as a bulwark defending order and civility from the encroaching evils of violence. Artegall learns the use of force from Astraea after he has mastered the theory of balance:

> Of all the which, for want there of mankind,
> She caused him to make experience
> Upon wyld beasts, which she in woods did find,
> With wrongfull powre oppressing others of their kind.   (i.7)

Both aspects of justice are crucial to Spenser's treatment of the virtue in Book 5.

a. Justice according to Aristotle

The sequence of Books 4 and 5 is partially explained by the close relationship of friendship and justice in Aristotle's view. Both seek to establish peace and concord in the community: 'unanimity, which seems akin to friendship, is the principal aim of legislators' (*Ethics* p. 167). But where friendship establishes bonds of love, justice is based on the law which seeks to hold rival claims in a fair balance.

Aristotle differentiates two kinds of justice: distributive and commutative. Each is distinguished by the different kind of balance, or proportion, it maintains. Distributive justice concerns the distribution of honours, or wealth 'which can be held by men in unequal proportions' (p. 96). Commutative justice is concerned with the fitting of punishments to crimes, attempting 'to equalize the wrong suffered and the wrong done' (p. 99). In the latter each term is exactly equal, the punishment balancing the crime, while the former allows for inequality, distributing to each his due according to his rights and status.

These terms became standard in the sixteenth century. For example, Sir Thomas Elyot:

Justice although it be but one entire virtue, yet is it described in two kinds or species. The one is named justice distributive, which is in distribution of honour, money, benefit, or other thing semblable; the other is called commutative or . . . corrective . . . Justice distributive hath regard to the person; justice commutative hath no regard to the person, but only considering the inequality whereby the one thing exceedeth the other, endeavoureth to bring them both to an equality. (pp. 159–60)

Justice as measure and balance, the fair apportioning of goods and punishments, is particularly fundamental to the opening cantos (i–iv) of Book 5.

Another distinction of importance for Book 5, made by Aristotle, is that between 'natural' and 'legal' or civil justice (*Ethics* pp. 106–7). The law of nature is universal and invariable; it is what all people in whatever time or place acknowledge in their conscience to be just. Civil justice is the particular set of laws established by a state for the running of its affairs and which will differ from state to state according to local customs. The laws of nature should, in the final analysis, take precedence over the laws of man.

The distinction is important for Book 5 because it is fundamental to the concept of equity. This is essentially the correcting or mitigating of particular laws of men by an appeal to the laws of nature, or of God. In the English legal system, it was recognized that a law might be found in particular circumstances to be inadequate: it might be not precise enough, or too harsh, or even too lenient. In such a case, appeal could be made to the monarch, whose justice overrode the particular laws of the state and who could dispense equity. In the sixteenth century, the equitable power of the monarch

Book 5

was invested in special courts of equity presided over by judges. A standard text book on English law in the sixteenth century defines equity in terms that seem close to Spenser's conception:

In some cases it is *good and even* necessary to leve the wordis of the lawe & to folowe that reason and Justyce requyreth & to that intent equytie is ordeyned that is to say to tempre and myttygate the rygoure of the lawe.[2]

At the same time as he learns the rules of balance and the use of force, Artegall is taught

> equitie to measure out along,
> According to the line of conscience,
> When so it needs with rigour to dispence.   (i.7)

The last line is ambiguous: it describes both equity's power to act with greater rigour than the letter of the law requires if conscience demands it, and its power to mitigate the law's rigour.

b. Elizabethan law and order

Clemency has an important place in the complete representation of justice, but it must not be confused with vain pity, which is a 'sickness of the mind' according to Sir Thomas Elyot (*The Governor* p. 119). Justice without mercy may be cruel, but to the Elizabethans mercy at the cost of justice was sheer folly likely to erode yet further the fragile bulwark against disorder. Quite what would happen if that bulwark fell is vividly conveyed by the homily *Concerning . . . Obedience* quoted at the head of this chapter. The homily was first printed in 1547, but it continued to be reprinted throughout Elizabeth's reign and was ordered to be read regularly from the pulpit. 'Take but degree away', said the Elizabethan Ulysses,

> And hark what discord follows . . .
> Force should be right, or rather right and wrong,
> Between whose endless jar justice resides,
> Should lose their names, and so should justice too.
> (Shakespeare, *Troilus and Cressida* I.iii.109, 116–18)

If order broke down a nightmare state of violence and injustice would follow.

   The Elizabethans' sense of the fragility of their civility was greatly increased by their embattled position as a small Protestant nation confronting a largely Roman Catholic continent. The Papacy and its instruments presented to horrified English eyes the spectacle of gross injustice abroad and the continual threat of usurpation and rebellion at home. The *Homily against Disobedience and Rebellion*, printed in 1571 after the Catholic-inspired Northern Rebellion in England, describes Catholicism as above all a threat to justice and peace. Intolerable were the

injuries, oppressions, ravenie, and tyranny of the Bishop of Rome, usurping as well against their naturall Lords the Emperours, as against all other Christian kings and kingdomes, and their continuall stirring of subjects unto rebellions against their Soveraigne Lords . . . and it may seeme more then marvayle, that any subjects would after such sort hold with unnaturall forraine usurpers against their owne soveraigne Lords, and naturall countrey.[3]

If Elizabethans felt their civility under such threat in the relative stability of England, how much more insecure and thus militant might they be expected to feel in Ireland, where large parts of the countryside were still inaccessible to English law in the 1590s. Inevitably Spenser's view of justice in practice must be influenced by what he saw and experienced there. His prose work, *A View of the Present State of Ireland*, reflects the hard-line views of the 'new English', men like himself who had come over in the 1580s and 1590s as Government officials or as colonizers (see pp. 6–8 above). Such men were exasperated by what they saw as the continuing savagery and lawlessness of Ireland in spite of English rule. Lacking the powerful authority of the monarch's presence, the Irish had grown so unruly that 'no laws, no penalties can restrain, but that they do in the violence of that fury tread down and trample underfoot all both divine and human things, and the laws themselves they do specially rage at and rend in pieces' (*View* p. 12). What was needed in the opinion of Spenser and like-minded men was authority, vigour and severity; order must be imposed 'by the sword . . . I mean the royal power of the prince, which ought to stretch itself forth in her chief strength, to the redressing and cutting off of those evils' (p. 95). If the Irish will not obey the civil laws, they must be forced into obedience by martial law pursued to the end, without 'vain pity'. Spenser is fully conscious of the seeming cruelty of his proposals, but he has a lively fear, shared with many of his contemporaries, of the consequences of lawlessness. A similar view of a harsh but necessary justice informs Book 5.

2. Historical allegory

It will be plain from this introduction that I believe Book 5 to be deeply concerned with issues of justice in Spenser's own time. All the books of *The Faerie Queene* confront the difficulties that beset virtue in practice, but this is particularly true of Book 5. In the Proem, Spenser claims to form his heroes 'to the antique use . . ./When Justice was not for most meed outhyred,/But simple Truth did rayne, and was of all admyred' (3). But it is clear that Artegall operates in a world which reflects Spenser's and our own fallen and depraved one:

> For that which all men then did vertue call,
> Is now cald vice; and that which vice was hight,
> Is now hight vertue, and so us'd of all:
> Right now is wrong, and wrong that was is right. (4)

In his own time Spenser found the battle between justice and its enemies fought out in epic fashion, and it was a struggle in which he was passionately involved. This is not to say that Book 5 can only be understood as a commentary on political events of the late sixteenth century. Spenser sees the events of his own time as exemplifying a universal struggle between justice and injustice, civility and tyranny. The universal issues are given specificity and intensity by being grounded in the particular.

Spenser saw the history of England in providential terms. In some respects, England under Elizabeth may have enacted struggles that recur in every period, but it was also unique, a time of culmination and promise. In Book 3, Merlin foretold a time of peace:

> Then shall a royall virgin raine, which shall
> Stretch her white rod over the *Belgicke* shore,
> And the great Castle smite so sore with all,
> That it shall make him shake, and shortly learne to fall.
>
> (3.iii.49)

That myth of the virgin queen, the godly Protestant monarch, preserver of justice at home and champion of those oppressed by tyrannous Catholic power abroad, pervades the second half of Book 5. Spenser is being vigorously political, giving visionary form to Protestant hopes associated with Leicester, Sidney and Essex, who tried to persuade Elizabeth to take a more active interventionist role abroad against the Catholic powers (see pp. 4–6 above). By 1595 it was clear that such hopes and policies would not be fulfilled under Elizabeth, and it is a measure of Spenser's realism that his poem recognizes the imperfection of Artegall's achievement even while celebrating what that achievement might have been (see p. 141 below).

It is easy to be clumsy in detecting historical allusions. Not all the episodes in Book 5 have particular reference to contemporary events.

When we do detect historical allusions, they must be put in the context of the poet's wider aims – whether his more universal exposition of justice, or his political vision of an idealized role for Protestant England. Read in this way, I believe the historical allegory gives an extraordinary vigour to the book, giving us a sense of an involved and committed Spenser tackling the exigencies of justice in the real world.

ARTEGALL

Describing the degeneration of world from a golden to a 'stonie' age (Proem 2), Spenser makes use of the classical myth of the world's beginnings described in the first book of Ovid's *Metamorphoses*, which tells us of the world's fall from its first golden, paradisaical age through four stages to the present iron age (*Metamorphoses* 1.89–127); this is symbolized by the rebellion of the Titans, a race of impious giants who raise a mountain to threaten the heavens and are hurled down by Jove's thunderbolts (1.151–62). The final degeneration of the world is marked by the departure of Astraea, goddess of justice (1.149–50).

The myth underlies Spenser's account of Artegall's training. Astraea lures him away to live far from human society in the woods (i.6). The harshness of Artegall's role is made clear by the imagery. He must be kept uncorrupted by society, but he must also learn to act with a ferocity untouched by fellow-feeling among 'wyld beasts' (i.7), a grim but commonplace image of lawless men and women (see p. 147 below). That Artegall's rigour is itself closely akin to savagery seems to be acknowledged by our first view of him in Book 4, where as the savage knight whose motto is '*salvagesse sans finesse*', he wreaks havoc at Satyrane's tournament until chastened by Britomart (4.iv.39–44). In Book 4, Artegall's ferocity is used for his own ends and becomes an instrument of disorder and even of injustice (4.iv.5–6); in Book 5, it is controlled and turned against those whose violence and injustice oppress others, latter-day versions of those giants, the Titans, whose rebellious disobedience threatened to extend the chaos of the iron age to the heavens themselves.

It is the thunderbolt-like sword Chrysaor, which Jove used to quell the Titans, that Astraea now gives to Artegall (i.9); his quest is against the greatest of the latter-day Titans, Grantorto (Ital. *gran torto*, great wrong), who holds the lady Irena (Gk *eirēnē*, peace) captive (i.3–4). In canto xii, Spenser will give more specific form to both Irena and Grantorto, but at this stage their names are simple and inclusive, containing the whole scope of justice. Appropriately, Grantorto's name has a particular legal resonance: a 'tort' in law is an injury done to a person or property.

At her departure, Astraea leaves Talus, 'made of yron mould,/Immoveable, resistlesse, without end' (i.12), appropriately formed to execute justice in an iron age. Talus is the executive power of Artegall, the force which alone makes law effective:

> vaine it is to deeme of things aright,
> And makes wrong doers justice to deride,
> Unlesse it be perform'd with dreadlesse might.
> For powre is the right hand of Justice truely hight.   (iv.1)

The iconography of Talus makes his nature clear. He combines the stern justice of the classical Talos with the flail and iron armour of the war-god Mars (Aptekar pp. 42–5). Aptekar describes his function as 'a bloodhound and a police helicopter, an executioner and an army' (pp. 41–2).

'EQUALL BALLANCE': CANTOS i–iv

Artegall was taught by Astraea 'to weigh both right and wrong/In equall ballance with due recompense' (i.7). The first four episodes of Book 5 develop the implications of this skill. Aristotle made it clear that the balances were delicate instruments, with the golden mean differently calculated for distributive and commutative justice. In the former, justice was achieved not by giving to each equal portions, but by suiting the portions to the quality and desert of each. In the latter, the punishment must be balanced to fit the crime (see p. 122 above).

1. Sir Sangliere and the Squire

In the trial of Sir Sangliere (i.13–30), we are reminded that before Artegall can demonstrate his skill with the balances he must use force. Sir Sangliere (Fr. *sanglier*, wild boar) is like those wild beasts amongst whom Artegall learns the necessity of force (i.7). He must be forced to face trial (i.21), and when judgement has been passed he must be forced to accept it (i.29). Artegall's adjudication has been designed to recall the most famous judgement of all, that of Solomon (1 Kings 3.16–28). The details are not realistic: Artegall offers to divide the living lady in two (26) as Solomon offered to part the child. The incident emblematically establishes Artegall as a judge like Solomon, gifted with a godly wisdom.

Like Solomon, Artegall offers to Sir Sangliere and the Squire an apparently equally balanced judgement, which would in fact be unfair. The device is a means to discover the truth which, once known, allows Artegall to balance the scales of justice more sensitively, giving to each what is his due: the Squire his living lady, Sir Sangliere the dead one.

2. Pollente, and the giant with the scales

Canto ii is balanced between two opposite extremes: the first half deals, in the story of Pollente and Munera, with the abuse of power (Lat. *pollens*, powerful) and wealth, while in the second half the giant champions the commons' attempts to eradicate all social inequalities. That these two abuses are connected is suggested by the common complaint in social commentary of the period that oppression by the rich is a direct cause of insurrection by the poor. John Christopherson, for example, is orthodox both in linking oppression with rebellion and in denying to the commons the right to take the law into their own hands:

Let us see what cause they have to rebell, that be sore oppressed with taxes, and tributes, with pollynge and pilling, with rentes raysed and with pastures enclosed: such perhappes have cause to complayne, but no cause at all to make rebellion.[4]

Pollente's villainies (5–6) are similar to those Christopherson ascribes to tyrannical landlords. While he abuses the rich, his agent against the poor is a shaven groom whose raw scalp (11) is a sign not only of his bondage (6), but also of his function: '*Poll and Pill*, lit. to make bare of hair and skin too; to ruin by depredation and extortion' (*New English Dictionary*). Munera (Lat. *munus*, gift, hence bribe) is a fit daughter for such a father. Like her literary ancestress, Lady Mede in Langland's *Piers Plowman*, she is seductively beautiful (10) and represents bribery, though Munera both uses her wealth to corrupt (justice particularly) and embodies its illegal accumulation in the hands of the powerful.

Artegall deals summarily, indeed ferociously, with these two, but Spenser does not evade the issue. Artegall's fight with Pollente links the two men together in their fury:

> There being both together in the floud,
>   They each at other tyrannously flew;
>   Ne ought the water cooled their whot bloud,
>   But rather in them kindled choler new.   (13)

128

Book 5

Artegall's training upon 'wyld beasts' (i.7) was not for nothing: power must be met by greater power, the tyranny of oppression by the force of justice. As Pollente's bleeding head must be hung up as a lesson 'to all mighty men' (19), so must Munera's golden hands and silver feet. Spenser's language emphasizes the cruelty of justice. Talus 'chopt off, and nayld on high' her hands and feet (26) and then takes her

> by the sclender wast,
> In vaine loud crying, and into the flood
> Over the Castle wall adowne her cast,
> And there her drowned in the durty mud. (27)

Even Artegall feels pity, though he knows better than to respond to it (25–6). The justice is severe and consciously so, part of the grim realism Spenser shared with his contemporaries:

Mercy . . . be one of the greatest virtues, wherewith a noble captaine may be endued: but to be used out of time, as occasion may fal out, hath greater resemblance to foolish pitie then to be call mercy, and is rather to be holden a vice then a vertue.[5]

At the opposite extreme to Pollente is the giant with the scales, whose impulse to weigh all things anew is in part a response to such oppression as Pollente's:

> Tyrants that make men subject to their law,
> I will suppresse, that they no more may raine;
> And Lordings curbe, that commons over-aw;
> And all the wealth of rich men to the poore will draw. (38)

However, the giant is a figure of false justice. He holds the balances, but he has no skill in their use, substituting a crude egalitarianism for the subtle measuring Aristotle taught should be used in the just distribution of goods: 'If the persons are not equal they will not have equall shares' (*Ethics* p. 97). Spenser inhabited a hierarchical world which extended beyond man to the whole cosmos; everything and everyone had their place in a scale from greatest to least. Justice consists in weighing like with like, of finding the right place on the scale, not in a spurious balance:

> But set the truth and set the right aside,
> For they with wrong or falshood will not fare;
> And put two wrongs together to be tride,
> Or else two falses, of each equall share;
> And then together doe them both compare.
> For truth is one, and right is ever one.
> So did he, and then plaine it did appeare,

> Whether of them the greater were attone.
> But right sate in the middest of the beame alone.   (48)

The whole of canto ii re-enacts such a balance, with the two wrongs of misuse of power and egalitarianism weighed against each other.

The egalitarian threat posed by the giant was a real and frightening one in the sixteenth century, associated with the excesses of the anabaptists at Münster in the 1530s.[6] The degree to which the giant challenges what was seen as a God-given order is evident in Artegall's lengthy replies, which are a tissue of biblical echoes, particularly from 2 Esdras 4 (see notes in Hamilton's edition on stanzas 35–43). If the giant will not reform he must be punished, and Artegall measures out the same punishment to him as befell Munera at the other end of the scale, 'So was the high aspyring with huge ruine humbled' (50).

The leader destroyed, the armed and 'lawless multitude' (52) of his followers is routed by the iron Talus (51–4). The image leaves us with a final grim reminder of the real world of the sixteenth century. The ragged, plebeian rebels are scattered as Ket's followers were at Dussingdale in 1549, or the followers of the Desmonds in Ireland in the early 1580s. Spenser compares them to ducks scattered by a falcon (54), suggesting that the silly, gullible commons would live peaceably enough were they not led astray by false leaders.

3. Marinell's tournament

When the giant put truth and falsehood together in his scales, he found falsehood would not stay put, 'but still it downe did slide,/And by no meane could in the weight be stayd' (ii.45). There is no mean between truth and falsehood; only the mind can distinguish false words from true through the delicate mechanisms of the ear: 'The eare must be the ballance, to decree/And judge, whether with truth or falshood they agree' (ii.47).

The tournament held to mark the marriage of Marinell and Florimell (canto iii) continually confronts the characters with choices between the true and the false. The tournament itself parallels in many of its details that of Satyrane in Book 4 (iv–v), but where that ended in discord this brings about concord. At the end of Satyrane's contest, False Florimell was triumphant. In Book 5, when her true paradigm is brought forward, she simply disappears, as the false did from the giant's scales:

> Then did he set her by that snowy one,
>   Like the true saint beside the image set,

Book 5

> Of both their beauties to make paragone,
> And triall, whether should the honor get.
> Streight way so soone as both together met,
> Th'enchaunted Damzell vanisht into nought. (iii.24)

In the cases of Braggadochio's shield and Guyon's horse, the truth is less startlingly obvious and the evidence must be weighed by the judicious mind. As at the earlier tournaments, Artegall is disguised, but this time his covering, the sun-like shield, in fact reveals his Osiris-like justice (vii.4) rather than his savagery (4.iv.39; 5.iii.10 and 14). He unmasks himself, bringing about the unmasking of Braggadochio and the general establishment of truth (iii.20–6).

The episode rights the final discords of Book 4 and also establishes complementary relations between Books 2 and 4. Seeing Brigliadore in the possession of Braggadochio, Guyon draws his sword to exact vengeance (iii.29). Righteous anger, as we saw in our discussion of Book 2, must have no personal motive (see p. 54 above). Artegall's insistence that Guyon's anger be submitted to the due process of justice (32) is as important as Guyon's insistence, a few stanzas later, that Artegall's choler be restrained by temperance (36). For both knights, public vengeance must be sharply distinguished from private wrath.

4. Amidas and Bracidas

No sooner has the friendship of Book 4 seemed finally consummated in the union of Marinell and Florimell, 'Enlincked fast' (iv.3), than Artegall meets a group who echo the darkest images of discord in Book 4:

> two comely Squires,
> Both brethren, whom one wombe together bore,
> But stirred up with different desires,
> Together strove. (iv.4)

Where friendship fails to bind individuals together in concord, justice must enforce a peace.

The case of Amidas and Bracidas develops another of the lessons Artegall tried to teach the giant in canto ii. A major piece of the latter's evidence of growing imbalance among the elements was the encroachment of the sea on the land: 'The sea it selfe doest thou not plainely see/Encroch upon the land there under thee' (ii.37). Artegall's answer was orthodox:

> What though the sea with waves continuall
> Doe eate the earth, it is no more at all:

131

> Ne is the earth the less, or loseth ought,
> For whatsoever from one place doth fall,
> Is with the tide unto an other brought:
> For there is nothing lost, that may be found, if sought.   (ii.39)

In canto iv, Artegall's judgement simply confirms what nature, providentially guided, has already distributed equitably (19). Spenser's
careful repetitions emphasize that Artegall is balancing like with like:

> Then *Artegall* thus to the younger sayd;
>> Now tell me *Amidas*, if that ye may,
>> Your brothers land the which the sea hath layd
>> Unto your part, and pluckt from his away,
>> By what good right doe you withhold this day?
>> What other right (quoth he) should you esteeme,
>> But that the sea it to my share did lay?
>> Your right is good (sayd he) and so I deeme,
> That what the sea unto you sent, your own should seeme.
>
> Then turning to the elder thus he sayd;
>> Now *Bracidas* let this likewise be showne.
>> Your brothers threasure, which from him is strayd,
>> Being the dowry of his wife well knowne,
>> By what right doe you claime to be your owne?
>> What other right (quoth he) should you esteeme,
>> But that the sea hath it unto me throwne?
>> Your right is good (sayd he) and so I deeme,
> That what the sea unto you sent, your own should seeme.
>>>> (17–18)

In this case the just mean is found exactly in the middle, 'For equall
right in equall things doth stand' (19).

RADIGUND

In canto ii, the giant undertook 'to repaire,/In sort as they were
formed aunciently' all the 'realmes and nations run awry' (32). In
canto iv, Artegall encounters a nation, ruled by a woman, so awry
that eventually Britomart quite legitimately repeals its laws and
restores it to its former state (vii.42). We can assume that Spenser
expects us to notice the differences. The giant supposed the original
state of all things to be absolute equality, but Britomart founds
her reform on the hierarchical order which to the Elizabethans was
ordained by God, and which included, except in exceptional circumstances, the subordination of women (see, e.g., 1 Timothy 2.12).

The question of women's authority was a pressing and controversial one for late sixteenth-century Englishmen, who had to come to terms with the reigns of Mary Queen of Scots and Mary Tudor as well as Elizabeth. The 'moderate Puritan' view followed Calvin in arguing that the rule of women was generally 'contrary to the legitimate course of nature', but that exceptions were possible:

The grace of God sometimes displayed itself in an extraordinary way, since, as a reproach to the sloth of men, he raises up women, endowed not after the nature of men, but with a certain heroic spirit, as is seen in the illustrious example of Deborah.[7]

Spenser seems to conform closely to this position:

> Such is the crueltie of womenkynd,
>   When they have shaken off the shamefast band,
>   With which wise Nature did them strongly bynd,
>   T'obay the heasts of mans well ruling hand,
>   .That then all rule and reason they withstand,
>   To purchase a licentious libertie.
>   But vertuous women wisely understand,
>   That they were borne to base humilitie,
> Unlesse the heavens them lift to lawfull soveraintie.   (v.25)

Heaven's extraordinary Grace seems much needed in the imperfect world of Book 5. While Artegall and his fellow-prisoners lead a life of shame and inaction, it is given to the exceptional Britomart to defeat Radigund and, herself reigning 'as Princess' for a space (vii.42), voluntarily to restore the commonwealth of the Amazons to men's rule (vii.42–3).

Radigund is both magnificent and destructive, a potentially queenly figure gone awry. She is dressed like Belphoebe (v.2–3; and cf. 2.iii.26–7) and shares her heroic singleness, though not, of course, her virtue. More extensively, she is compared with Britomart. Both women are martial in appearance and courage, and both have a superficially similar effect on Artegall. As he fought with the unknown Britomart in Book 4, Artegall sheared away her 'ventayle', revealing her beauty, which 'Like to the ruddie morne appeard in sight,/Deawed with silver drops, through sweating sore' (4.vi.19). Overcome by the sight, he submits to a providential love to which Britomart, finally agreeing, 'yeelded her consent/To be his love, and take him for her Lord' (4.vi.41). Fighting with Radigund, Artegall snatches off her helmet, revealing her beauty, obscured with blood and sweat but 'like as the Moone in foggie winters night' (v.12). Again he submits, this time to vain pity and to an unjust inversion of the hierarchy with Radigund as master and wooer. Where Britomart reluctantly, and in spite of her love, acknowledged the necessity of Artegall's quest and gave him permission to depart (4.vi.42–4), Radigund's illicit love holds Artegall in prison, delaying his quest with nearly fatal results (xi.39).

The most vivid image of unnatural inversion in the episode is that of Artegall and his fellow-prisoners clothed in gowns and spinning like diligent maidens (v.22–3). Spenser compares Artegall's indignity to that of Hercules (24), whose shameful subjection to Omphale (Spenser names her 'Iola') was a familiar Renaissance emblem of man's loss of virtue when dominated, usually sexually, by women (Aptekar pp. 177–8). Artegall's fault is not that of sexual infatuation (vi.2), but his captivity is shamefully emasculating, destroying his power to act as the instrument of justice: his sword is broken (21), he gives up his shield (16), and he willingly obeys his captor, 'Serving proud *Radigund* with true subjection' (v.26). The unlikely combination of the last two words (repeated in stanza 18) points to the shameful irony of Artegall's position, pursuing his own dishonour through a misguided notion of honour.

Artegall's errors are vain pity and a narrow-minded legalism. At the sight of Radigund's face, he was 'Empierced . . . with pitifull regard' (v.13), all the less excusable because he knew well what she was and what she had done. This is that vain pity which in Sir Thomas Elyot's opinion 'contained neither justice nor yet commendable charity, but rather thereby ensueth negligence, contempt, disobedience, and finally all mischief and incurable misery' (*The Governor* p. 120). Artegall also agrees to Radigund's conditions of battle, 'That if I vanquishe him, he shall obay/My law, and ever to my lore be bound' (iv.49). Thus Artegall, Gloriana's instrument of justice, Astraea's deputy, submits himself to Radigund's false laws, which flout in every respect those laws of nature and God which are the foundation of justice (see pp. 122–3 above).

From this self-inflicted impotence, Britomart rescues the Knight of Justice, enabling him to return to his quest. Her actions systematically reverse Artegall's errors: to Radigund's unjust conditions she replies with disdain and silence (vii.28); to Radigund herself she is pitiless, hewing off her helmet and head at one stroke (vii.34). Finally, Britomart shows herself worthy of her exceptional status by replacing Radigund's laws with a justice based on the laws of nature and of God (vii.42). To Radigund's followers, Britomart shows an allowable clemency (vii.36). This is not vain pity because it puts no one in jeopardy. 'If ye ask me what mercy is', wrote Elyot, 'it is a temperance of the mind of him that hath power to be avenged, and it is called in Latin *clementia*, and is always joined with reason' (*The Governor* p. 119).

THE TEMPLE OF ISIS

In reforming Radigund's commonwealth, Britomart exercised equity, the prerogative of the monarch who may override the specific laws of the state in favour of the more fundamental laws of nature and God. It is with this aspect of justice that Britomart is identified in the Temple of Isis, when in her dream she finds herself assuming the identity of the goddess who 'in her person cunningly did shade/That part of Justice, which is Equity' (vii.3).

The Temple is both a deeply soothing and a disturbing place, an area of stillness amidst the pressing problems and harsh action of Book 5, but the site also of Britomart's violent and metamorphic dream. The Temple itself reflects an achieved balance and order, with Isis existing in peaceful and united harmony with Osiris; they are like the moon and sun 'For that they both like race in equall justice runne' (4). Talus, that symbol of the harshness with which law must be imposed on a recalcitrant world, is excluded. The priests are ordered, chaste and temperate:

> they mote not taste of fleshly food,
> Ne feed on ought, the which doth bloud containe,
> Ne drinke of wine, for wine they say is blood,
> Even the bloud of Gyants, which were slaine,
> By thundring Jove. (10)

They are the antithesis of those turbulent rebellious Titans who challenged the authority of Jove himself, the types of injustice (cf. i.9). The orderliness of the Temple is complemented by its clarity. Each detail of clothing and of the Idol's appearance is explained to us without ambiguity (4–11).

Amidst such order and transparency, Britomart can trust and sleep. Her dream is all that the Temple is not. It precipitates us from one strange transformation to the next, some violent, some sexually disturbing. The crocodile, we were told, represents guile and force (7), but now it becomes first Britomart's defender, swallowing up the 'outragious flames' which suddenly threaten to consume her Temple (14), and then her suitor:

> Tho turning all his pride to humblesse meeke,
> Him selfe before her feete he lowly threw,

> And gan for grace and love of her to seeke:
>   Which she accepting, he so neare her drew,
>   That of his game she soone enwombed grew,
>   And forth did bring a Lion of great might.   (16)

The priest who interprets her dream tells Britomart the crocodile is both Artegall and Osiris (22). Britomart herself is both onlooker and actor (13), idol, wife and mother (15–16), suppressor and lover of the crocodile. The dream is a dense mingling of the many levels and aspects of Britomart's and Artegall's significance.

The Artegall that is figured in Britomart's dream is not unfamiliar: it is the Artegall who was trained on 'wyld beasts' (i.7) and whose justice must be exercised in a fallen and predatory world. We have already seen that Artegall's ferocity is a weapon that can be used justly and unjustly, a form of savagery when used for illegitimate ends, as in Satyrane's tournament, but necessary severity when used for justice. Similarly, the ingenuity and policy that are wise when used to trap Sir Sangliere (i.26–8) or to temporize with Clarinda and Radigund (v.56) may easily become 'forged guile' (vii.7) when used to subvert justice. The methods of practical justice are powerful and dangerous in the wrong hands; the crocodile can be both an instrument of subversion and the founder of a dynasty.

Even in the right hands, practical justice needs some restraint, and this is equity's role. The monarch's authority is greater than that of the law and can overturn it or supplement it. Equity is not the same as mercy, or clemency, as is made clear in a later comment on the Mercilla episode:

> For if that Vertue be of so great might,
>   Which from just verdict will for nothing start,
>   But to preserve inviolated right,
>   Oft spilles the principall, to save the part;
>   So much more then is that of powre and art,
>   That seekes to save the subject of her skill,
>   Yet never doth from doome of right depart:
>   As it is greater prayse to save, then spill,
> And better to reforme, then to cut off the ill.   (x.2)

The first 'Vertue' is equity, which dispenses with the law when it is found to be unjust in a particular case; the second is mercy, which, while acknowledging the law's justness, nevertheless seeks to reform rather than to punish. In practice, however, equity was often merciful in effect, tempering the rigour of the law (see p. 123 above). It is this aspect of equity that Spenser chooses to stress in the dream of the Temple of Isis. The crocodile now restrained and sleeping under

Isis' foot shows that 'clemence oft in things amis,/Restraines those sterne behests, and cruell doomes of his' (vii.22).

Reconciled, the crocodile and Isis, Artegall and Britomart, shall 'joyne in equall portion' of Britomart's realm (23). They will enjoy that state of achieved balance, between justice and equity, ferocity and mildness, which Isis and Osiris exemplified at the beginning of the episode (4), but only for a while. Merlin has already foretold Artegall's fate, 'Too rathe cut off by practise criminall' (3.iii.28). Britomart's dream has many aspects: it is an allegory of justice, an allegorical account of a love match, and a prophecy of a dynastic union from which will come the Tudor line, symbolized by the royal lion (16). The contrast between the static calm of the Temple itself and the dream is that between the representation of an ideal justice and the turbulent process by which it is achieved in history.

FORCE AND GUILE: DOLON, THE SOULDAN AND MALENGIN

Before arriving at the Temple of Isis, Britomart comes, again at evening, upon an aged knight who seems 'bent/To peace' (vi.19). He is Dolon (Lat. *dolus*, guile, deceit), and the shelter he offers to Britomart proves to be a place of traps. To some extent the incident prefaces Britomart's troubled dream of Artegall in the Temple. The guile of Dolon seems to image her fears of Artegall's faithlessness, which she sees as a form of self-betrayal:

> Ye guilty eyes (sayd she) the which with guyle
> My heart at first betrayd, will ye betray
> My life now to. (vi.25)

The trapped bed (vi.27) may be an image of Britomart's sense of sexual treason.

The episode has, however, another dimension. Dolon attacks Britomart thinking she is Artegall, who in the Pollente episode killed one of his sons (ii.11 and vi.33). The linking of the two episodes brings together those two arch-enemies of justice 'forged guile,/And open force' (vii.7), for Pollente's name pointed to the violence of his nature (see pp. 128–9 above). Sir Thomas Elyot cited a venerable truism when he wrote that 'injury, which is contrary to justice, is done by two means, that is to say, either by violence or by fraud' (*The Governor* p. 168; see Aptekar pp. 108–24). In the two episodes which follow the Temple, Spenser explores particular aspects of these two forms of injustice.

While there may be some historical reference to plots against Elizabeth's life in the Dolon episode,[8] Spenser begins in canto viii an extended sequence of historical allegory in which Protestant England's struggles against her Roman Catholic enemies are imaged in terms of confrontations between the just ruler, Mercilla, and the forces of injustice at home and abroad.

The Souldan is a figure of 'lawlesse powre and tortious wrong' (viii.51, and also 30) whose wife and counsellor is Adicia (Gk *adikia*, lawlessness). He threatens Mercilla's subjects and 'Seekes to subvert her Crowne' (18). The incident is normally taken to refer to Philip II of Spain's Armada against England in 1588. The Souldan's chariot 'hye,/With yron wheeles and hookes arm'd dreadfully' (28) suggests the great armed galleons of the Spanish fleet. In defeat, the Souldan is compared to Phaeton, who stole the sun-god's chariot and, driving it out of control, 'This lower world nigh all to ashes brent' (40). The image neatly parodies Philip II's personal emblem, or *impresa*, which depicted the sun-god soaring across the heavens in his chariot.[9] It is the sight of the truly 'sunlike' brightness of Arthur's unveiled shield (41) that drives the Souldan's horses astray, shattering his chariot. The detail recalls the circumstances of the Armada's defeat, scattered, seemingly through the intervention of Divine Grace, by wind and tempest, so that most of the ships were wrecked and shattered in their flight round the coast of Scotland and Ireland.

Spenser deploys the forces of justice against the Souldan with considerable care. Arthur and Artegall take on complementary roles, Artegall acting with policy, closely akin to guile, but used here against the unjust (25), while Talus stays with Arthur, who seems to assume the role of forceful executioner:

> But the brave Prince for honour and for right,
> Gainst tortious powre and lawlesse regiment,
> In the behalfe of wronged weake did fight:
> More in his causes truth he trusted then in might. (30)

In fact, Arthur's might proves ineffective – 'Yet could the Prince not nigh unto him goe,/That one sure stroke he might unto him reach' (37) – and it is Divine Grace, symbolized by Arthur's unveiled shield, that subdues the Souldan. Only then can the undisguised Artegall control Adicia's wrath and punish her followers 'with finall force' (50). The episode seems to spell out the limits of human justice's weapons of force and guile; against such an enemy as the Souldan, figuring Philip II, the agent of Antichrist in English eyes,

Book 5

Grace must aid human justice. With such aid, Arthur and Artegall go far beyond Elizabeth's achievement in 1588, destroying not only the Armada, but the Souldan himself.

Malengin's name indicates his guileful nature (ix.5, and see 3.i.53). The episode is paired with that of the Souldan: both malefactors attack Mercilla's subjects, and both are defeated by Arthur and Artegall with the help of Mercilla's ambassador, Samient. The two just knights again use a combination of force and guile, though in this case Artegall and Talus take the forceful part (ix.8–9, 15), sufficient against this less dreadful and more domestic enemy. As the Souldan clearly represented the threat of Roman Catholic force from abroad, it seems probable that Malengin shadows its guileful operations at home, the covert activity of the Jesuits. Such a reading of the episode is by no means uncontroversial, though the details of Spenser's description are suggestively close to contemporary descriptions of the Jesuits as 'a rabble of vagrant runagates' (cf. 10), shrouding 'like foxes in holes and coverts' (cf. 6), who 'in disguised habits . . . transformed themselves at plesure like unto Protews' (cf. 16–19).[10]

MERCILLA

The culmination of Book 5 is the description of Mercilla's palace, an exemplary place of justice as the Houses of Holiness and of Alma were exemplary places of holiness and temperance. Mercilla herself is a superlative figure, shadowing an idealized Elizabeth:

> Most sacred wight, most debonayre and free,
> That ever yet upon this earth was seene,
> Or that with Diademe hath ever crowned beene.   (ix.20)

The throne on which she sits is decorated with the lions and fleur-de-lis which figured on Elizabeth's coat of arms, and at her feet she has a sword, 'Whose long rest rusted the bright steely brand' (30), which has been identified with a rusty sword which Elizabeth herself, with a sense of symbolism, kept as an emblem of her peaceful reign (see note in Hamilton's edition on stanza 30).

As we might expect, the episode is intensely political, figuring Elizabeth's trial of Mary Queen of Scots in 1586. The episode is out of strict chronological sequence if the Souldan episode celebrates the defeat of the Armada in 1588, but, dramatically, it has been carefully arranged. Our approach to Mercilla/Elizabeth is conditioned by our experience of the threats which seek to undermine her and her people – one of force, the other of guile, both Roman Catholic. When we finally arrive at Mercilla's palace, magnificent, civilized and orderly, a place of peace and justice (24), we have been made aware of its vulnerability. The knowledge affects our response to Duessa as Mary Queen of Scots, the symbol, and for long the excuse, for all treasonable Roman Catholic activity within England and attempts at invasion from abroad. Duessa implies the Souldan's 'tortious' force and Malengin's craft.

The significance of Duessa/Mary must be fully grasped if we are to understand Spenser's distinction between the vain pity Arthur momentarily feels (46) and the mercy Mercilla embodies. Sir Thomas Elyot called mercy 'a temperaunce of the mind of him that hath power to be avenged' (*The Governor* p. 119). He is quoting from Seneca, who in *De Clementia*, the main authority on the subject in the sixteenth century, advises the prince to show neither cruelty nor vain pity, that 'failing of a weak nature that succumbs to the sight of others' ills'.[11] The merciful prince will mitigate the punishment 'if he can in safety' (p. 415). He must proceed with scrupulous justice in trying and proving the fault, and if considerations of safety make punishment necessary he will sign the death warrant 'after great reluctance, after much procrastination' (p. 435). Mercilla proceeds exactly as Seneca said she ought, even to the (conveniently historical) procrastination (ix.50; x.4). When she finally signs, it is done without anger or vengeance, 'even then ruing her wilfull fall,/With more then needfull naturall remorse' (x.4).

Mercilla figures Elizabeth, but she is also the quintessential monarch fulfilling the first duty of kings 'to doe equitie and righteousnesse' (1 Kings 10.9). As judge, the monarch's chief attribute should be mercy: 'nothing more entirely and fastly joineth the hearts of subjects to their prince or sovereign than mercy and gentleness' (*The Governor* p. 119). Mercilla is actively engaged in judgement in a palace which is also a court of law (36). The door stands open to the people, but there is no laxness; Awe keeps out 'guyle, and malice' (22). There is a grim warning in the seditious poet whose tongue is nailed to a post (25–6), an image all the more personal and shocking when it is remembered that Spenser begins and ends the three books published in 1596 with indications of his own difficulties with those in power, particularly Elizabeth's secretary, Lord Burleigh (4.Proem 1; 6.xii.41) and that he places this warning in a book that is at times subtly critical of Elizabeth and her policy (see pp. 141–5 below). The detail grimly reminds us of the severity of the law even in this idealized place of justice.

Order and Degree lead the knights to Mercilla's throne of justice, a rich emblem of her authority (27–33). The cloth of state above her throne is like a cloud with spreading wings recalling biblical descriptions of God's 'Mercyseat' (Exodus 25.20 and Leviticus 16.2; see Hume p. 136), indicating the divine source of Mercilla's power. In its gloss on 1 Kings 10.9, the Geneva Bible comments that 'it is a chiefe signe of Gods favour, when godly and wise rulers sit in the throne of Justice'. Mercilla's trial of Duessa is both godly and wise. Evidence is heard on both sides, counsel is taken, and a judgement arrived at that respects both equity and the law. Mercilla's procrastination in carrying out the judgement is, as we have seen, just what would be expected of a merciful sovereign.

ELIZABETH'S JUSTICE ABROAD: BELGE, BOURBON AND GRANTORTO

Having brought us to a vision of perfect justice at home, Spenser turns our attention to its extension abroad. In so doing, Spenser makes it clear that his vision is that of the militant, evangelical Protestants whose hopes in the 1580s were focused on Leicester and his nephew, Sir Philip Sidney. Writing of those heady and hopeful visions many years later, Sidney's friend Fulke Greville cast Elizabeth in a heroic mould. She vowed, he wrote, to repair 'our *Saviours Militant Church*, through all her Dominions; and as she hoped, in the rest of the World, by her example. Upon which Princelike resolution, this She-*David* of ours ventured to undertake the great *Goliath* among the *Philistins* abroad, I mean *Spain* and the *Pope*.'[12]

Elizabeth herself was never particularly influenced by this ideal, and by 1596 it must have seemed a vain dream. Spenser's recognition of the gap between the militant Protestant vision and the realities of Elizabeth's stop-gap measures is perhaps hinted at by the division of cantos x–xii between Arthur and Artegall. Arthur, the divinely assisted embodiment of national aspirations, carries out the Protestant vision, perfecting the historical facts of Elizabeth's bungled operation in the Netherlands to provide Mercilla and justice with a glorious and final victory against Spain, as his earlier victory against the Souldan went beyond England's actual achievement. Artegall, the representative of justice in a contingent, fallen world, achieves victories that are less unambiguously glorious and less complete.

1. Belge

For Leicester and those visionary Protestants who gathered round him in the 1580s, the Netherlands was a suffering neighbour calling out for aid against the tyrannous persecution of its Roman Catholic rulers. Elizabeth's failure to intervene decisively seemed to such Protestants a scandal which in 1585 looked as though it might be rectified. With the fall of Antwerp to the Spanish forces imminent, Elizabeth agreed to send over a sizeable force with Leicester at its head. Antwerp fell before it arrived, and there followed a year of military setbacks for the English, made yet more ignominious by political wrangling between Leicester and the Queen, and Leicester and the Netherlanders. The crusade petered out in 1587 with Leicester's return to England, to the relief of almost everyone, and having gained nothing. But that was not how it should have been. Sir Philip Sidney, who died in the Netherlands, roused his troops with a visionary statement of their task:

Wherein hee declared what cause they had in hand, as Gods cause, under, and for whom they fought, for her Majestie . . . against whom they fought, men of false religion, enemies to God and his Church: against Antichrist, and against a people whose unkindnes both in nature and in life did excell, that God would not leave them unpunished.[13]

The basic facts of the Netherlands campaign are visible through Spenser's fiction – Belge's distress, her loss of all but five of her seventeen children, the United Provinces (x.7–8), the fall of Antwerp (x.25) – but he soon departs from them. Antwerp is unhistorically regained (x.38–9), Belge comforted, Geryoneo, son of the three-bodied giant Geryon, a figure for Spanish power (Aptekar p. 146) is killed (xi.14), and finally, in a fight that recalls St George's defeat of the dragon in Book 1, Arthur defeats the idolatrous monster, the inquisitorial power of Roman Catholicism in Belge's land (xi.19–33).

2. Bourbon and Grantorto

It is left to Artegall to reflect the imperfect achievements of history. In the Bourbon episode particularly (xi.43–65), Spenser considerably embellishes the historical facts, but his version, while flattering to England, nevertheless imitates the difficulties and disappointments of a real as opposed to an idealized world.

As Artegall hurries forward to rescue Irena from Grantorto at the eleventh hour (xi.43), he comes across Sir Bourbon beset by a rude and lawless rout of men who hold his lady, Flourdelis, in their brutish hands (xi.43–4). The names are transparent. Bourbon represents the Protestant Henry Bourbon of Navarre, the lawful heir to the French throne. His accession was fiercely opposed by a grouping of die-hard

Catholics within France called the Catholic League. Their rebellion within France was supported financially and militarily by Spain. Henry eventually gained Paris and the crown by abjuring the Protestant faith, thus winning over to his side more moderate Catholics. Historically England played a relatively minor role, sending troops and money to assist Henry both before and, reluctantly, after his conversion.

These facts are apparent through Spenser's fiction: Bourbon's shield, given him by Redcrosse (xi.53), is laid aside in the hope that it will gain him Flourdelis (xi.54); Flourdelis, promised to Bourbon, is seduced by Grantorto (xi.50) and proves reluctant to return to her rightful lord (xi.60–4). Artegall's decisive role somewhat exaggerates the importance of the English intervention, but Spenser does not disguise the very imperfect resolution of the crisis: a Catholic monarch united with a reluctant France 'nor well nor ill apayd' (xi.64).

While it is from a rude and plebeian rout that Artegall rescues Bourbon, the arch-villain of both this and the Irena episode is Grantorto. His name marks him as the greatest of the 'tortious' tyrants who appear throughout Book 5. He combines within himself the evils of guile and of force: he tricked Irena 'by guilefull treason and by subtill slight' (xi.39) and seduces Flourdelis with many a 'guilefull word' (xi.50), but when he appears to fight Artegall he is the embodiment of violence:

> Of stature huge and hideous he was,
>   Like to a giant for his monstrous hight,
>   And did in strength most sorts of men surpas.   (xii.15)

His size associates him with the rebellious Titans.

Rebellion and the threat of Roman Catholic invasion were the twin horrors of Elizabethan England, the one threatening all law and established order from within the country, the other bringing the forces of Antichrist to the borders. It is this awful combination of evils that Grantorto represents historically. In France, Henry Bourbon was opposed by the Catholic League and Spain, a lawless combination of rebellion and Roman Catholic intervention. In Ireland, the same combination seemed yet more tyrannous in effect.

Irena's name means peace (see p. 126 above), but also Ireland (*Ierna* is the classical name for Ireland). To English eyes, Ireland was in bondage to everything that threatened peace and justice, the quintessential example of a 'savage nation' crying out for the liberation of law and civility (*View* p. 1; and see pp. 6–8 above). Grantorto himself embodies the violence of the Titans and the last iron age of lawless bloodshed, but he is also a particular image of Irish violence:

> Who came at length, with proud presumpteous gate,
>   Into the field, as if he fearelesse were,
>   All armed in a cote of yron plate,
>   Of great defence to ward the deadly feare,
>   And on his head a steele cap he did weare
>   Of colour rustie browne, but sure and strong;
>   And in his hand an huge Polaxe did beare.   (xii.14)

The armour is distinctive, made up of the steel cap, long coat of mail and axe of the Irish mercenary foot soldiers, the Galloglasses, used so often in uprisings.

The abiding English fear was of an alliance between the rebellious Catholic Irish warlords and an invading Papal or Spanish force. Just such a combination occurred during the Desmond Rebellion (1579–83), which Spenser witnessed at first hand, and whose violent suppression he vividly describes in the *View* (pp. 104–8). Elizabeth's deputy on that occasion was Lord Grey, who, like other of her officials in Ireland, was accused of using excessive severity. Owing to the Queen's displeasure, Lord Grey returned before he had completed his tour of duty in Ireland. Spenser defends him with warmth in the *View*, stressing the havoc caused by what he considers the Queen's vain pity:

All suddenly turned topsy turvy, the noble Lord [Grey] eftsoons was blamed, the wretched people pitied . . . upon which all former purposes were blanked, the governor at a bay, and not only all the great and long charge which she had before been at quite lost and cancelled, but also all that hope of good which was even at the door put back and clean frustrate.

(p. 106)

Artegall also suffers such reversals and is vulnerable to such accusations. We are made aware of the cruelty that accompanies the suppression of the rebellion in France (xi.65), while in Ireland Spenser has Artegall restrain Talus from his 'rage'; it is not 'for such slaughters sake/He thether came' (xii.8). But some slaughter, in Spenser's view, inevitably accompanies the restoration of peace. Talus is a necessary instrument in reforming the 'ragged commonweale':

> that same yron man which could reveale
> All hidden crimes, through all that realme he sent,
> To search out those, that usd to rob and steale,
> Or did rebell gainst lawfull government;
> On whom he did inflict most grievous punishment.   (xii.26)

144

Artegall, too, must leave before his task is done (27), and he is exposed, on his return, to the slanderous attacks of Envy, Detraction and the Blatant Beast (28–43). 'Most untruly and maliciously do these evil tongues backbite and slander', wrote Spenser of Lord Grey's treatment by English opinion (*View* p. 108). Artegall's experience is that which habitually greeted the more zealous implementers of the Queen's justice in Ireland. The twentieth century is not alone in being shocked by the force which, in Spenser's view, necessarily accompanies justice in a fallen world.

Spenser ends Book 5 with the frenzied and disturbing image of the two monstrous and demonic hags with their hundred-tongued beast baying at Artegall, who rides patiently on, restraining Talus from action. Artegall's power is external; he can bind those who break the law, but he cannot reform those whose resolute ill will is confined to their thoughts or expressed only in words. Artegall's failure to complete his reform of the 'ragged common-weale' is perhaps not entirely due to his recall. To complete the task, by teaching men to love good as well as to obey the law, requires the skills of Sir Calidore, the Knight of Courtesy.

Chapter 6

BOOK 6

INTRODUCTION

1. Courtesy

These three on men all gracious gifts bestow,
    Which decke the body or adorne the mynde,
    To make them lovely or well favoured show,
    As comely carriage, entertainement kynde,
    Sweete semblaunt, friendly offices that bynde,
    And all the complements of curtesie:
    They teach us, how to each degree and kynde
    We should our selves demeane, to low, to hie;
To friends, to foes, which skill men call Civility.   (6.x.23)

Colin Clout's description of the gifts of the three Graces unfolds the
virtue of courtesy as it is conceived by Spenser. The gifts range from
an outer comeliness of manner and appearance to the skill of 'Civility', whose significance goes far beyond mere politeness: 'This I call
the civil life', wrote the sixteenth-century writer, Thomas Starkey,
'living togidder in good and politic order, one ever ready to do good
to another, and as it were conspiring togidder in all virtue and
honesty.'[1] Spenser's courtesy draws for its meaning on a number of
related qualities: civility; humanity, as defined for example by Sir
Thomas Elyot, who gives it three parts, benevolence, beneficence
and liberality (*The Governor* p. 121); the arts of courtesy set out in such
Italian 'courtesy books' as Castiglione's *Il Libro del Cortegiano* (1528),
and courtesy as the word came to Spenser from its use in the Middle
Ages with its 'sense of individual integrity in relation to the group
. . . of self-control and moderation, of active goodwill and kindness
to others'.[2] In order to understand more fully the significance
courtesy has in Book 6, we need to examine some of its tributary
meanings in a little more detail.

The Graces give the skill of civility to men, and courtesy, so
Spenser's narrator tells us, is the 'roote of civill conversation' (i.1),
a phrase which means 'an honest commendable and vertuous kinde
of living in the world'.[3] Thomas Starkey was typical in seeing civility as the pinnacle of human achievement in the world: 'to this all

men are born and of nature brought forth: to commune such gifts as
be to them given, each one to the profit of other, in perfit civility'
(p. 22). Such social harmony rests firmly on a foundation of law and
order without which men 'had yet remained in their old rudeness and
lived like wild beasts in the woods' (p. 22). A similar perception
informs Spenser's *View*, whose programme is by 'tempering and
managing of this stubborn nation of the Irish, to bring them from
their delight of licentious barbarism unto the love of goodness and
civility' (p. 11). Spenser's imagery makes clear that, before achieving
civility, the Irish must be curbed and restrained by the forces of law
and order. The gentle arts of courtesy rest firmly on the necessary
harshness of Artegall in Book 5.

The Graces bestow 'friendly offices that bynde' (x.23), that well-
wishing, and well-doing which binds men together in mutual love
and obligation. Spenser's description of the Graces and their gifts
owes much to Seneca's discussion of liberality in his essay *De
Beneficiis*. 'How else do we live in security', Seneca asks,

if it is not that we help each other by an exchange of good offices? It is only
through the interchange of benefits that life becomes in some measure
equipped and fortified against sudden disasters. Take us singly, and what are
we?[4]

Such well-wishing and well-doing are, for Seneca, 'the chief bond of
human society' (p. 19), the basis, in fact, of civility. Like Starkey,
and Spenser in the *View*, Seneca's emphasis on mutual benevolence
rests on an awareness of the alternative, the life of 'wild beasts in the
woods', dominated by selfishness, rapacity and danger.

The delightfulness and the significance of benevolence are
developed by Sir Thomas Elyot in terms that are very close to those
Spenser uses of courtesy:

When I remember what incomparable goodness hath ever proceeded of this
virtue benevolence, merciful God, what sweet flavour feel I piercing my
spirits, whereof both my soul and body to my thinking do conceive such
recreation, that it seemeth me to be in a paradise, or other semblable place
of incomparable delights and pleasures. First I behold the dignity of that virtue, considering that God is thereby chiefly known and honoured both of
angel and man. As contrariwise the devil is hated and reproved both of God
and man for his malice, which vice is contrarious and repugnant to
benevolence . . . God is all goodness, all charity, all love, which wholly be
comprehended in the said word benevolence.   (p.122)

In similar terms, at the beginning of Book 6, Spenser shifts our mood
from the harshness of the Book of Justice by discoursing of the
'delightfull land of Faery', whose ways are

> sprinckled with such sweet variety,
> Of all that pleasant is to eare or eye,
> That I nigh ravisht with rare thoughts delight,
> My tedious travell doe forget thereby.   (Proem 1)

It seems certain that it is the thought of his new subject, courtesy, rather than his long 'travell' through Book 5, that has produced such imaginative recreation. Elyot stressed the divine origins of benevolence, and for Spenser courtesy is the fairest flower of virtue, deriving 'From heavenly seedes of bounty soveraine' (Proem 3). Spenser uses the language of myth, but it is clear that his virtue is close to Elyot's benevolence. They share, too, a common enemy, malice, the vice of Elyot's devil and the weapon of Spenser's Blatant Beast (see e.g., i.9).

Whatever its origins and its nature, courtesy derives its name from the Court: 'Of Court it seemes, men Courtesie doe call,/For that it there most useth to abound' (i.1). Its finest exemplar in the Faery Court is Calidore,

> In whom it seemes, that gentlenesse of spright
> And manners mylde were planted naturall;
> To which he adding comely guize withall,
> And gracious speach, did steale mens hearts away.   (i.2)

The art of manners and the nature of the perfect courtier were topics much written about in the sixteenth century. One of the most famous of the writers was Castiglione, whose ideal courtier was to have 'noblenesse of birth, wit and disposition of person, and grace of countenance' and also 'the understanding to frame all his life and to set forth his good qualities generally in company with all men without purchasing him selfe envy'.[5] Such qualities as nobleness of birth and a good understanding are gifts of fortune and nature, but the general emphasis of Castiglione's work, and of others like it, is on the acquisition of the arts needed to present oneself to the best advantage, to impress. In Castiglione's view, even a certain deception is in order: 'That may bee saide to be a verie arte, that appeareth not to be arte, neither ought a man to put more diligence in any thing than in covering it' (p. 46). Such arts may come perilously close to that false courtesy which is 'nought but forgerie,/Fashion'd to please the eies of them, that pas' (Proem 5). Spenser makes it clear that Calidore, whose name in Greek means beautiful or good gift, is endowed by nature with the main elements of his courtesy: 'gentlenesse of spright/And manners mylde were planted naturall' (i.2). To these he adds the arts of pleasing behaviour ('comely guize') and eloquence, not to dazzle, still less to deceive, but to communicate his genuine, natural courtesy.

Calidore's gentility of nature and manner reflects his gentle birth; he is a knight. The degree to which high birth is essential for a gentleman is an issue much debated in the courtesy books and it is of great importance in Book 6, in which a person's origins often tell us much about his or her nature; those nobly born usually act with a noble spirit and vice versa. More illuminating for Spenser's ideas than the courtesy books is Protestant thought about vocations, that is the calling of each of us to a particular place and role in life. Perkins compares the providentially guided world to clockwork:

Behold here a notable resemblance of God's speciall providence over mankinde, which is the watch of the great world, allotting to every man his motion and calling: and in that calling, his particular office and function. Therefore it is true that I say, that God himeselfe is the author and beginning of callings. This overthroweth the heathenish opinion of men, which thinke, that the particular condition and state of man in this life comes by chance, or by the bare wil and pleasure of man himself.

(A Treatise of Vocations, in *Workes* I, 750)

In such a scheme the gifts of nature should be appropriate to a person's birth and calling. The arts of courtesy may refine and move men to fulfil their calling benevolently and graciously, but by themselves they cannot make a man what he is not called to be.

2. The romance mode of Book 6

In Book 6, the mode of chivalric romance with its knights and quests is mixed with a different, and for Spenser, a new kind of narrative writing, that of Greek or pastoral romance. This form enjoyed a vogue in the sixteenth century, with such Greek romances as Helidorus' *Aethiopica* or Longus' *Daphnis and Chloe* (both written in the third century AD) influencing Sir Philip Sidney's *Arcadia* and, indirectly, Shakespeare's *The Winter's Tale*. A summary of typical narrative motifs in the Greek romances helps us to see Spenser's debt for many of his own episodes:

In these works, the characters are exposed as babies, suckled by animals, brought up by shepherds, and suffer, with endless rhetorical complaints, all the pangs of love; together or separated, the lovers are shipwrecked, attacked by pirates, captured by robbers, wooed by lustful men . . . imprisoned, beaten, enslaved, intended for sacrifice, and endure the apparent deaths of their beloveds; in the end they are reunited with chastity intact, discover their true parents, marry, and, presumably, live happily ever after.[6]

The same writer points out that Spenser tends to imitate those incidents in Greek romance 'which seem to emphasize the role of chance and fortune in men's lives' (p. 255). Such words as 'by chance' (e.g., i.4; viii.46), 'by fortune' (e.g., iv.2), 'as fortune now did fall' (iv.15), 'by strange occasion' (v.11) re-echo through the book, as knights come by chance upon others, those in great danger are luckily rescued, and separated friends are unexpectedly reunited. . The effect is undoubtedly to create 'an image of a world in which unexpected misfortune seemingly cannot be avoided . . . in which all men must at some time be dependent on the courtesy of others' (Culp p. 258), but that is only part of the story. Fortune, however blind it may seem, has a way in Book 6 of bringing all right in the end. Behind the characters' confused perception of chance events, we may detect the same providential pattern that, finally, Lady Claribell's handmaid perceives in the history of Pastorella:

> streight she gan to cast
> In her conceiptfull mynd, that this faire Mayd
> Was that same infant, which so long sith past
> She in the open fields had loosely layd
> To fortunes spoile, unable it to ayd.
> So full of joy, streight forth she ran in hast
> Unto her mistresse, being halfe dismayd,
> To tell her, how the heavens had her graste,
> To save her chylde, which in misfortunes mouth was plaste.
> (xii.16)

The bounty and guidance of a beneficent heaven are seen throughout Book 6, not only in the gifts of nature bestowed upon men, but also through the intertanglements of the narratives, which bring rescuers to victims in the nick of time and restore those who are lost to those who search for them.

Elizabethan imitations of Greek romance developed particularly its pastoral setting, with its traditional connotations of innocence and restoration (see, e.g., *As You Like It* II.i.1–18). Spenser's Meliboe is conventional; having spent ten years pursuing his youthful ambition at Court, he longs for

> this sweet peace, whose lacke did then appeare.
> Tho backe returning to my sheepe againe,
> I from thenceforth have learn'd to love more deare
> This lowly quiet life, which I inherite here.   (ix.25)

Book 6 mixes Greek romance and pastoral motifs with *The Faerie Queene*'s more usual mode of chivalric romance, with its motifs of knights, quests and armed combat. The effect of such juxtaposition of the two modes has been described by Humphrey Tonkin: 'Chivalric romance . . . depends upon guidance, on forward movement through a perilous countryside. Pastoral romance depends upon redemption, the healing powers of the natural world, on passivity in the midst of plenty' (Tonkin p. 19). The two modes seem frequently to come into conflict in Book 6: Calidore dubiously decides to abandon his quest and stay with the shepherds (canto x), and in many smaller episodes places of retreat and repose are broken into, accidentally or aggressively, by those who represent and belong to the 'perilous countryside' of chivalric romance. In Book 6, places where individuals enjoy the vulnerable delights of civility, the dalliance of love, the tending of sheep, the contemplation of the Graces, are repeatedly threatened and disturbed by manifestations of a more urgent and aggressive world.

JUSTICE AND COURTESY: CANTOS i–ii

Book 6 is closely linked to Book 5; courtesy's hopes depend on the achievements of the law.[7] At their meeting at the beginning of Book 6, Calidore acknowledges his relationship with Artegall: 'But where ye ended have, now I begin' (i.6). Calidore's quarry, the Blatant Beast, has, with Envy and Detraction, already attacked Artegall (5.xii.37), whose refusal to act against these foes indicates that the Blatant Beast's weapons of 'spight and malice' (i.9) are beyond the capacity of the law. Starkey is helpful: 'law of itself be not able to bring man to his perfection, nor give him perfit reason and virtue withal' (quoted Horton p. 80, footnote 19). Law is necessary for the preservation of civility, but it cannot make men civil. For that the arts of Calidore are needed.

Book 6 starts with two episodes which suggestively parallel the first two incidents of Book 5. The Crudor/Briana (6.i.11–47) and Pollente/Munera (5.ii.4–28) narratives follow a similar pattern: in both a tyrant and his lady, assisted by a servant, molest passers-by. As befits the more serious oppression and evil represented by Pollente and Munera, Artegall's punishment is savage and final (5.ii.18, 26–7). Crudor's and Briana's behaviour is rooted in discourtesy rather than inveterate opposition to justice, and there is room for reform:

> they that breake bands of civilitie,
> And wicked customes make, those doe defame
> Both noble armes and gentle curtesie.
> No greater shame to man then inhumanitie.

> Then doe your selfe, for dread of shame, forgoe
>> This evill manner, which ye here maintaine,
>> And doe in stead thereof mild curt'sie showe
>> To all, that passe.   (i.26–7)

Briana's discourtesy is to passers-by: Crudor's is to Briana herself, in the harsh conditions he makes for returning her love (15). Like Artegall, Calidore must use the sword, but his more characteristic weapons are graceful behaviour and eloquence. Calidore corrects the discourteous pair, meeting Briana whose name means 'shrill voice' (see note in Hamilton's edition on stanza 14, line 16) with gentle eloquence (26–8) and instructing Crudor (Lat. *crudus*, cruel, raw – suggesting an uncivilized man) in the civilized code of knighthood (41–2).

Similarly parallel, but adapted to their respective books, are the narratives of Tristram (6.ii.3–38) and Sir Sangliere (5.i.13–30). In both, a knight, tiring of his own lady, tries to take another man's love by force and then punishes his own. In both, his accuser is a squire whose vulnerability may seem at first sight no match against the power of the knight. The 'Squire in squallid weed' of Book 5 (i.13) is protected by the law in the person of Artegall, who establishes the truth, protects the weak and punishes the offender in an episode that exemplifies the skills of a justicer. In Book 6, the knight is guilty of extreme discourtesy rather than murder, and it is the squire who punishes him, by killing him, against the 'law of armes' (ii.7). Like Artegall, Calidore must discern the facts behind the appearance, but where in Book 5 the emphasis was on the astuteness of Artegall's judgement, in Book 6 it is on Calidore's courteous listening (ii.8, 13) and on his willingness to set aside the letter of the law of arms when he learns the facts of the knight's behaviour.

Artegall's and Calidore's spheres of action differ, though both are concerned with the breakdown of social bonds and obligations. Artegall establishes and defends the law, while Calidore must know how, in certain circumstances, to set it aside. By showing mercy to Crudor, Briana, at least, is drawn into the circle of gratitude and generosity that is the mark of true courtesy (i.45–6). In the case of Tristram, the codified law of arms must be set aside in favour of the natural law of courtesy which motivates the squire's actions.

Courtesy too can be codified, teaching ladies and knights 'to beare themselves aright/To all of each degree, as doth behove' (ii.1), but more felicitously it is a gift of nature:

> Thereto great helpe dame Nature selfe doth lend:
>> For some so goodly gratious are by kind,

152

Book 6

> That every action doth them much commend,
> And in the eyes of men great liking find;
> Which others, that have greater skill in mind,
> Though they enforce themselves, cannot attaine. (ii.2)

Tristram is an example of one endowed with gracefulness both by nature (ii.24) and by education (31). Revealingly, his perfect poise of natural and cultivated courtesy has been nurtured far from the Court (30–1), which, though it gives its name to the virtue (i.1), may also be the source of its corruptions (Proem 5). But Tristram's life of retirement does not give scope to the nobility of his nature. He aspires to the calling to which he was born, that of a knight (32–3), the embodiment of gentility of mind as well as of birth. In the fictional romance world of Book 6, nobility of birth is truly an indication of the gift of a noble spirit, though it does not guarantee the gifts of fortune.

CALEPINE AND TURPINE

1. Turpine's discourtesy

Much of the significance of Book 6 depends on carefully developed parallels and contrasts of episodes and characters. One of the most important of these is the relationship between Calidore and Calepine. They are linked by the first element in their names, which in Greek means 'beautiful' or 'good'. Calidore's name means beautiful or good gift; the second element in Calepine's name is less clear, perhaps suggesting the English verb 'pine' (see note in Hamilton's edition on iii.27). From canto iii (26) until canto ix, Calidore disappears from the narrative in pursuit of the Blatant Beast and it is Calepine who dominates the central cantos. It seems clear that the two knights are in some way complementary.

The relationship between them is to some extent clarified by the pairing of the stories of Aladine and Priscilla (ii.40–iii.19) and of Calepine, Serena and Turpine (iii.20–51). The discourteous knight killed by Tristram came upon Aladine and Priscilla in a glade of the wood 'in joyous jolliment/Of their franke loves, free from all gealous spyes' (ii.16) and rudely broke in upon them, wounding Aladine and causing Priscilla to flee into the wood for fear (18–20). Calidore finds the pair and assists them, demonstrating the generosity and the restorative powers of courtesy. As he tells Priscilla, it is no shame to carry a wounded knight:

153

> Faire Lady let it not you seeme disgrace,
> To beare this burden on your dainty backe;
> My selfe will beare a part, coportion of your packe.   (ii.47)

Nor does he disdain to set aside the strict, literal truth in order to restore Priscilla without loss of reputation to her father:

> Fearelesse, who ought did thinke, or ought did say,
> Sith his own thought he knew most cleare from wite.
> So as they past together on their way,
> He can devize this counter-cast of slight,
> To give faire colour to that Ladies cause in sight.   (iii.16)

Like Guazzo (quoted above, p. 146), who thought it 'commendable to coyne a lye at some time, and in some place, so that it tend to some honest ende' (I, 97), Calidore puts generosity before a strict legalism.

Scarcely has Calidore left Priscilla than he, like the discourteous knight, disturbs an unarmed knight resting 'In covert shade . . ./To solace with his Lady in delight' (iii.20). Calidore's inadvertent rudeness is not, of course, on a par with that of the discourteous knight and he is soon forgiven. But while he rests 'with delightfull pleasure' (22) with Calepine, Serena is attacked and wounded by the Blatant Beast (24). Calepine and the wounded Serena are less fortunate than Priscilla and the wounded Aladine; they encounter in their extremity not the courteous Calidore, who has gone belatedly in pursuit of the Blatant Beast, but Turpine, the most discourteous of knights.

The episodes shift the narrative from Calidore to Calepine, from celebration of the achievements of courtesy to a demonstration of discourtesy and its effects. As courtesy is most clearly seen when more is given than is deserved, so discourtesy is most exposed when it is a response to vulnerability, and even necessity is refused. The vulnerable role is given to Calepine. The more his care for Serena makes him dependent on the courtesy of others, the more cruel seems Turpine's discourtesy. Calidore retains the more heroic role of courtesy's champion.

Calepine's main function is to suffer at the hands of Turpine. The rhyming of their names elegantly reflects their pairing, the behaviour of the one in striking contrast to that of the other. Turpine's name means shameful (Lat. *turpis*) and this is his dominant characteristic. His knightly status does not in this case indicate nobility of mind. Spenser made a feature of Calidore's willingness humbly to bear the burden of the wounded Aladine (ii.47), and Calepine similarly does not hesitate to put the wounded Serena on his horse while he walks unceremoniously by her side (iii.27–8). Turpine refuses such aid with a stiff, legalistic arrogance:

> Perdy thou peasant Knight, mightst rightly reed
> Me then to be full base and evill borne,
> If I would beare behinde a burden of such scorne.   (iii.31)

His statement distorts the narrator's 'The gentle minde by gentle deeds is knowne' (iii.1); Turpine's understanding of gentility pays attention only to the appearance of social superiority without any of its moral substance. He fears the shame of compromising his social status and thus exposes his shamefulness.

The true difference between shameful grandeur and noble misery is made clear to us in the speaking pictures that juxtapose Turpine and his lady 'at bord' in their inhospitable castle (iii.42) with Calepine and Serena outside:

> So downe he tooke his Lady in distresse,
> And layd her underneath a bush to sleepe,
> Cover'd with cold, and wrapt in wretchednesse,
> Whiles he him selfe all night did nought but weepe,
> And wary watch about her for her safegard keepe.   (44)

Calepine feels shamed by being forced to bear Turpine's abuse without retaliation (iii.35–6, 47), and shameful indeed is his attempt in his utmost extremity to hide behind his lady's back (49), but it is Calepine's courtesy that has thus exposed him to unknightly recourses. The greater burden of shame is Turpine's for attacking the defenceless pair. Quite different is Turpine's recourse to a similar stratagem when in cowardly flight from Arthur he hides under his lady's skirts, shaming all knights 'with this knightlesse part' (vi.33).

2. The Savage Man

In his greatest need a providential fortune (iv.2, 15) brings to Calepine's aid an ally who is all that Turpine is not. Turpine has the status, the material possessions, the outward appearance of a knight while his nature is thoroughly base. The 'salvage man' appears little more than a beast, naked (iv.4) and without knowledge of arms nor, till now, of 'gentlesse' (3), but even in his savage breast Calepine's plight moves pity (3), telling us much about the worse savagery of the 'civilized' Turpine. The fundamental distinction between true baseness of behaviour and a mere physical appearance of baseness is again before us. The Savage Man does not hesitate to bestow all he has on Serena and Calepine, giving them willing service (12, 16).

What he offers them is 'base and meane' (15), but its bare sufficiency, graced by his hospitality, creates a primitive idyll in contrast to their previous night's lodging (see iii.44):

> To whom faire semblance, as he could, he shewed
> By signes, by lookes, and all his other gests.
> But the bare ground, with hoarie mosse bestrowed,
> Must be their bed, their pillow was unsowed,
> And the frutes of the forrest was their feast. (iv.14)

The forest has so far proved a beneficent place in Book 6. Its shades provide privacy (albeit vulnerable) for Aladine and Priscilla, and for Calepine and Serena, and within its confines Tristram and the Savage Man lead lives more virtuous than Turpine's in his castle. But the forest also harbours the Blatant Beast. Canto iv contrasts two images of the forest, both of which develop the themes of nature and nurture: the Savage Man, noble by nature and, in fact, by birth (v.2), though ignorant and brutish by nurture, and the 'cruell Beare' (17) from whose jaws Calepine rescues a little baby whom he then bestows for nurture on the wife of Sir Bruin, whose name is that commonly used of the brown bear.

The 'cruell Beare' is an image of the ferocity of savage nature; his 'bloodie jawes' (17) clamp the baby, and he turns on Calepine with 'greedie force/And furie' (20). Calepine attacks him with a ferocity which is in some respects savage: he uses not the weapon of civilization, the sword, but his hands, throttling the bear to death (22). When Calepine turns to the baby, Spenser's language shifts from the ferocious to the tender:

> Then tooke he up betwixt his armes twaine
> The litle babe, sweet relickes of his pray;
> Whom pitying to heare so sore complaine,
> From his soft eyes the teares he wypt away,
> And from his face the filth that did it ray. (23)

Like the Savage Man, but unlike the bear, Calepine can be savage in battle but gentle when his help is needed. The same combination of savagery and gentility is suggested by the name and history of Sir Bruin. His bear-like nature has been used for good, to subdue 'a foule feend' (31), 'a great Gyant, called *Cormoraunt*' (29) and to maintain his land, once gained, 'with peaceable estate,/And quietly' (30). The gentleness which controls the ferocity of Calepine, the Savage Man and Sir Bruin is seen to be the source of civilization, albeit a civilization that must be won and defended. Sir Bruin's fragile civilization is now threatened for want of an heir.

Book 6

The 'spotlesse spirit' (35) of the foundling child now bestowed on him is a blank. Good nurture may guide and direct the unformed child and turn him into either of those high achievements of civilization, a knight or a philosopher (35). But foundlings often prove to have a special genius – evidence that, as men's callings and gifts are god-given, 'the Gods', for exceptional purposes, use exceptional means:

> Therefore some thought, that those brave imps were sowen
> Here by the Gods, and fed with heavenly sap,
> That made them grow so high t'all honorable hap.　　　(36)

3. Arthur's intervention

Working still by juxtaposition of examples which show differing aspects of his central theme of nature and nurture, Spenser brings together the Savage Man, with his 'gentle' but 'undisciplynd' mind (v.i), and Arthur, the poem's outstanding example of nobility of nature, of birth and of nurture (see 1.ix.3–5). The prince and Timias come across the Savage Man courteously adjusting the harness of Serena's horse (v.10), though his act appears sinister to Timias, who discourteously intervenes (v.25). The Savage Man replies as his nurture prompts him:

> Gnashing his grinded teeth with griesly looke,
>> And sparkling fire out of his furious eyne,
>> Him with his fist unwares on th'head he strooke,
>> That made him downe unto the earth encline.　　　(26)

It is perhaps such a glimpse of his undisciplined spirit that makes Arthur reluctant to take the Savage Man as his companion (vi.18). The contrast between the two is evident once they enter Turpine's castle. Arthur is cautious and gives the occupants of the castle a chance to show hospitality (vi.20–1). The Savage Man's response to the sight of the porter laying hands on Arthur is impetuous and savage:

> And running streight upon that villaine base,
> Like a fell Lion at him fiercely flew,
> And with his teeth and nailes, in present vew,
> Him rudely rent, and all to peeces tore.　　　(22)

Arthur converts his victory over Turpine into a display of mercy far beyond the base knight's desert (vi.31, 36), while the Savage Man shows no mercy either to Turpine's men (vi.38) or to Turpine himself (40) until restrained by Arthur. Set against Arthur's courteous generosity, the Savage Man's 'gentle mynd' (v.i) is not enough; it teaches him only to succour the vulnerable. He knows nothing of the more difficult and God-like skill of benevolence to a foe.

But if the Savage Man falls short of Arthur's perfect courtesy, he nevertheless continues to compare well with Turpine, who lacks even the ferocity of a savage but untutored nature. His

> faintnesse and foule cowardize,
> Is greatest shame: for oft it falles, that strong
> And valiant knights doe rashly enterprize,
> Either for fame, or else for exercize,
> A wrongfull quarrell to maintaine by fight;
> Yet have, through prowesse and their brave emprize,
> Gotten great worship in this worldes sight.
> For greater force there needs to maintaine wrong, then right.   (35)

Arthur's words anticipate the next episode in Turpine's narrative, his meeting with the two 'youthly' knights who, merely for the adventure, 'In which they mote make triall of their might' (vii.5), undertake to attack Arthur for the craven Turpine. Misled they may be, but in contrast to Turpine there are at least signs of nobility of nature in their courage. This is confirmed by the surviving 'youthly' knight's, Sir Enias' (viii.4), response to Arthur's mercy (vii.12). Calidore had instructed Crudor in the benefits of courtesy: 'Who will not mercie unto others shew,/How can he mercy ever hope to have?' (i.42). Now we see this enacted. Arthur's mercy to Sir Enias produces a return of benevolence. Arthur, exposed to danger in his unprotected sleep (vii.18–19), is protected by Sir Enias' sense of obligation to him, 'the gentle knight/Would not be tempted to such villenie,/Regarding more his faith' (vii.23). Sir Enias' gentle response contrasts with that of Turpine, who, though under a similar obligation, is impervious to gratitude (22). If courtesy will not work on Turpine, then force must; mercy is not extended to him a second time (26–7).

Turpine's irredeemable baseness of nature and of manners is complemented by his lady, Blandina (Lat. *blandiri*, to soothe, to flatter). Earlier this lady's behaviour had seemed placatory (iii.32, 42), but in fact it consists of a merely superficial manipulation of the forms of courtesy:

> For well she knew the wayes to win good will
> Of every wight, that were not too infest,
> And how to please the minds of good and ill,
> Through tempering of her words and lookes by wondrous skill.
>
> Yet were her words and lookes but false and fayned.   (vi.41–2)

Book 6

Such skill is that 'forgerie,/Fashion'd to please the eies of them, that pas' (Proem 5) against which Spenser warned us. Blandina's self-serving sophistication is grafted on to a nature as base as Turpine's.

4. Serena's fortune

Serena's name seems to pair her with Blandina, as Calepine was paired with Turpine. Her name in Latin means clear, cloudless, serene, suggesting that we should find in her a genuine peacefulness as opposed to Blandina's mere false appearance of peace-making. But Serena's name belies her fortune and her state of mind for much of her narrative. She is caught by the Blatant Beast (iii.24), suffers with Calepine the miseries of Turpine's persecution, finds herself at the mercy of the Savage Man, is apparently abandoned by Calepine (v.4), and finally flees into 'wylde deserts' (viii.35) when her current protector, Timias, falls victim to Disdain (vii.50). Her state of mind during these misfortunes is far from serene (see, e.g., iii.45, iv.9, viii.33).

At two points in her narrative she does achieve a certain serenity of mind, and these are also the moments when she is in fact most vulnerable. As she wanders about the fields in the mild weather that echoes her name and suggests her state of mind (iii.23), she is taken by the Blatant Beast. Later, in the 'wylde deserts', she lies down to sleep. Spenser's language lulls us into the security Serena herself feels and then abruptly catapults us into her real danger:

> There whilest in *Morpheus* bosome safe she lay,
> Fearelesse of ought, that mote her peace molest,
> False Fortune did her safety betray.   (viii.34)

Our sense of the irony of Serena's fearlessness on this occasion is increased by our memory of her terror when confronted with the Savage Man in canto iv. On that occasion she was 'fearefully aghast' (9), though the Savage Man proved courteous and loyal. The danger that now disturbs her peace is 'a salvage nation' (viii.35) whose natures are as bad as that of the Savage Man was good. They represent man in his lowest and most depraved form, whose society is based on 'stealth and spoile' (viii.35) and whose religion is a superstitious cannibalism (38). As these savages survey their victim with a lustful appetite, Spenser's language disconcertingly echoes the sensual language of the biblical Song of Solomon:

> Her goodly thighes, whose glorie did appeare
> Like a triumphall Arch, and thereupon
> The spoiles of Princes hang'd, which were in battel won.   (42)

Thy necke is as the towre of David built for defence: a thousand shieldes hang therein, and all the targets of the strong men.

(Song of Solomon 4.4)

The Geneva gloss tells us that the Song shows the 'perfect love of Jesus Christ' to the faithful soul, whom he enriches 'of his pure bounty and grace without any of her deservings'. Spenser's language, by implication, sets the depraved lustful religion of the cannibals, about to sacrifice Serena, against the true religion of Christ, whose sacrifice of love was of a quite different kind.

In spite of the 'wretched stormes' (viii.47) which seem to overcast her fortunes, Serena's narrative in fact shows a beneficent providence. At her moments of greatest need she is rescued, as she is now from the savage nation by Sir Calepine, driven to the spot 'by chaunce, more then by choyce' (46). The faith Serena earlier showed when she commended herself 'To Gods sole grace' (iv.10) is amply justified by her narrative. Serena's name in relation to her fortunes does prove significant. She epitomizes the reiterated examples throughout the book of the dangers of repose, of an unwary serenity; but she also serves to prove, within the romance fiction of the book, that such trust and innocent repose are divinely protected, whatever their vulnerability to the discourtesies of men.

THE BLATANT BEAST

Elyot wrote that, while benevolence is the characteristic virtue of God, 'the devil is hated and reproved both of God and man for his malice, which vice is contrarious and repugnant to benevolence' (see p. 147 above). In Spenser's poem, the Blatant Beast, by contrast to the 'heavenly seed' of courtesy (Proem 3), derives from Hell,

> Where he was fostred long in *Stygian* fen,
> Till he to perfect ripenesse grew, and then
> Into this wicked world he forth was sent,
> To be the plague and scourge of wretched men:
> Whom with vile tongue and venemous intent
> He sore doth wound, and bite, and cruelly torment.

(i.8; cf. Proem 4)

In canto vi, the Hermit gives the Blatant Beast a slightly different, though still Hellish, genealogy. Its mother is Echidna, who seems from the front

> A faire young Mayden, full of comely glee;
> But all her hinder parts did plaine expresse
> A monstrous Dragon, full of fearefull uglinesse.

(vi.10)

Book 6

Its father is 'cruell *Typhaon*', known for his 'tempestuous rage' (vi.11). This variation comes, suggestively, just before Arthur's encounter with Turpine and Blandina, faint reflections of the infernal malice of the Blatant Beast's parentage. However craven Turpine himself, the power which he commands attacks Arthur with strokes 'That on his shield did rattle like to haile/In a great tempest' (vi.26), while his lady shows on the surface 'courteous glee', but falseness and malice come behind (vi.41–2). Turpine and his lady, it seems, are two of the many manifestations of the Blatant Beast in this world.

We only gradually build up a full understanding of the Blatant Beast's significance. It is spiteful and malicious (i.9), its wounds those of infamy (vi.1), and it uses its poisonous tongue 'Gainst all, both good and bad, both most and least' (vi.12), whereas courtesy maintains and observes the decorums of distinctions, teaching us how to behave 'to low, to hie;/To friends, to foes' (x.23). It seems to attack innocent victims, Artegall, Serena and Timias; only gradually do we realize that those it bites contribute in some way to their own suffering. The benevolent Hermit shows Serena and Timias, by the art of words, not of medicine, how to cure themselves:

> If therefore health ye seeke, observe this one.
> First learne your outward sences to refraine
> From things, that stirre up fraile affection;
> Your eies, your eares, your tongue, your talke restraine
> From that they most affect, and in due termes containe. (vi.7)

The Blatant Beast signifies the malice, spite or infamy of others that causes loss of honour or reputation, but for the venom to work there must be some fault, however mild.

Serena was bitten as she wandered through the pleasant fields, 'as liking led/Her wavering lust after her wandring sight' (iii.23). The language suggests the dangers of such an unreflecting pursuit of delight. She is exposed in a moment of incautious sensual repose, as so many others are in Book 6. Where Priscilla was rescued from a similar lapse by the courteous Calidore, who restored her without loss of reputation to her parents (iii.15–19), Serena is not so fortunate, and the wound of the Blatant Beast to her reputation is left to fester.

Timias' fault is of a similar kind. The long narrative of his love for Belphoebe, which began in Book 3 (v) and continued in Book 4 (vii–viii), is now concluded. Timias (Gk *timē*, honour) has found 'happie blisse' (6.v.12) with Belphoebe, but however virtuous their love, it is susceptible to infamy, and, more seriously, it keeps Timias in the forest, spending his days hunting, instead of by Arthur's side in the selfless but supremely honourable duties of knight errantry. Unlike Tristram (ii.32–3), Timias seems content with such recreation until attacked by the Blatant Beast and its three companions, the first two of which, *Despetto* (Despite) and *Decetto* (Deceit), seem to represent aspects of the malignity of others, while the third, the 'spightfullest' (v.13), *Defetto* (Fault), may allude to imperfections in Timias himself. Arthur's rescue of him from his enemies restores him to his calling as a squire, but damage has been done and lingers both in the bite of the Blatant Beast and in the state of Timias' affections. His response to the open love of Arthur (v.23) seems to refer more to his regret at leaving Belphoebe than to his feelings at refinding his master:

> But shedding few soft teares from tender eyne,
> His deare affect with silence did restraine,
> And shut up all his plaint in privy paine. (24)

Serena and Timias are unsound within and without, in virtue and in reputation, when they arrive at the Hermit's cell. The Hermit speaks to them with authority because he is their antithesis, a man sound in reputation and virtue. Spenser emphasizes this point by telling us about him twice from different points of view:

> And soothly it was sayd by common fame,
> So long as age enabled him thereto,
> That he had bene a man of mickle name,
> Renowmed much in armes and derring doe: (v.37)

> For whylome he had bene a doughty Knight,
> As any one, that lived in his daies,
> And proved oft in many perillous fight,
> Of which he grace and glory wonne alwaies,
> And in all battels bore away the baies. (vi.4)

The first account tells us of his reputation, the second of the fact. This is no knight who retires for recreation in the prime of manhood, but one who turns from the active to the contemplative life when his strength has gone. Even in his retirement he gives willingly of his gifts to the suffering Serena and Timias.

MIRABELLA

Mirabella is not bitten by the Blatant Beast, but she suffers from two of its manifestations; 'foule *Infamie*, and fell *Despight*' (vii.34) are her accusers before Cupid. The second is an aspect of her own behaviour (vii.30, or viii.21). Though of 'meane parentage', she is endowed with 'wondrous giftes of natures grace' (vii.28), but she misuses them to cause suffering and fuel her own pride (29). She is merciless, inviting the grim logic of which Calidore warned Crudor: 'Who will not mercie unto others shew,/ How can he mercy ever hope to have?' (i.42). When brought to trial, her weeping is 'of no man mercifide' (vii.32). Cupid, however, does show some mercy and responds to her pleas for 'mercie' (36) by mitigating in some degree what remains a severe though just sentence (vii.37).

In the midst of the serious and painful romance narratives of Timias, Turpine and Serena, the story of Mirabella seems strangely out of place, an old-fashioned Court of Love narrative told in a simple allegorical manner. The effect is partly to lighten the mood and prepare our minds for the topic of love shortly to be more fully developed in the narrative of Calidore's wooing of Pastorella (canto ix). But this account of a mythical god's justice and its effects is, I believe, deliberately set apart in manner from the Christian frame of reference of the romance narratives. Mirabella must follow through the logic of her transgression and its punishment to the bitter end. She is unable to accept the grace offered by Arthur:

> Nor heavens, nor men can me most wretched mayd
> Deliver from the doome of my desart,
> The which the God of love hath on me layd,
> And damned to endure this direfull smart,
> For penaunce of my proud and hard rebellious hart.
>
> (viii.19; and see 30)

The language is religious, but the logic of law and penance is distant from the Protestant vocabulary of Grace. Mirabella cannot free herself from disdain and scorn because by this time they are aspects of herself: she is punished by her own self-disdain.

The situation with Timias and Sir Enias, both of whom also fall victim to Disdain and Scorn, is different. In both cases, Arthur's love, which overlooks blame, is an important detail. Seeing Sir Enias, who had not long before tried to kill him, made captive by Scorn, Arthur intervenes 'to save his friend from jeopardy' (viii.12). His action is fully effective. Timias is also freed by Arthur, but he is unwilling to make himself known so overwhelmed is he by shame (27). Arthur's response is as unjudgementally loving as it was when he refound him in the forest after his long period of truancy with Belphoebe: he 'him did oft embrace, and oft admire,/Ne could with seeing satisfie his great desire' (viii.27; and see v. 23). It seems probable that, like Mirabella, both Sir Enias and Timias are punished by their own self-disdain and self-scorn for past errors. Unlike Mirabella, they occupy a Christian frame of reference and can be freed by the Christ-like benevolence of Arthur.

CALIDORE AND THE SHEPHERDS

1. The pastoral idyll

The pastoral idyll of cantos ix and x is preceded and concluded by two grim episodes, the cannibals (canto viii), and the brigands (cantos x and xi). The songs, the simple hospitality and the security of the shepherds contrast with the darkness (viii.48; x.42) and horror of the framing episodes. The effect is to stress the vulnerability as well as the delight of the idyll. It seems to us, as to Calidore, a place of temporary sweetness and rest.

We have learned throughout the book, however, that such repose is perilous, morally and physically. While pursuing the Blatant Beast, Calidore had not rested himself, 'For dread of daunger, not to be redrest,/If he for slouth forslackt so famous quest' (ix.3). When he does 'forslack' the quest, the narrator sternly points out his moral failing:

> Who now does follow the foule *Blatant Beast*,
>> Whilest *Calidore* does follow that faire Mayd,
>> Unmyndfull of his vow and high beheast,
>> Which by the Faery Queene was on him layd. (x.1)

Calidore is wrong to abandon the quest, but his attraction to the innocent delights of the shepherds' life seems hard to condemn. The shepherds seem to represent that 'lowly stalke' (Proem 4) from which courtesy blossoms. They show a simple hospitality to Calidore (ix.6, 16–17), they are pious (6 and 21), and, in Meliboe's case at least, content with their humble lot (20–5). But such a life, for all its virtues, is not that to which Calidore is called. To Meliboe, each man's vocation is given him by heaven and contentment lies in his willing acceptance of it: 'It is the mynd, that maketh good or ill,/That maketh wretch or happie, rich or poore' (30). Calidore distorts Meliboe's words to make of them an excuse for abandoning his quest:

> Since then in each mans selfe (said *Calidore*)
>> It is, to fashion his owne lyfes estate,
>> Give leave awhyle, good father, in this shore
>> To rest my barcke. (31)

Calidore falls victim to that 'heathenish opinion of men which thinke,

that the particular condition and state of man in this life comes by
. . . the bare wil and pleasure of man himselfe' (see p. 149 above).

Yet, as the narrator acknowledges, 'Ne certes mote he greatly
blamed be,/From so high step to stoupe unto so low' (x.3). In spite
of his truancy, he receives from the shepherds many gifts: an example
of simple courtesy in Meliboe, a glimpse of Colin's vision in canto
x, and above all Pastorella's love. His love for Pastorella is virtuous
and apparently providential. She, we discover, is a foundling (ix.14)
whose 'rare demeanure' makes her, in Calidore's eyes, 'a Princes
Paragone' (ix.11). We subsequently learn of course that her birth is
indeed noble (xii.15). Pastorella's mind aspires beyond her rustic
suitors (ix.10), but this, we can see in retrospect, reflects her gifts of
birth and her destiny; it is not, like Mirabella's disdain for her
suitors, an effect of selfish arrogance (cf. viii.21).

Love, the narrator tells us in Book 3, is a 'sweet fit'

> that doth true beautie love,
> And choseth vertue for his dearest Dame,
> Whence spring all noble deeds and never dying fame.   (3.iii.1)

In striving to please Pastorella, Calidore exerts himself 'With all kind
courtesies, he could invent' (ix.34), with increasing success. His first
attempts at a courtly courtesy move her not at all: 'His layes, his
loves, his lookes she did them all despize' (35). Doffing his armour,
he humbles himself not only in doing her service but in commending
his loutish rival (37, 39–44) and in so doing sows the seeds of love
(45–6). However, not until Pastorella, attacked by a lion and abandoned by the loutish Coridon, is rescued by Calidore (x.35–7), does
he win a full return of his love: on this occasion love inspires 'noble
deeds' rather than graceful manners. But Calidore's response to
her favour still seems unworthy. Like Aladine and Calepine he tries
to enjoy his love hidden from the sight of others, even using the
cowardly Coridon for that end, 'That by his fellowship, he colour
might/Both his estate, and love from skill of any wight' (x.37; and
cf. ii.16; iii.20).

Calidore's mildly aberrant secrecy is exceeded far by the brigands
who carry Pastorella and the other shepherds to

> hollow caves, that no man mote discover
> For the thicke shrubs, which did them alwaies shade
> From view of living wight, and covered over:
> But darkenesse dred and daily night did hover
> Through all the inner parts, wherein they dwelt.   (x.42)

The isolation of the place reflects the uncivility of the men, who, like

the cannibals, prey on others for a living (x.39). Such a place of evil
and darkness seems to Pastorella like Hell itself, 'where with such
damned fiends she should in darknesse dwell' (x.43), or a kind of
death (xi.23, 50). From such a negation of life and humanity,
Pastorella is rescued by the power of love, first by the brigand
captain, whom love so inspires that 'minding more her safety then
himselfe,/His target always over her pretended' (xi.19) and, more
effectively, by Calidore, for whom love and his duty as a knight at
last coincide. The image of Calidore setting out for the rescue
corrects all that was amiss in his behaviour: this time he is guided by
God, he uses Coridon for honourable ends, and he wears his knight's
armour below his shepherd clothes:—

> So forth they goe together (God before)
>   Both clad in shepheards weeds agreeably,
>   And both with shepheards hookes: But *Calidore*
>   Had underneath, him armed privily.   (xi.36)

2. Colin Clout and the Graces

Places of retirement and privacy have repeatedly been places of
moral and physical peril throughout Book 6, yet its core canto
celebrates a retreat where the Graces themselves, the source of true
courtesy, dance for Colin Clout. Calidore interrupts Colin's 'blisse'
(x.29) as he interrupted Calepine and Serena's (iii.21), but the two
cases are quite different. Calepine like Calidore is a knight, called
to a life of active questing in the world; Colin is a poet whose inspiration and imagination must be nurtured in retirement. The distinction
between the two callings helps to explain the sudden vanishing of the
Graces at Calidore's approach: in spite of his truancy, a glimpse of
the visionary perfection of the Graces is one of the gifts a benevolent
providence bestows on Calidore through the shepherds, but no more
than a glimpse is possible for a knight whose calling is to a life of
action.

As love inspires Calidore's return to heroic virtue, so it inspires
Colin's vision. In the midst of the circling rings of 'naked maidens
lilly white' (x.11) and the Graces themselves, 'handmaides of *Venus*'
(15) is a mere 'countrey lasse' (25), and it is to her alone that Colin
pipes (15); his gifts of imagination and music can transform the
ordinary into the divine. But, although cultivated in retirement,
Colin's gifts extend beyond the private to the public. Colin sees not
only his transformed love, but the nature of the Graces themselves,
and, reluctantly but courteously, he communicates his vision to

166

Calidore. Wholly delightful as his private vision of his love is, Colin must turn from it to assume the calling of poet as teacher. Comparing the poet to the lawyer, Sidney wrote that the latter

> doth not endeavour to make men good, but that their evil hurt not others; having no care, so he be a good citizen, how bad a man he be: . . . so is he not in the deepest truth to stand in rank with these [poets] who all endeavour to take naughtiness away and plant goodness even in the secretest cabinet of our souls. *(Apologie* p. 106)

Poetry's civilizing power relates it closely to courtesy.

Poets 'plant goodness in . . . our souls' by creating a golden world *(Apology* p. 100). For Colin's vision Spenser employs his most golden art, setting it in an earthly paradise, 'mount *Acidale*' (6–9), associated in Greek mythology with Venus and the Graces. The dance of the maidens and Graces around Colin's love outgoes the similar circle of rustic shepherds around Pastorella (ix.8), as that in turn transformed the image of the savage circle of the cannibals around Serena (viii.39). We move from the gaze of lust, to the admiration of earthly charms, to a visionary perfection. It is in this setting that Colin unfolds the nature and the gifts of the Graces (22–4).

I have discussed the implications of the Graces' gifts in my introduction to Book 6 and through the narratives. A word needs to be said about the Graces' appearance and their dance. Colin himself explains each detail of the vision:

> Therefore they alwaies smoothly seeme to smile,
>   That we likewise should mylde and gentle be,
>   And also naked are, that without guile
>   Or false dissemblaunce all them plaine may see.
>   Simple and true from covert malice free:
>   And eeke them selves so in their daunce they bore,
>   That two of them still froward seem'd to bee,
>   But one still towards shew'd her selfe afore;
> That good should from us goe, then come in greater store. (24)

The dance is ambiguous. In the first (1596) edition of the poem, line 7 reads 'two of them still *forward* seem'd to bee' (my italics), which is in conflict with the forward-looking Grace of the eighth line. The ambiguity of their position, whether two coming towards us, or two going away, is echoed by the ambiguity of the last line. Common sixteenth-century usage would allow 'then' to mean 'than', so that, with an alteration to the punctuation, the last line could read 'good should from us goe than come, in greater store'. The ambiguities are, I think, fruitful. The Graces may come towards us, or go from us 'in greater store'. In Book 6, the good that is given is often doubly rewarded (the good comes towards us 'in greater store') whether by providence, or by the gratitude of the recipients (e.g., i.46; vii.21–3). On the other hand, we should give (the Graces should go from us) 'in greater store' than we expect to receive.

THE CAPTURE OF THE BLATANT BEAST

Restored to the integrity of his knightly calling, Calidore returns to his quest (xii.22). The measure of his truancy is the damage the Beast has done in his absence. The evil it represents, infamy that feeds on its victims' faults, has been carried to the very heart of the nation's spiritual life, the Church. Spenser's language of monks and images (24–5) makes it clear that he alludes to the evils of Roman Catholicism, whose notoriety provoked the extreme reaction of wholesale demolition of churches and secularization of church land (see notes in Hamilton's edition on stanzas 23 and 25).

Spenser now, for the first time, describes the Blatant Beast's appearance, which consists mainly of mouth in which are iron teeth and the tongues of many beasts (27), among them those of serpents:

> That spat out poyson and gore bloudy gere
> At all, that came within his ravenings,
> And spake licentious words, and hatefull things
> Of good and bad alike, of low and hie. (28)

The details take us back to the final episodes of Book 5, in which the Blatant Beast's companion, Envy, spat out of her mouth a 'halfe-gnawen snake' (5.xii.39) whose bite wounded Artegall. Traditionally Envy was associated with the many-headed Hydra, whose defeat was one of Hercules' labours (Aptekar pp. 206–14). The Blatant Beast itself is now likened to the Hydra (32). The final episode links Books 5 and 6 as the earliest episodes did. Artegall, a second Hercules throughout his quest (Aptekar chaps. 10–12), will not, or cannot, overcome Envy. That is for Calidore, whose particular weapons of courteous behaviour and, particularly, words are more appropriate antidotes to the Beast's many tongues. Spenser uses another Herculean analogy for Calidore: he drags the captured and muzzled Beast behind him on a chain as Hercules did Cerberus when he brought him from Hades to the light of day (35). The image faintly recalls another iconographical association of Hercules, as Eloquence, who held his listeners' ears as though with chains of gold and silver (Nohrnberg p. 376, and footnote 174). But the Blatant Beast is not a willing follower of Calidore, and his binding relies on force rather than eloquence. Honest words are weak instruments; even Colin Clout's eloquence charms rather than instructs Calidore (x.30). More powerful are the Blatant Beast's 'licentious words' (28) and calumnies, which, when he again gets loose, ravage the works of 'gentle Poets' (40) and particularly 'this homely verse' (41).

Chapter 7

THE *MUTABILITIE CANTOS*

> From these kind *turns* and *circulation*
> *Seasons* proceed and *generation*.
> This makes the spring to yield us flowers,
> And melts the clouds to gentle showers.
> The *summer* thus matures all seeds
> And ripens both the corn and weeds.
> This brings on *autumn*, which recruits
> Our old, spent store with new fresh fruits.
> And the cold *winters* blustering season
> Hath snow and storms for the same reason.
> This *temper* and wise *mixture* breed
> And bring forth every living *seed*.
> And when their *strength* and *substance* spend
> (For while they *live*, they drive and tend
> Still to a *change*,) it takes them hence
> And shifts their *dress*; and to our sense
> Their *course* is over, as their *birth*:
> And hid from us, they turn to earth.
> But all this while the *Prince* of life
> Sits without *loss*, or *change*, or *strife*:
> Holding the *reins*, by which all move;
> (And those his *wisdom, power, love*
> And *justice* are;)[1]

INTRODUCTION

1. The *Mutabilitie Cantos*

The 'Two Cantos of Mutabilitie', with a fragmentary third, were
first published in 1609, ten years after Spenser's death, with the note
that they 'both for Forme and Matter, appeare to be parcell of some
following Booke of the *Faerie Queene*, under the Legend of *Constancie*'.
No more is known about them than that. Even the division into cantos may not be by Spenser himself. The stanza form, the theme and
the mode of these cantos all suggest that they are a continuation of
the main poem, possibly the 'core cantos' of a seventh book, with as
rich a mixture of philosophy, myth and allegory as the Garden of
Adonis (3.vi) or Colin Clout's vision of the Graces (6.x). There are,

however, problems with such a view. Unlike the 'core cantos' of other books, they take up two cantos, not one, and there are no knights or such figures as could carry the narrative beyond the confines of Arlo Hill. The *Mutabilitie Cantos* are complete in themselves, with Mutability's challenge and trial, the Faunus episode and the poet's final prayer relating closely to one another as parts of a magnificently inclusive meditation on, and celebration of, time and flux. Rather than as fragments of a seventh book, it is tempting to see them as an epilogue to the poem, a final comment on all that has gone before, moving us from the things of this world to those of the next;[2] or as a gesture to indicate the impossibility of completeness, 'offered in lieu of any continuation of the poem' (Nohrnberg p. 85).

2. Mutability

Mutability is one of the great topics of Western literature, and Spenser draws for his version on a wide range of established traditions. His methods, as always, are thoroughly eclectic, gathering material, images, motifs, from the past to transform them into his own, richly allusive whole. Such renewal of the past is part of the very process of mutability and of its opposite, permanence. Spenser is ever conscious that writing itself, working through change, may defeat time's depredations. His own 'great dame *Nature*' (vii.5) derives, as Spenser himself tells us, from Chaucer and beyond him from Alain de Lille (vii.9). Like theirs, Spenser's is 'vicaire of the almyghty Lord' (*Parliament of Fowls* l. 379) and sits in judgement over a process whose orderly outcome will ensure the perpetual renewal of the cycle of the seasons and of generation.

Mutability moved the Elizabethans to an eloquence that was both elegiac and celebratory, typified by Shakespeare's image of 'summer's green all girded up in sheaves/Borne on the bier with white and bristly beard' (Sonnet 12); time is a bringer of harvest and of death. Such paradoxes are part of the traditions which Spenser inherits. For Boethius, in his very influential *Consolation of Philosophy* (sixth century AD), change itself changes according to the perspective from which it is viewed. To mortals in the midst of flux, all seems capricious, subject to the Wheel of Fortune, which ensures, like Mutability's great cycles, that 'nothing here long standeth in one stay' (vii.47). Philosophy teaches Boethius to look beyond, to the perspectives of fate and providence which resolve the apparent flux into a preordained, God-guided pattern (Book 4, prose 6). Seen from this perspective, mutability becomes not a threat to order, but the source of nature's abundance, celebrated by Philosophy in the song from which I quote at the head of this chapter, in which change is in the hands of God, who 'Sits without *loss*, or *change*, or *strife*'. Seen as providence, flux becomes an ordered flexibility revealing God's infinite beauty, though often experienced by mortals as death and disorder. 'It is the Nature of all created beings, to hasten unto their change and fall', wrote Justus Lipsius in *De Constantia* (1583), yet 'I apprehend no beauty any where in this great frame without variety, and a distinct succession and change of things.'[3]

The great poet of change was Ovid, whose *Metamorphoses* (first century AD) transforms, in a seemingly infinite variety of examples, the central motif of matter's protean instability. Ovid puts his theme into the mouth of Pythagoras: 'Nothing is constant in the whole world. Everything is in a state of flux, and comes into being as a transient appearance.'[4] The planets and seasons, the ages of men and of nations, all are included in the ceaseless mutability. Ovid translates this philosophy into story after story, some comic, some tragic, of an animate nature in which rivers appear as nymphs and mortal men and women may become birds or trees or rocks. As part of that process of continual change, Spenser transforms Pythagoras' evidence of continual flux into his own poetry to form part of Mutability's own case (vii.18–31; cf. *Metamorphoses* 15.199–251). Spenser himself reworks Ovid's matter throughout the *Mutabilitie Cantos*, most notably producing an Ovidian myth of his own in the story of Faunus and Molanna.

VERSIONS OF THE FALL: CANTO vi

Mutability's ascent from 'hellish dungeons' (vi.27) to the earth, and from thence to the sphere of the moon (8) and even to '*Joves* high Palace' (23) is a form of fall, re-enacting that high aspiring ascent which, according to Ovid (*Metamorphoses* 1.151–62), her ancestors, the Titans, attempted by heaping up huge mountains in order to bring disorder to the very heavens. This is not, understandably, the version of the Titans' fall which Mutability uses for her case (vi.26–7; vii.16), but it was the best-known version and would have been in every reader's mind. The rebellion of the Titans was seen as the primal challenge to order and justice (cf. 5.i.9), the classical equivalent of Satan's aspiration and fall.

The seriousness of Mutability's effect is suggested by some of the language:

> For, she the face of earthly things so changed,
>   That all which Nature had establisht first

> In good estate, and in meet order ranged,
> She did pervert, and all their statutes burst:
> And all the worlds faire frame (which none yet durst
> Of Gods or men to alter or misguide)
> She alter'd quite, and made them all accurst
> That God had blest.　　　　　　　　　　　　　　(5)

In this view, she is the agent, even perhaps the instigator, of the Fall of man and the loss of Paradise. But, paradoxically, when Spenser describes Mutability herself, he abandons such a grim and tragic note. She and the gods are comic figures, robustly physical. Mutability climbs to Cynthia's sphere (8) and lays hold of that goddess 'To pluck her downe perforce from off her chaire' (13). Cynthia stoutly replies, and 'Bade her attonce from heavens coast to pack' (12). The language is mock-heroic, mixing grandeur with colloquialism, and no tragedy, beyond Cynthia's temporary eclipse (14–15), ensues from the Titaness' boldness, in spite of Jove's intention:

> With that, he shooke
> His Nectar-deawed locks, with which the skyes
> And all the world beneath for terror quooke,
> And eft his burning levin-brond in hand he tooke.
>
> But, when he looked on her lovely face,
> In which, faire beames of beauty did appeare,
> That could the greatest wrath soone turne to grace
> (Such sway doth beauty even in Heaven beare)
> He staide his hand.　　　　　　　　　　　　　　(30–1)

The parenthetical line in stanza 31 slyly reminds us of Jove's notorious susceptibility to beauty. On Jove, too, Mutability has a demonstrable effect and he changes his mind. The comedy gives us a benign superiority to both Jove and Mutability, allowing, for a while, the grim implications of change with which the canto began to remain half hidden.

As befits his theme, Spenser digresses from the story of Mutability, to

> tell how *Arlo* through *Dianaes* spights
> (Beeing of old the best and fairest Hill
> That was in all this holy-Islands hights)
> Was made the most unpleasant, and most ill.　　　(37)

Spenser changes his muse (37), his subject and his mode, from mock-heroic to a simple pastoralism, but change reveals order and this tale too is to be about a fall and a paradise lost in which, once again, Cynthia (who is also Diana) will be implicated. Where, in the first part

173

of canto vi, we moved from a note of tragedy to one of comedy, in the tale of Faunus we move from comedy to at least a hint of grimmer realities.

Spenser has borrowed details from a number of Ovidian tales for this episode, most important being the grim tale of Actaeon, a young huntsman who while out with his hounds accidentally comes upon Diana bathing in a secret pool. As a punishment for seeing her naked, Diana sprinkles him with drops from the pool which transform him into a stag and he is torn to pieces by his own hounds (*Metamorphoses* 3.138–252). Spenser's version seems in many ways a parody. Not the noble Actaeon, but the foolish wood god Faunus, peeps from his hiding-place at the naked Diana, betraying himself with a foolish laugh:

> There *Faunus* saw that pleased much his eye,
> And made his hart to tickle in his brest,
> That for great joy of some-what he did spy,
> He could him not containe in silent rest;
> But breaking forth in laughter, loud profest
> His foolish thought. A foolish *Faune* indeed.   (46)

Faunus' punishment is reminiscent of Actaeon's, though less tragic in its outcome (50, 52). Faunus' vulgar intrusion into Diana's privacy is clearly reminiscent of Mutability's. Both reveal their earthy understandings, unable to raise their minds to the decorum of the heavens, and Faunus' humiliation prefigures Mutability's. But both represent a principle of vitality, in Faunus' case particularly sexual vitality. Diana's maidens, against their will, cannot geld Faunus, because 'that same would spill/The Wood-gods breed, which must for ever live' (50). Where Diana and her maidens are virginal, denying sexual pleasure, Faunus furthers it, promising, and keeping his promise, to Molanna to make her the lover of Fanchin (44, 53).

It is Faunus who transforms Molanna's fall to a fertile resolution (53). The course of her stream from its source in 'two marble Rocks' (41) to the 'pleasant Plaine' (53) it waters, imitates her career from chaste companion to the lofty Diana to wife of Fanchin. Diana's response to her transgression, though lawful and chaste, is apt to seem destructive and indeed tragic. She stones Molanna and abandons the lovely Arlo:

> Them all, and all that she so deare did way,
> Thence-forth she left; and parting from the place,
> There-on an heavy haplesse curse did lay,
> To weet, that Wolves, where she was wont to space,
> Should harbour'd be, and all those Woods deface,
> And Thieves should rob and spoile that Coast around.   (55)

Molanna's fertility pours itself out in a savage land of disorder and crime, the Ireland whose wasted riches Spenser mourns in *View* (e.g., p. 19). Those riches are wasted by Faunus' and Molanna's un-reflecting self-gratification, but Diana is not Jove, still less the God of Nature, and it is difficult not to see her action, with whatever implications for Elizabethan policy in Ireland, as creating a worse disorder than it punishes.

NATURE'S COURT OF LAW: CANTO vii

Nature's entry restores Arlo, indeed gives it a new splendour:

> And thither also came all other creatures,
>   What-ever life or motion doe retaine,
>   According to their sundry kinds of features:
>   That *Arlo* scarsly could them all containe;
>   So full they filled every hill and Plaine:
>   And had not *Natures* Sergeant (that is *Order*)
>   Them well disposed by his busie paine,
>   And raunged farre abroad in every border,
> They would have caused much confusion and disorder.   (vii.4)

God's vicar, Nature, achieves what eluded Spenser and his fellow-colonizers, the miraculous transformation of Ireland into a place of abundance and order. With her entry, too, Spenser's style changes, rising 'in bigger noates' (1) to imitate the splendour and decorum of the occasion. Nature herself is rendered mysterious and comprehen-sive by the language of paradox:

> Great *Nature*, ever young yet full of eld,
> Still mooving, yet unmoved from her sted;
> Unseene of any, yet of all beheld.   (13)

In the presence of such a deity, even Mutability transforms herself from a bold parvenu to the mistress of infinite richness and beauty, unfolded, inevitably, in a self-revealing order.

The centrepiece of Mutability's case is the pageant of the seasons (28–31) and the months of the year (32–43), and like all her evidence it turns against her. Sherman Hawkins has pointed out that the cycle of the months was traditionally regarded as the best evidence of God's divine plan, especially when it begins, as Mutability's does, in March, the month of the Annunciation, the beginning of the church year.[5] Mutability's proof of endless change becomes, as the months pass by 'in order' (32), a demonstration of God's plan. Each month brings with it the delights of its season, accompanied by labourers who work cheerfully to fulfil the cycles of sowing and harvest, youth, age and birth. Even Mutability's curse of age and death seems, in this pageant, softened by the fantasy of February's chariot and his readiness to begin the cycle anew:

> And lastly, came cold *February*, sitting
>> In an old wagon, for he could not ride;
>> Drawne of two fishes for the season fitting,
>> Which through the flood before did softly slyde
>> And swim away: yet had he by his side
>> His plough and harnesse fit to till the ground,
>> And tooles to prune the trees, before the pride
>> Of hasting Prime did make them burgein round:
> So past the twelve Months forth, and their dew places found.   (43)

In the *Consolation*, Philosophy teaches Boethius that a hidden order, not immediately apparent to the ignorant understanding of mortals, but accessible through reason and faith, guides our world of degeneration and injustice according to a good and providential plan (Book 4, prose 6). It is that ability to look beyond the mere senses that Mutability lacks. Like Faunus she sees and responds sensually, not rationally: 'But what we see not, who shall us perswade?' (49). It is on this principle that she marshals her evidence. Jove's case is more metaphysical:

>> But, who is it (to me tell)
> That *Time* himselfe doth move and still compell
> To keepe his course?   (48)

Such dry reasoning carries no weight with Mutability. Nature, however, does not rely on her senses, 'But with firme eyes affixt, the ground still viewed' (57). Her judgement, given in just two stanzas, confirms the perspective of providence whose instrument is fate, but introduces a new element, the promise of an end to time:

> I well consider all that ye have sayd,
>> And find that all things stedfastnes doe hate
>> And changed be: yet being rightly wayd
>> They are not changed from their first estate;
>> But by their change their being doe dilate:
>> And turning to themselves at length againe,
>> Doe worke their owne perfection so by fate:
>> Then over them Change doth not rule and raigne;
> But they raigne over change, and doe their states maintaine.

> Cease therefore daughter further to aspire,
>> And thee content thus to be rul'd by me:

176

> For thy decay thou seekst by thy desire;
> But time shall come that all shall changed bee,
> And from thenceforth, none no more change shall see. (58–9)

Even Mutability recognizes such final authority and is 'put downe and whist' (59).

In the final stanzas, the voice of the poet is that of the regenerate Christian who longs, as does Redcrosse on the Mount of Contemplation after his view of the glorious New Jerusalem, never to 'turne againe/Backe to the world, whose joyes so fruitlesse are' (1.x.63). Redcrosse's rejection of the world comes just one stanza after he has asked with regret 'But deeds of armes must I at last be faine,/And Ladies love to leave so dearely bought?' (1.x.62). But Mutability transforms love and success into loss and death. Both aspects are evident throughout the *Mutabilitie Cantos*; however, in the two final stanzas we are made strikingly aware of their effect on the poet and his poem. In the *Mutabilitie Cantos*, Spenser has harnessed and imitated Mutability's vitality and creative energy, her copiousness and variety of effect, to produce a work of great beauty, but it is left 'unperfite': the cantos are an emblem of both her splendour and her destructiveness. Only in the achieved stillness of the 'Sabaoth' God, resting after his six completed days of creation, could Spenser ever hope to find rest and perfection:

> For, all that moveth, doth in *Change* delight:
> But thence-forth all shall rest eternally
> With Him that is the God of Sabbaoth hight:
> O that great Sabbaoth God, graunt me that Sabaoths sight.
>
> (viii.2)

NOTES

Introduction

[1] The following account is based on A. C. Judson, *The Life of Edmund Spenser* (Baltimore, Md, 1945). This is the standard life.

[2] Helena Shire, *A Preface to Spenser* (London, 1978) p. 10. Her introduction contains a brief account of the life, largely, though not entirely, based on Judson.

[3] Bryskett gives a highly fictional account of conversations between himself and other English officials and gentlemen in Ireland, including Spenser, in his *A Discourse of Civill Life* (1606).

[4] The best discussion of the *View* in the context of contemporary political thought on Ireland is Nicholas Canny, 'Edmund Spenser and the Development of an Anglo-Irish Identity', *The Yearbook of English Studies* 13 (1983) 1–19.

[5] A useful and easily available history of the period is J. E. Neale, *Queen Elizabeth I* (Harmondsworth, 1960). For further reading on domestic politics, see Wallace T. MacCaffrey, *Queen Elizabeth and the Making of Policy, 1572–1588* (Princeton, NJ, 1981), and, on foreign affairs, R. B. Wernham's two books, *Before the Armada: the Growth of English Foreign Policy, 1485–1588* (London, 1966), and *After the Armada: Elizabethan England and the Struggle for Western Europe 1588–1595* (Oxford, 1984). On the religious history of the period, see A. G. Dickens, *The English Reformation* (London, 1967), and Claire Cross, *Church and People 1450–1660*, Fontana History of England (London, 1976).

[6] See Eleanor Rosenberg, *Leicester, Patron of Letters* (New York, 1955).

[7] Quoted by D. B. Quinn, in *The Elizabethans and the Irish* (Ithaca, NY, 1966) pp. 35–6. This is a useful and compact account of Irish society and the Elizabethan view of it.

[8] For the 'race' as a biblical metaphor of the Christian life, see Hume p. 64.

[9] Judith Dundas, *The Spider and the Bee: the Artistry of Spenser's Faerie Queene* (Urbana, Ill., 1985) p. 174. See also a very useful account of the narrative styles of the poem by John Webster, 'Oral Form and Written Craft in Spenser's *Faerie Queene*', *Studies in English Literature* 16 (1976) 75–93. Also Paul Alpers, 'Narration in *The Faerie Queene*', *Journal of English Literary History* 44 (1977) 19–39.

1 Book 1

[1] Barbara Lewalski, *Protestant Poetics and the Seventeenth-Century Religious Lyric* (Princeton, NJ, 1979) pp. 20–3, describes what she calls the 'paradigm of salvation' briefly and clearly.

Notes

[2] John Lydgate, *The Legend of St. George* in *The Minor Poems*, ed. H. N. MacCracken, Early English Text Society, Extra Series, 107 (London, 1911) stanza 3. I have modernized the medieval *thom* of the original.

[3] In Alexander Barclay, *The Life of St. George*, ed. W. Nelson, Early English Text Society, Original Series, 230 (London, 1955) p. 112.

[4] *Virgil*, ed. and trans. H. Rushton Fairclough, 2 vols., Loeb Classical Library (Cambridge, Mass. and London, 1916, rev. 1935) I, pp. 240–1.

[5] Examples are given by D. Douglas Waters in 'Errour's Den and Archimago's Hermitage: Symbolic Lust and Symbolic Witchcraft', in *Critical Essays on Spenser from ELH* (Baltimore, Md, 1970) pp. 160–2.

[6] John Bradford, 'A Comparison Between The Old Man and The New', in *Sermons and Meditations*, ed. A. Townsend, Parker Society (Cambridge, 1848) pp. 297–8.

[7] E.g., Hume pp. 104–5, and Carole V. Kaske, 'The Dragon's Spark and Sting and the Structure of Redcrosse's Dragon-Fight; *The Faerie Queene* 1.xi–xii', *Studies in Philology* 66 (1969) 609–38.

2 Book 2

[1] *The Book of Vices and Virtues*, ed. W. Nelson Francis, Early English Text Society, Original Series, 217 (London, 1942) p. 148.

[2] Geoffrey Whitney, *A Choice of Emblemes* (1586), selected and ed. John Horden, Scolar Press Facsimile (London, 1969) p. 181. See the discussion of Occasion in Alpers pp. 209–14.

[3] The quotation is from a gloss on a sixteenth-century version of the emblem, quoted by A. D. S. Fowler in 'Emblems of Temperance in *The Faerie Queene*, Book II', *Review of English Studies* 11 (1960) 143–9 (p. 148). For a more cautious discussion, see Nelson p. 190.

[4] Susan Snyder, 'Guyon the Wrestler', *Renaissance News* 14 (1961) 249–52.

[5] Quoted, with his interpolations, from Merritt Y. Hughes, 'Burton on Spenser', *Publications of the Modern Language Association of America* 41 (1926) 545–67 (p. 566).

[6] Cesare Ripa, *Iconologia* (1593), introd. Erna Mandowsky (Hildesheim, 1970) p. 482. (This is a facsimile reproduction of the Rome, 1603 edition.)

[7] E.g., Alpers pp. 240–75 interprets details of the garden as emblems of avarice and erring heroism. A. Kent Hieatt argues that the garden shows 'the final intemperance of human desire for or infringement upon the realm of the divine': 'Three Fearful Symmetries and the Meaning of *Faerie Queene* II', in *A Theatre for Spenserians*, ed. J. M. Kennedy and J. A. Reither (Manchester, 1973) pp. 19–52 (p. 41).

[8] Atalanta is snared by apples given to Hippomenes by Venus: see Lotspeich p. 40. Acontius trapped Cydippe with an apple on which was written a false oath to Artemis which the goddess then enforced: see Ovid, *Heroides* 21, esp. ll. 151–86.

[9] Henry Bullinger, *Decades*, 4 vols., Parker Society (Cambridge, 1849) I, 300.

3 Book 3

[1] In *Complete Poetry and Selected Prose*, ed. John Hayward (London, 1929) pp. 346–7.

2 In *Complete Prose Works, Volume II: 1643–1648*, ed. E. Sirluck (New Haven, Conn., 1959) p. 251.

3 For a suggestive discussion of the function of the sea in this book, see Daniel M. Murtaugh, 'The Garden and the Sea: the Topography of *The Faerie Queene* III', *Journal of English Literary History* 40 (1973) 325–38.

4 See A. Bartlett Giamatti, 'Proteus Unbound: some Versions of the Sea God in the Renaissance', in *The Disciplines of Criticism: Essays in Literary Theory, Interpretation, and History*, ed. P. Demetz *et al.* (New Haven, Conn., 1968) pp. 437–75.

5 From *Wisdom of the Ancients* 13, in *The Philosophical Works*, trans. Ellis and Spedding, ed. J. M. Robertson (London, 1905) p. 838.

6 Baldassare Castiglione, *The Book of the Courtier*, trans. Sir Thomas Hoby (1561), Everyman Library (London, 1928) p. 319.

7 *Vives: On Education* (1531), trans. Foster Watson (Cambridge, 1913) p. 127.

8 Pierre Charron, *Of Wisdome: Three Bookes*, trans. Samson Lennard (London, [1608]) p. 83.

4 · Book 4

1 E.g., Chaucer, *Knight's Tale* l. 1131. Aristotle describes the love of brothers as having the characteristics of virtuous friendship (p. 185).

2 The suggestion that in Timias' story Spenser is glancing at Sir Walter Raleigh's fall from Elizabeth I's favour after his marriage to one of the royal Maids of Honour seems plausible. For the evidence, see O'Connell pp. 114–24. Spenser handles Belphoebe/Elizabeth's responsibility for Timias/Raleigh's state with tact, but not uncritically.

3 See John M. Steadman, 'Spenser's House of Care: a Reinterpretation', *Studies in the Renaissance* 8 (1960) 207–24, and 'The "Inharmonious Blacksmith": Spenser and the Pythagoras Legend', *Publications of the Modern Language Association of America* 79 (1964) 664–5.

5 Book 5

1 *Certaine Sermons or Homilies Appointed to be Read in Churches in the Time of Queene Elizabeth I (1547–1571)*, introd. M. E. Rickey and T. B. Stroup, Scholars Facsimiles and Reprints (Gainesville, Fla, 1968) p. 69.

2 Christopher St German, *Doctor and Student* (1523), ed. T. F. T. Plucknett and J. L. Barton, Selden Society (London, 1974) p. 97.

3 *Homilies* p. 313.

4 John Christopherson, *An Exhortation To All Menne To . . . Beware of Rebellions* (1554), The English Experience, 580 (Norwood, NJ, 1973) sig. Dvʳ.

5 Barnaby Riche, *Allarme to England, foreshewing what perilles are procured, where the people live without regarde of Martiall lawe* (London, 1578) sig. Biiiᵛ.

6 Norman Cohn, *Pursuit of the Millennium* (London, 1970) pp. 261–80.

7 Quoted by James E. Phillips, Jr, in 'The Background of Spenser's Attitude Toward Women Rulers', *Huntington Library Quarterly* 5 (1941–2) 5–32 (p. 9). This and the same writer's 'The Woman Ruler in Spenser's

Notes

Faerie Queene', *Huntington Library Quarterly* 5 (1941–2) 211–34, are essential reading on this topic.

8 See René Graziani, 'Elizabeth at Isis Church', *Publications of the Modern Language Association of America* 79 (1964) 376–89 (pp. 387–9).

9 René Graziani, 'Philip II's Impresa and Spenser's Souldan', *Journal of the Warburg and Courtauld Institutes* 27 (1964) 322–4.

10 For readings of the episode as referring to the Jesuits, see Bennett p. 189, and Douglas A. Northrop, 'Spenser's Defence of Elizabeth', *University of Toronto Quarterly* 38 (1969) 277–94 (p. 281). The quoted descriptions are by Sir Walter Mildmay, quoted MacCaffrey p. 145, and by Raphaell Holinshed and George Whetstone, quoted Northrop p. 281.

11 *De Clementia*, trans. J. W. Basore, Loeb Classical Library (Cambridge, Mass. and London, 1928) p. 439.

12 Fulke Greville, *Life of Sir Philip Sidney* (1652) (Oxford, 1907) p. 165.

13 John Stow, *The Annales, or Generall Chronicle of England* (London, 1615) p. 732. For a detailed discussion of the episode in relation to Leicester's Netherlands campaign, see R. C. Strong and J. A. Van Dorsten, *Leicester's Triumph* (Leiden and London, 1964).

6   Book 6

1 Thomas Starkey, *A Dialogue Between Reginald Pole and Thomas Lupset*, ed. Kathleen M. Burton (London, 1948) p. 27. Although not printed until the nineteenth century, the *Dialogue* was written between 1533 and 1536.

2 D. S. Brewer, 'Courtesy and the Gawain-Poet', in *Patterns of Love and Courtesy; Essays in Memory of C. S. Lewis*, ed. J. Lawlor (London, 1966) pp. 54–85 (p. 79).

3 *The Civile Conversation of M. Steeven Guazzo*, trans. G. Pettie and B. Young (1581–6), 2 vols. (London, 1925) I, 56.

4 *De Beneficiis*, trans. J. W. Basore, Loeb Classical Library (Cambridge, Mass. and London, 1935) p. 241.

5 *The Book of the Courtier* p. 94.

6 Dorothy Woodward Culp, 'Courtesy and Fortune's Chance in Book 6 of *The Faerie Queene*', *Modern Philology* 68 (1971) 254–9 (p. 255).

7 See P. C. Bayley, 'Order, Grace and Courtesy in Spenser's World', in *Patterns of Love and Courtesy*, ed. Lawlor, pp. 178–202, and Horton pp. 76–99 and 112–23.

7   The *Mutabilitie Cantos*

1 Boethius, *Consolation of Philosophy* Book 4, metre 6, trans. Henry Vaughan (*c.* 1650), in *Henry Vaughan: the Complete Poems*, ed. Alan Rudrum, Penguin English Poets (Harmondsworth, 1976) pp. 357–8.

2 For the Mutabilitie Cantos as a retrospective comment on the preceding poem, see William Blissett, 'Spenser's Mutabilitie', in *Essays in English Literature presented to A. S. P. Woodhouse*, ed. Millar MacLure and F. W. Watt (Toronto, 1964) pp. 26–42.

3 Quoted by Victor Harris in *All Coherence Gone* (Chicago, 1949) p. 105.

4 Ovid, *Metamorphoses*, trans. Mary M. Innes, The Penguin Classics (Harmondsworth, 1955) p. 339.

[5] Sherman Hawkins, 'Mutability and the Cycle of the Months', in *Form and Convention in the Poetry of Edmund Spenser*, ed. William Nelson (New York, 1961) pp. 76–102 (pp. 88 and 90). This is a very fine discussion of canto vii.

SELECT BIBLIOGRAPHY

I list only those books which I can, on the whole, recommend to those wishing to embark on an exploration of the extensive scholarship on *The Faerie Queene*. Those wishing to go further should consult Waldo F. McNeir and Foster Provost, *Edmund Spenser: an Annotated Bibliography 1937–1972* (Pittsburgh, Pa, 1975) and its updates in copies of the *Spenser Newsletter* (available from the Department of English, Duquesne University, Pittsburgh, PA 15219, USA) from volume 11 (Winter, 1980) on.

Annotated editions of 'The Faerie Queene'

The Faerie Queene, ed. A. C. Hamilton, Longman Annotated English Poets (London and New York, 1977). The best edition. The notes are generally reliable and invaluable. Contains an extensive bibliography.

The Faerie Queene, ed. T. P. Roche, Jr, Penguin English Poets (Harmondsworth, 1978). Useful, brief introduction and notes to each book.

Works: a Variorum Edition, ed. E. A. Greenlaw, F. M. Padelford, C. G. Osgood, *et al.*, 10 vols. (Baltimore, Md, 1932–49). Each book of *The Faerie Queene* has its own volume, which contains summaries of, and quotations from, all scholarship on the poem up to the Variorum's publication. Much that it contains is out of date, but it is always worth consulting.

'The Faerie Queene' I, II, and the 'Mutabilitie Cantos', and Selections from the Minor Poems, ed. Robert Kellogg and Oliver Steele (New York, 1965). Summarizing introductions and fairly full notes.

The Mutabilitie Cantos, ed. S. P. Zitner (London, 1968). Informative and helpful introduction and notes.

Background and sources

A. Bartlett Giamatti, *The Earthly Paradise and the Renaissance Epic* (Princeton, NJ, 1966). Useful introduction to the topic, with a chapter on Spenser.

H. G. Lotspeich, *Classical Mythology in the Poetry of Edmund Spenser* (Princeton, NJ, 1932). Cites Spenser's probable sources for each reference, with a brief explanation.

Isabel Rivers, *Classical and Christian Ideas in English Renaissance Poetry: a Students' Guide* (London, 1979). Brief informative chapters, with contemporary quotations, on such topics as 'The Golden Age', 'Protestant Theology', 'Allegory', etc.

Jean Seznec, *The Survival of the Pagan Gods*, trans. B. F. Sessions (Princeton, NJ, 1953). Fascinating account of the ways classical mythology reached the Renaissance. Most illuminating on the kind of learning Spenser inherited.

Rosemond Tuve, *Allegorical Imagery: some Medieval Books and Their Posterity*

(Princeton, NJ, 1966). Learnedly places Spenser in the context of medieval writing on the vices and virtues, and the tradition of allegorized romance.

Books on 'The Faerie Queene'

Paul J. Alpers, *The Poetry of 'The Faerie Queene'* (Princeton, NJ, 1967). An important book, which did much to show readers that it was not enough to abstract the moral of the allegory but that close attention should be paid to the poetic effects of the poem. Tends to be too dogmatic on how we ought to read.

Jane Aptekar, *Icons of Justice: Iconography and Thematic Imagery in Book V of 'The Faerie Queene'* (New York, 1969). Best study of Book 5. Invaluable on iconography, but almost entirely ignores historical allegory.

Peter Bayley, *Edmund Spenser: Prince of Poets* (London, 1971). A useful introduction to the poet and his work. Best on Books 5 and 6.

Josephine Waters Bennett, *The Evolution of 'The Faerie Queene'* (Chicago, 1942). Enquires into order of composition of poem. Often fascinating and informative, though many of her suggestions should be treated with scepticism.

Harry Berger, Jr, *The Allegorical Temper: Vision and Reality in Book II of Spenser's 'Faerie Queene'* (New Haven, Conn., 1957). Only full-length study of Book 2. A close and subtle reading, though in my view it should be treated with caution, particularly in its emphasis on Guyon as a distinct and psychologically complex personality.

Donald Cheney, *Spenser's Image of Nature: Wild Man and Shepherd in 'The Faerie Queene'* (New Haven, Conn., 1966). Studies dichotomy of Spenser's images of 'harsh' and 'soft' nature. His most extended discussion is of Book 6.

T. K. Dunseath, *Spenser's Allegory of Justice in Book Five of 'The Faerie Queene'* (Princeton, NJ, 1968). Interprets Book 5 almost entirely in terms of Artegall's psychology and ignores historical allegory. Nevertheless, helpful at times.

Maurice Evans, *Spenser's Anatomy of Heroism: a Commentary on 'The Faerie Queene'* (Cambridge, 1970). Early chapters usefully and reliably set the poem in the context of a number of contemporary assumptions about poetry. Later chapters offer interpretations of each book.

Alastair Fowler, *Spenser and the Numbers of Time* (London, 1964). A study of traditional number symbolism and its possible importance for the organization of *The Faerie Queene*. Exciting but unreliable.

A. Bartlett Giamatti, *Play of Double Senses: Spenser's 'Faerie Queene'* (Englewood Cliffs, NJ, 1975). An introduction for students. Part 1 offers some brief, useful chapters on Spenser's continental and English predecessors.

A. C. Hamilton, *The Structure of Allegory in 'The Faerie Queene'* (Oxford, 1961). A study of the allegorical mode of the poem which particularly emphasizes the importance of the 'literal', surface level.

R. A. Horton, *The Unity of 'The Faerie Queene'* (Athens, Ga, 1978). Looks afresh at the overall design of the poem. Thorough and, on the whole, sensible.

Anthea Hume, *Edmund Spenser: Protestant Poet* (Cambridge, 1984). Authoritative account of Spenser's Protestantism. Particularly useful for Books 1 and 2.

Frank Kermode, *Renaissance Essays: Shakespeare, Spenser, Donne* (London, 1971). Contains three essays on *The Faerie Queene*, particularly Books 1 and 5, which stress the need to recover sixteenth-century contexts and attitudes. All three take particular interpretations too far.

C. S. Lewis, *The Allegory of Love* (Oxford, 1936). Contains a classic chapter on *The Faerie Queene* which discusses the poem in the contexts of the Italian epic and the 'courtly love' tradition. Many of its conclusions have now been questioned.

C. S. Lewis, *Spenser's Images of Life*, ed. A. Fowler (Cambridge, 1967). A series of essays on the iconography of episodes and topics. Originally designed as undergraduate lectures.

Isabel G. MacCaffery, *Spenser's Allegory: the Anatomy of Imagination* (Princeton, NJ, 1976). Not for beginners, but an informed and sensitive exploration of the topic of imagination, which she sees as central to the poem.

William Nelson, *The Poetry of Edmund Spenser: a Study* (New York, 1963). A useful introduction to the complete works. Individual chapters on each book of *The Faerie Queene*, which concentrate on explaining the allegory.

James Nohrnberg, *The Analogy of 'The Faerie Queene'* (Princeton, NJ, 1976). A vast accumulation of facts and ideas more or less relevant to the poem. Much gold to be found in its labyrinths.

David Norbrook, *Poetry and Politics in the English Renaissance* (London, 1984). Contains a much-needed and vigorous account of Spenser's political engagement in Book 5.

Michael O'Connell, *Mirror and Veil: the Historical Dimension of Spenser's 'Faerie Queene'* (Chapel Hill, NC, 1977). Only recent book-length study of historical allegory in the poem. Useful on Book 1, but disappointing on Book 5.

Patricia A. Parker, *Inescapable Romance: Studies in the Poetics of a Mode* (Princeton, NJ, 1979). Contains a stimulating chapter on Spenser which uses some of the techniques of modern American deconstructionist criticism.

William Renwick, *Edmund Spenser: an Essay on Renaissance Poetry* (London, 1925). An early but thoroughly reliable introduction, which places Spenser in the context of contemporary theories about poetry. Particularly informative about Spenser's continental models.

Thomas P. Roche, Jr, *The Kindly Flame: a Study of the Third and Fourth Books of Spenser's 'Faerie Queene'* (Princeton, NJ, 1964). The only full-length study of Books 3 and 4. An important book, particularly illuminating on Spenser's use of emblematic material.

Humphrey Tonkin, *Spenser's Courteous Pastoral: Book Six of the 'Faerie Queene'* (Oxford, 1972). Sophisticated and stimulating study of Book 6. Not an introduction.

Kathleen Williams, *Spenser's 'Faerie Queene': the World of Glass* (London, 1966). Chapters on each book. Particularly sensitive to the way the poem seems to imitate the flux of experience, through which the reader works towards a realization of order.

INDEX OF CHARACTERS
AND EPISODES

References in bold type are to discussions of key episodes.

Index

Index